The Governance of Climate Change
Science, Economics, Politics and Ethics

The Governance of Climate Change

Science, Economics, Politics and Ethics

Edited by
David Held, Angus Fane-Hervey and Marika Theros

polity

Individual chapters © their authors 2011; this collection © Polity Press, 2011

First published in 2011 by Polity Press

Polity Press
65 Bridge Street
Cambridge CB2 1UR, UK

Polity Press
350 Main Street
Malden, MA 02148, USA

ISBN-13: 978-0-7456-5201-6
ISBN-13: 978-0-7456-5202-3(pb)

A catalogue record for this book is available from the British Library.

Typeset in 10.5 on 13 pt Swift
by Servis Filmsetting Ltd, Stockport, Cheshire
Printed and bound in Great Britain by MPG Books Group Limited, Bodmin, Cornwall

The publisher has used its best endeavours to ensure that the URLs for external websites referred to in this book are correct and active at the time of going to press. However, the publisher has no responsibility for the websites and can make no guarantee that a site will remain live or that the content is or will remain appropriate.

Every effort has been made to trace all copyright holders, but if any have been inadvertently overlooked the publisher will be pleased to include any necessary credits in any subsequent reprint or edition.

For further information on Polity, visit our website: www.politybooks.com

Contents

Notes on Contributors

Ulrich Beck is the *British Journal of Sociology* Visiting Centennial Professor at the London School of Economics and Political Science (LSE) and Professor of Sociology at the Institute of Sociology, University of Munich. His recent publications include *World at Risk* (2008), *Cosmopolitan vision* (2007) and *Power in the Global Age* (2005).

Alex Bowen is a principal research fellow at the Grantham Research Institute on Climate Change and the Environment at the LSE. He has previously served as a Senior Economic Advisor to the UK Stern Review on the Economics of Climate Change, a Senior Policy Advisor at the Bank of England, and Head of Policy Analysis and Statistics at the UK's National Economic Development Office.

Robert Falkner is a senior lecturer in international relations at the London School of Economics and a senior research fellow at LSE Global Governance. He is also an associate of the Grantham Research Institute on Climate Change and the Environment at the LSE and of the Energy, Environment and Development Programme at Chatham House. He is the author of *Business Power and Conflict in International Environmental Politics* (2008).

Ian Goldin is the Director of the James Martin 21st Century School at the University of Oxford. He previously held positions as Vice President of the World Bank (2003–6), Director of Development Policy at the World Bank (2001–3), Chief Executive of the Development Bank of Southern Africa (1996–2001) and advisor to President Nelson Mandela. He has published over fifty articles and twelve books, including *Globalisation for Development: Trade, Finance, Aid, Migration and Ideas* (reprinted 2007) and *The Economics of Sustainable Development* (1995).

David Held is the Graham Wallas Chair in Political Science and co-Director of the Centre for the Study of Global Governance at the LSE.

His recent publications include *Cosmopolitanism: Ideals and Realities* (2010), *Globalisation/Anti-Globalisation* (2007), *Models of Democracy* (2006) and *Global Covenant* (2004).

Angus Hervey is a Ph.D. candidate and the Ralph Miliband Scholar at the LSE, where he is conducting doctoral research on the political economy of tropical deforestation in Africa. He is co-author of *The Scramble for Africa in the 21st Century: A View from the South* (2006).

David King is the Director of the Smith School of Enterprise and Environment at the University of Oxford. He has served as the UK Government's Chief Scientific Advisor and Head of the Government Office of Science from October 2000 to December 2007 and as President of the British Science Association from 2008 to 2009. He has published more than 500 papers on chemical physics and science and policy, and has co-authored (with G. Walker) *The Hot Topic: How to Tackle Global Warming and Still Keep the Lights On* (2008).

Martin Manning is the Director of the New Zealand Climate Change Research Institute at the School of Government at the Victoria University of Wellington. He has led research programmes at the National Institute of Water and Atmospheric Research covering atmospheric chemistry and the carbon cycle for ten years, and represented New Zealand on the Intergovernmental Panel on Climate Change (IPCC). He is the author of over forty peer-reviewed scientific research papers plus numerous book contributions and reports.

Michael Mason is a senior lecturer in the Department of Geography and Environment and an associate of the Grantham Research Institute on Climate Change and the Environment at the LSE. He has authored *Environmental Democracy* (1999) and *The New Accountability: Environmental Responsibility across Borders* (2005).

David Miliband is a British Labour Party politician who has been the Member of Parliament (MP) for South Shields since 2001. He was the Secretary of State for Foreign and Commonwealth Affairs from 2007 to 2010.

Ed Miliband is a British Labour Party politician who is currently the leader of the Labour Party and the Leader of the Opposition of the UK. He has been the Member of Parliament (MP) for Doncaster North since 2005. He served in the Cabinet from 2007 to 2010, first as the Minister for the Cabinet Office and Chancellor of the Duchy of Lancaster, and then as Secretary of State for Energy and Climate Change.

Baroness Onora O'Neill is a professor of philosophy at the University of Cambridge. She is a former President of the British Academy and chairs the Nuffield Foundation. In 2003, she was the founding President of the British Philosophical Association (BPA). She was created a Life Peer in 1999 and has served on the House of Lords Select Committees on Stem Cell Research and the BBC Charter Review, and is currently serving on the Select Committee on Genomic Medicine. Some of her recent books include *Rethinking Informed Consent in Bioethics*, with Neil Manson (2007), *Autonomy and Trust in Bioethics* (2002) and *Bounds of Justice* (2000).

James Rydge is a post-doctoral researcher at the Grantham Research Institute on Climate Change and the Environment at the LSE. Prior to that he worked at the Bank of New York in London, and was a research fellow and lecturer in finance at the University of Sydney.

Peter Singer is Ira W. DeCamp Professor of Bioethics in the University Center for Human Values at Princeton University, and Laureate Professor at the University of Melbourne, in the Centre for Applied Philosophy and Public Ethics. He is the founding President of the International Association of Bioethics, and co-founder and President of The Great Ape Project. His books include *Animal Liberation* (1975), *Practical Ethics* (1979), *Rethinking Life and Death* (1994) and, most recently, *The Life You Can Save* (2009).

Hannes Stephan is a post-doctoral fellow at Keele University and is affiliated with the ESRC Centre for Climate Change Economics and Policy (CCCEP). He has published on global environmental governance, with special attention to international organizations and the EU's leadership role.

Joost van Loon is Professor of Media Analysis at Nottingham Trent University and Editor-in-Chief of *Space and Culture*, a journal that brings together critical interdisciplinary research in cultural geography, cultural studies, architectural theory, ethnography, communications, urban studies, environmental studies and discourse analysis. He is author of *Media Technology: Critical Perspectives* (2007) and *Risk and Technological Culture: Towards a Sociology of Virulence* (2003).

John Vogler is Professor of International Relations at Keele University. He is a member of the CCCEP and serves as Convenor of the British International Studies Association Environment Working Group. He has written numerous articles on international environmental politics, co-edited *The Environment and International Relations* (1996) and *The International Politics of Biotechnology* (2000), and authored *The Global Commons* (2000).

Editors' Introduction

In the last decade the problem of climate change has moved from the realm of scientific research and environmental advocacy into mainstream political and economic policy discussions at all levels of governance. Yet, as politicians and citizens become increasingly aware of the threat that climate change poses to human societies, the debate has become more fractious and the level of rhetoric has increased. It also appears more and more apparent that progress in combating climate change has stalled. This presents something of a paradox – the more we become aware of the level of the threat posed by anthropogenic climate change, the less we seem capable of acting to prevent it.

There are a number of reasons for this. While the nature of the threat is quite well understood, thanks to scientific research and sustained advocacy on behalf of environmental groups and increasingly from private business, the way in which the issue has been framed has alienated significant sections of society, and has failed to convince many of the necessity of taking concerted action. Structural problems are apparent too. Democratic countries find it difficult to translate policy commitments into policy outcomes, and the entrenched interests of a relatively small proportion of state and non-state actors have paralysed or blunted many of the efforts to limit greenhouse gas (GHG) emissions and to develop pathways to sustainable energy usage. The atmosphere is a shared resource, and countries have failed to set aside national interests in favour of the common global good. International efforts have not been helped by existing international institutions either, which appear increasingly outdated and unfit for purpose. There has been a failure of collective action that has profound implications.

The lack of concerted action is understandable, but not inevitable. For what is at stake is a fundamental reorganization of the way in which modern industrial economies are constituted – the kind of change that involves the same level of disruption as previous watershed developments such as the industrial revolution, the development of the internal combustion engine and the information technology revolution. Yet, given our relatively recent awareness of just how serious a threat it poses, we are only just starting to appreciate what is at stake. Climate change involves not only physical changes in the weather, sea levels, food production, water, but also major political and social upheavals, such as struggles over scarce resources, market fluctuations and migration.

This book is an attempt to further stimulate the debate about these issues by bringing together scholars and practitioners from a number of different fields to discuss the nature of climate change and its wide-ranging implications. It begins by reflecting on the science. David King sets out a selection of the scientific evidence on climate change, and frames it within the larger context of population growth, demographic shifts and health pandemics. Martin Manning, a lead author of the most recent IPCC report, follows in chapter 2 by looking at the gaps between science and society. He explains how scientific research, despite showing the clear and possibly even understated threat posed by climate change to human society, has failed to overcome opposition from vested interests opposed to reductions in GHG emissions and from a relatively small minority who hold strong personal viewpoints. The economic and technological context is provided in chapter 3 by Ian Goldin, head of the James Martin 21st Century School at Oxford. In a wide-ranging piece on 21st-century challenges, he explores how globalization and greater interdependence amongst societies have brought with them new types of existential risks, such as climate change, which threaten our way of life.

Alex Bowen and James Rydge then look more closely at some of the key elements of the economics of climate change in chapter 4. They describe the scale of the potential impacts of climate change and how the associated risks shape economic analysis. They explore central economic issues such as greenhouse gas externalities, market failures that allow GHG emissions to grow, and key policy instruments that aim to encourage emission reductions. In chapter 5, two of the book's co-editors, David Held and Angus Hervey, analyse the political barriers to combating climate change. They contend that structural obstacles to effective policy have to be understood at both the domestic and global levels. Exploring the strengths and weaknesses of different types of political associations in relation to climate change, they argue that an effective approach must include greater space for deliberative principles and a policy mix that can operate effectively both within and across borders. A sociological perspective is provided in chapter 6 by Ulrich Beck, from Munich University, and Joost van Loon, from Nottingham Trent, who argue for a new type of thinking about climate change based on a shared recognition of a 'world risk society', and a politics anchored in cosmopolitan principles.

The volume also includes contributions from two well-known philosophers, Baroness Onora O'Neill and Peter Singer. In chapters 7 and 8, they engage with some of the deeper social and ethical questions posed by climate change. The former points out how the pursuit of both social justice and sustainability requires trade-offs and serious decisions that have an impact on the wellbeing of both people and the environment, while the latter presents an ethical case for urgent action. They are followed by Michael Mason in chapter 9 who explores what climate change means in the context of modern liberal theories of justice, and asks how this might apply to a specific case, namely, the implications of climate change for Palestine.

The final section looks toward the future with contributions from both the sons of Ralph Miliband, after whom the lecture series which gave rise to this book was named. David Miliband presents his vision for a global deal on climate change, placing particular emphasis on the role of the EU, while Ed Miliband outlines his views on a new politics for climate change, based on long-term sustainability and ethical concerns rather than the politics of 'now', which lies at the heart of so many of the challenges outlined in this book. The book concludes with a piece by Robert Falkner, John Vogler and Hannes Stephan, who explore in greater detail why climate policy has failed at the global level, and advocate what they call a 'building blocks' approach for the future.

Running throughout the volume are four key underlying questions, around which there is some controversy.

How settled are the debates about climate change?

In the lead-up to the negotiations at Copenhagen in 2009 it looked like both the scientific and economic arguments had been settled. The IPCC, having recently received its Nobel prize, was unchallenged as the definitive authority on the subject, and had delivered its verdict on the existence and seriousness of anthropogenic climate change, while Nicholas Stern's 2007 report had shown that the costs of taking immediate action were relatively minor compared to the costs of waiting and doing nothing. It looked like the debate was finally ready to move on from arguing about whether climate change was real or not to arguing about what to do about it. Yet somehow, since the breakdown of the Copenhagen negotiations, both the scientific and economic arguments for doing something about climate change have taken a number of steps backwards. Media outlets across the world have revelled in the various 'Climategate' stories, and a series of polls reveal a public that seems unwilling to incur costs and take the word of politicians and scientists at face value.

This is all the more surprising since, as both King and Manning point out, the nature of the climate change problem is by now very well understood. There is a critical mass of scientific research and opinion incorporating analysis from geologists, climatologists and paleontologists, among others, that points overwhelmingly to the conclusion that the average global temperature is climbing, and that it is due to the emission of greenhouse gases. Worryingly, as noted by King, Manning and Goldin, there is also a massive amount of inertia in the present climate, thanks to the earth's oceans which take more time to register and absorb temperature rises. This means that by far the majority of the effects of increased emissions are still to come. This is an important point, and one to which little attention has been paid by sceptics.

Why then, given the overwhelming nature of the evidence, is scepticism making a comeback? There are a number of reasons. One is that the nature of science in this area lends itself to criticism. The general public is not used to uncertainty amongst scientists, yet climate science, by its nature, is unpredictable. The complexity of the different factors involved at a global scale means that scientists are unwilling to make specific predictions, and instead revert to ranges and estimates. The complexity of the problem also means that data can be contradictory, with changing states and tipping points, and with the potential for non-linear feedback processes that can't be accounted for by linear models. King mentions the example of methane hydrates emissions from regions around the Arctic, which, because they cannot be estimated, are not factored into models. However, as Manning points out, while it is important to consider uncertainties in science, an objective approach must consider the full range of potential causes and not simply focus on the one we might prefer.

It also seems that the issue has until now been framed largely in the wrong way, a criticism made by Beck and van Loon, who show that environmentalists have either advocated a romantic return to pre-industrial activities or offered a too negative view of the problems at hand. The same point is raised by King, who suggests there is a need to reframe the debate in terms of risk avoidance rather than in terms of certainty. As he says, a passenger would not board an aeroplane once informed that it had only an 80 per cent chance of landing. In the case of climate change, the potential for catastrophe is far higher than that. The next step then, is to take on board the nature of the challenge politically. This requires a fundamental transformation of economic systems, the biggest since the rise of the industrial age.

Yet, as Bowen and Rydge suggest, such a transformation will not emerge from competitive markets left to their own devices. This is due to the continued plentiful supply of fossil fuels, multiple market failures and some policy failures. Their discussion of the various risks implied by climate change, the scale of the problem, and the actions required places a strong emphasis on the notion of risk and uncertainty. A failure to see the problem in these terms is likely to result in poor policy choices that do not adequately reflect the seriousness of the threat. The authors conclude that:

> While traditional economic techniques such as project cost–benefit analysis and other marginal analysis techniques are useful as a guide, the primary analysis must consider how to bring about large changes in our economic structures, in particular a transition away from high-carbon to low-carbon growth, while always maintaining the flexibility to accommodate changes in our understanding of the science, economics and ethics of climate change.

Why is climate change such a difficult problem to solve?

Climate change is an incredibly complex problem, and a very difficult policy issue to address. In addition to the debate about its physical effects and the economic costs and benefits of addressing it, climate change also involves questions of power, social justice and distribution. Ian Goldin explains how globalization has led to an explosion of growth and wellbeing, but also creates new types of risk and vulnerabilities. Because we are more integrated than before, and interdependent, the threat from existential risks such as health pandemics, nuclear terrorism and climate change has become more serious. The rise of such challenges reveals that no one country or community alone can provide the solution. This is because climate change is a problem at the global scale, transcending physical and political boundaries. As Beck and van Loon point out, the types of risks mentioned by Goldin are not only transcending, but also 'de-bounding', because they eventually transform boundaries themselves. They do so spatially (across nation-states), temporally (different timescales) and socially (accountability, responsibility, liability).

At the national level, it can be argued, as Held and Hervey do, that modern liberal democracies suffer from a number of structural characteristics that prevent them from tackling climate change. These include short-term decision-making based on electoral cycles, self-referring decision-making that downplays externalities and cross-border spillover effects, and greater interest group concentration and pluralism that tends to cater to narrow interests and can lead to a gridlock in public decision-making. Another problem is that the issue of climate change spans both the domestic and the international domains. Institutional fragmentation and competition between states can lead to it being addressed in an ad hoc and dissonant manner. And, even when the global dimension of a problem is acknowledged, there is often no clear division of labour among the myriad of international institutions that seek to address it: their functions frequently overlap, their mandates conflict and their objectives often become blurred

The ethical implications of climate change are profound as well. This is an area that has not received enough attention. Goldin shows how climate change is taking place in an era of rising inequality, with vast disparities in the living conditions of people around the world. This is coupled with the prospect of population growth and major demographic shifts in the future. Climate change is, accordingly, occurring in the context of ever-growing demands for resources, in a world in which they are increasingly scarce. The distributional questions are therefore crucial – who gets what, how, and when? O'Neill attempts to better understand this question by unpacking the terms 'social justice' and 'sustainability'. She suggests that both are highly indeterminate, because they can be realized in many ways. While it may possible in theory to aim for equal opportunities and equal outcomes, not all specific configurations of these are possible. Similarly, you can at least in theory have sustainable growth and sustainable agriculture – but at certain points choices will be needed. Moreover, if we aim for both social justice and sustainability, we shall need to aim not merely for a configuration of each that is internally coherent, but for a configuration of the two that is coherent: we might find that we have to trade off some forms of equality for some forms of sustainability. Unless we recognize this, we are only playing with the rhetoric of social justice and sustainability, rather than thinking seriously about either.

Singer makes a distinctive and bold ethical argument, suggesting that, since we are aware of the threat implied by climate change, we are also obliged to counteract it. Knowledge of the consequences of climate change together with an understanding of the atmosphere as a shared resource means that the actions of those with high carbon footprints in industrialized countries are curbing the rights of people in developing nations. GHG emissions involve rights violations, and citizens of relatively rich, industrialized countries therefore have an obligation to lead a carbon neutral lifestyle. Mason also suggests that our current ways of thinking about and dealing with social justice and sustainability are inadequate. Climate vulnerability generates issues about the bounds of justice, including duties to those deemed most vulnerable to present and future climate hazards. However, in his overview of the dominant liberal theories of justice (the social contract and capabilities approaches), he argues that they do not fit the bill. Climate vulnerability falls outside moral parameters of Rawlsian justice because of uncertainty about the cumulative impact of climate change, since previous generations were unable to recognize the climate harm being caused by carbon-intensive development. The capabilities approach also fails to grasp the profile of climate change, especially the non-substitutable nature of the environment's sink capacity. There is no priority accorded to the conditions necessary for human survival as opposed to human development, and no distinction made between the present vulnerable and the future vulnerable. Liberal theorists, despite wishing to bring the least advantaged into the fold of moral concern, are found wanting when confronted with the problem structure of climate change.

What works and what doesn't in the mitigation and adaptation of climate?

At the level of global governance there has so far been a failure to generate a sound and effective international framework for managing global climate change, whilst at the level of the state solutions have been weak and have struggled to transcend the normal push and pull of partisan politics. A number of this volume's contributors, including King, Goldin and both the Milibands, suggest that tackling climate change can only be achieved via a comprehensive global agreement. This strategy, predicated on the idea of negotiating a comprehensive, universal and legally binding agreement, prescribes top-down policies based on agreed principles. However, as Falkner, Vogler and Stephan show, attempts to reach a global deal have failed because of deep fissures on climate politics. Major powers are interested in narrow national interests and in avoiding costly commitments to emission reductions. Major emitting countries also lack domestic support to create a basis for international commitments, particularly in the US. This has been compounded by a changing global economic system. A shift in the power centres of the world economy, driven largely by the rise of the East, has weakened the bargaining power of the traditionally dominant Western countries, who had become used to dictating their priorities in international deals. The Copenhagen Conference demonstrated that this is no longer the case. As Falkner, Vogler and Stephan point out, the US/China bilateral relationship is increasingly coming to define world politics – and with the lion's share of GHG emissions, they now hold primary responsibility for taking action on climate change.

In terms of specific policy options, efforts thus far have not been convincing. According to its supporters (including Singer and King from this volume), cap-and-trade makes the most sense of the options available, because it allows for greater certainty about eventual emissions levels and provides better incentives for producers. At this point, it also appears to be the approach most likely to be adopted at the global level, with a European Union Emission Trading System (EU ETS) already in place, and a successful precedent in the form of markets for sulphur in the United States. However, cap-and-trade has not led to substantial emission reductions, nor is it likely to in the future. It is too easily manipulated, and susceptible to special interests. An alternative, or supplementary, approach is to put a price on GHG emissions via carbon taxation. However, taxes do not allow certainty over how big future GHG reductions will be, since estimates are imprecise and there is a long lag time between policy output and actual outcomes. They are also hard to coordinate internationally, and developing countries are unlikely to agree to such arrangements, which impose economic burdens on crucial industries without offering the offsetting gain of being able to sell emissions permits. Moreover, in the current economic and political climate, and especially in the wake of the financial crisis and future austerity cuts, carbon taxation seems politically unattractive and unrealistic.

What is the right policy mix for the future, and can a viable coalition be found?

Climate change, if taken seriously, implies a political paradigm shift. It requires an alliance of multiple state and non-state actors, motivated by a sense of what Beck and van Loon call a 'world risk society'. This is not a matter of abolishing or undermining nation-states but of bolstering their capacity to act effectively. What is needed is a 'cosmopolitan *realpolitik*' which could empower societies and states. The task is to analyse and explore how global risks can be deployed as mobilizing forces to help us encounter climate change realities and find solutions. What can unite human beings faced with such challenges? According to Beck and van Loon, the answer is to develop an understanding of the world as a community of global risks that threaten our existence. A new approach must overcome false alternatives of retreat or accommodation, and instead must develop via a cosmopolitan philosophy which opens up a moral and political space that can give rise to a civic culture of responsibility that transcends borders and conflicts.

In terms of actual steps, the first requirement is to agree on targets. Despite the pessimism surrounding the failure of negotiations over climate change in Copenhagen, this is one thing which was largely agreed upon. Most countries have converged on a target of keeping the global temperature rise to less than 2 degrees Celsius, although a number of African countries during the negotiations insisted on even lower targets. In addition, most of the major emitters, including the EU and the US, have set national targets of varying degrees. The next step is to ensure that such commitments are likely to be carried out. Putting a price on GHG emissions (whether through tradable permits or taxes) will not be enough on its own to deliver the needed reductions. What is ultimately required is a fundamental overhaul of energy systems through transformative technologies that require a combination of factors to succeed – not only market incentives, but also applied scientific research, early high-cost investments, regulatory changes, infrastructural development, information instruments and public acceptance.

At the international level, it will require coordination and participation, and the reform of global institutions. The current system is not adequate for the task, a point raised by a number of authors in this volume. Of course, this is easier said than done. It is unclear whether it can be achieved in time, or whether it is possible at all. Falkner, Vogler and Stephan argue for an alternative 'building blocks' approach, which recognizes that a functioning framework for climate governance is unlikely to be constructed all at once, in a top-down fashion. They suggest there is no need for a comprehensive legally binding treaty. Rather, we should engage in an ongoing process that seeks to build an overall international framework for action from the bottom up. Climate issues can be disaggregated into different areas, and countries can focus on the here and now, and on what can be realistically done at national level. Economic change can be initiated via the creation of incentives, the promotion of efficiency and technological breakthroughs. This approach doesn't ignore international politics but recognizes the need for it to reflect domestic politics and priorities. Ultimately, the aim is to create a coherent governance architecture out of separate and partial agreements. Such an approach is not without precedent – trade policy provides an example of how it can work.

Taken together, the chapters in this book provide a comprehensive overview of climate change and the immense challenges it poses for the way human society is organized. The issues raised span all areas of human understanding and endeavour. There are very few moments in history in which humankind has been faced with such pressing questions which go to the heart of how we relate both to each other and to our environment. Climate change contextualizes the place of human beings and clarifies that they are but one element in a highly complex and vulnerable world. This is one reason why it invokes such controversy and intense questioning. While it is unlikely that the controversy can be entirely put to rest, the overwhelming scientific consensus is that if we do not act now, and act together across borders, we will store up more problems than we solve. This book explains why acting now in relation to climate change is scientifically rational, economically sensible and ethically desirable. Yet it also highlights how extraordinarily difficult it is to produce a clear and coherent political and economic response in a world of divided communities and competing states.

Part 1

THE CHALLENGE OF CLIMATE CHANGE

1
The Challenge of Climate Change

David King

I want to start this chapter with a very simple idea: we have an enormous knowledge base. It has been developing rapidly over the previous 200 years. Then the computer revolution came along and we suddenly created the ability to retain our high level of sophistication and analysis for very complex phenomena involving enormous amounts of data. I would like to use that as a starting point. My thesis is going to be that, having this knowledge capability very largely cocooned into our universities, we have a rather poor system of moving that understanding into policy decision-making.

I have had eight years in government to become aware of this. I find in principle that in the private sector there is often a better understanding (examples range from the high-tech manufacturing sector to the insurance industry and venture capital) of managing opportunities and risks. There is, in short, a better understanding of the state of knowledge relevant to what these industries are doing than you often find in governments around the world.

My first example is an admittedly dramatic one but it's one that I was involved in: the tsunami of 26 December 2004. The latter took place in a part of the world where there was no early warning system in place and, as a result, those of us watching it on television sets were aware that the tsunami was moving across a part of the planet, while those potentially affected were not. Eight hours later, the tsunami killed a number of people off the Kenyan coast. No warning mechanism was in place to see that the risk was managed. I, in turn, was asked to make a report to the Prime Minister on this matter. And, when I went to the United Nations and asked why there wasn't an early warning system in place, I was told this was a random and unexpected event because tsunamis generally happen in the Pacific Ocean.

Given the sudden propagation of the wave, the people just off the coast of Banda Aceh, where the Sumatran trench runs and where the phenomenon originated, could not have been rescued: they were too close and things happened far too quickly for us to do anything. But what about the people in Sri Lanka? What about those in India? As the tsunami made its way across the ocean, 230,000 people died. My estimate is that 150,000 lives would have been saved with an early warning system in place.

But delving into the topic from a scientific point of view, was the tsunami really random and unforeseeable? The seismologists who study where volcanoes are, how plate tectonics work, and how the plates carry the great continents around are fully aware of the fact that, when two plates are in collision, there can be a section that gets 'stuck'. The collision rate is slow, the plates move at about the rate of growth of one's fingernails but nevertheless, since they carry an enormous mass, when a section gets stuck we know that great quantities of energy will be discharged. The longer it takes, the more pressure builds up, and, eventually, the bigger the event is going to be. So, as a matter of fact, the seismological community had predicted that a tsunami would occur along the Sumatran trench and said it would create a tsunami of Force 9. That was the prediction by the scientists: the tsunami was not unforeseen; people were in fact waiting for one.

To fully understand the extent of awareness of the imminent nature of the danger, we can recall how, in the summer of 2004, one Oxford scientist and one Californian scientist went on a trip to Sri Lanka, Indonesia and India to try to persuade the governments they needed an early warning system. They couldn't find a mechanism for talking to somebody powerful enough to take on the idea of spending $30 million – that is all it would have cost – on the project. Now the point I want to make is: there is now an early warning system in place. We have learnt nothing in moving the state of knowledge to the decision-making process since 1985 when the previous big tsunami occurred off the Peruvian coast. In 1979, seismologists had said the next big tsunami was likely to occur off the Peruvian coast. My point is very simple, the knowledge is available: we understand enough to predict where these events will occur and with what force.

Going back to my initial theme – that is, knowledge and how well we use it – I suspect many in the academic community are feeling that economic modelling on a purely linear basis, which doesn't include the possibility of non-linear, sudden events – an individual revolution or an economic collapse, a catastrophe – is hardly worth the computer time that is spent on it. But, the fact of the matter is that we know enough to include feedback terms – that is, non-linear terms – in modelling processes. The next task we should embrace is to think hard about causality and impacts that lead into catastrophic events that build up over long periods of time: the tsunami was simply an illustration of this latter point.

Striking a more positive note, we should also avoid being excessively pessimistic. Through the nineteenth and twentieth centuries there were a remarkable series of improvements in human well-being. Going back to the Enlightenment, the Reformation or the more recent Industrial Revolution, all these historical periods have witnessed amazing transformations which can be measured in terms of increased life expectancy.

Life expectancy at the beginning of the twentieth century was around forty to forty-five years in most parts of the world. Today, it is more than seventy in most of the same places. If we wanted to describe the trend in life expectancy changes, we would conclude that in many parts of the world it is simply increasing linearly with time. That, in itself, is already a startling piece of information. In the United Kingdom, life expectancy is around eighty, and still increasing. I am going to attribute the UK's progress to our infrastructure; to our cultural systems; to the revolutions that have occurred in science, agriculture, civil engineering, the cleaning-up of water provision, medicine and so on. I am also going to suggest that the British Empire enabled many of these developments in Europe to spread rapidly around the world. From the latter point of view, we see the benefits still playing through in many distant parts of the world.

This is the upside aspect of the twentieth century: a massive transformation in wellbeing. Yet as we move into the twenty-first century, we find that we are building up another sort of catastrophe resulting from this very good picture. The problem naturally arises from the fact that there is a necessary follow-through from increasing lifespan massively in short periods of time (e.g. 100 years) – namely, population explosion. Nation by nation, you find that, as wellbeing improves, female fecundity is eventually reduced to a level which is matched by the mortality rate. But before this is achieved, population growth is rapid. So, for example, during the Middle Ages in this country, out of seven or eight children born to each woman, only two would survive into maturity, and two is precisely the number needed for a stable population. But if, on the other hand, you have a sudden improvement in wellbeing and all seven or eight children survive into maturity, they will – excuse the scientific term – form breeding pairs. In turn. each of these breeding pairs will produce seven or eight children that will survive and form breeding pairs of their own, and so on. The result is easy to predict: an explosion.

Generally, population dynamics are altered by improved wellbeing and by factors such as female education and empowerment. As they improve, female fecundity comes down and the population growth rate tends to drop to zero. This is roughly where Europe is today. In other parts of the world, growth rates have recently approached a

fecundity of 2 (and hence no population growth): the whole continent of South America is down to an average of 2.3, and so rapidly
approaching that equilibrium level. Other parts of the world are still
experiencing a high rate of growth.

We started the twentieth century at roughly 1.5 billion human
beings. We ended the century, after adding 1 billion every twelve years,
at 6 billion. We are now at 6.8 billion. By 2028 we'll be at 8 billion, and
the best current population forecast puts us at 9 billion by mid twenty-
first century. That's the challenge. The 9 billion people are also all
aspiring to experience the sort of standard of living enjoyed in western
Europe and the United States. So we not only have another 50 per cent
to be added to the population as we move forward in time, but we also
have increased demand for resources per head.

My suggestion is that this contains the seeds of a whole series of
necessary changes. If we use the knowledge of the problem at hand
to guide our decisions, we might be able to cope with it. If we don't,
it will lead to a series of potential catastrophes. I am going to suggest
that we should mainly focus on a few of these challenges, with this
large global population being at the core of our future problems. On
the other hand, it must be clear from the start that simple population containment is only a very small part of the solution. Given the
dynamics of population growth, and provided you have an increase
in female education and empowerment and access to contraceptives,
population containment comes without the necessity of direct inter-
vention on reproductive activity.

The challenges I wish to highlight – including fresh water provision,
energy and mineral resources, food production and climate change –
cannot be approached linearly, as if they were not interrelated. Each
one of them is strongly related to the others. In sum, we have to treat
this as a complex problem that demands complex answers.

Take the example of water resources. The state of Victoria in Australia
is one of the breadbaskets of the country because of increased desertification (after an impressive seven successive years of drought). The area
is now witnessing a process of population loss through migration. The
farmers are packing their bags, and one-third of the freshwater provision to supply the human population in the state is now provided from
desalination. So one might think that there's a technological solution. Desalination comes through and solves the problem. However,
desalination is an energy-intensive process. Hence the former problem
of water security becomes one of energy security and supply. What
seemed a simple question of providing one resource in a given place
turned out to have an impact on a different issue, and on a different
scale.

Perhaps one could argue that Australia has lots of coal and can therefore afford to burn coal to produce the desalinated water. But to burn coal means to accelerate climate change, and the latter is exactly what brought us the desertification process. Again, linear solutions do not work well for non-linear problems: a linear solution to one problem might create a feedback on a presently secondary variable of the current problem and eventually reinforce the causes of the main problem we were targeting. We need to be very, very careful as we tackle these problems so that we don't get into these positive feedback loops, because they are the ones leading to the kind of catastrophe that we should be trying to avoid.

We could say quite a lot about water supplies but the obvious thing is that, as the human population increases, the demand for fresh water increases as well. Yet, with an increasing human population, we increase water contamination. So, given a stable fresh water supply around the planet, decreasing fresh water supply after contamination crosses over with increasing water demand from the augmented population. Where's the crossover point? About 2040–5: approaching mid century. But that's a global crossover point based on an average count of water available. Locally, people run out of water much sooner. That is, there will be places in which water supplies will run out much sooner than mid twenty-first century. To put the matter bluntly, the presence of water no longer matches local population dynamics. We will increasingly get high population growth in areas where water supplies are scarce. We will go back to desalination, and the latter, as we have seen, will feed into the causes of our problems.

A further illustration is food production. An increased population with higher standards of living clearly needs more food. A simple solution to that problem is to increase the amount of land you put into food production. If this is not locally possible everywhere, one can also imagine a global market operating to transport the food to areas where people need it. But, of course, shipping food around the world contains the risk of threatening the biodiversity of local ecosystems. If, on the other hand, we want to tackle the problem of food production more directly, we will need to seek different production techniques to implement worldwide. I believe intensive agriculture is needed for the improvement in food production volumes that we require. In turn, if we intensify production to a greater degree, we might be able to set aside land to manage and protect biodiversity. So, technological solutions such as genetically modified organisms (GMOs) are available, although whether they are socially acceptable, of course, is another question.

As we move forward with a planet where there are limited resources available and a rapidly rising demand, there is a clear potential for increased conflict. Of course, the more powerful you are, the more likely you are to secure resources, wherever they may be, for the purposes of your own population. For example, we have been mining in Africa for a long time: we need the mineral resources. Recent developments involve the Chinese appearing in Africa, for many of the same reasons. China doesn't have platinum – it doesn't have copper either; and of course it needs all such resources. Potential for conflict, I think, is enormous.

A further issue is climate change. Rising sea levels means less land available and, eventually, the flooding of many coastal cities. As we know, many important and densely populated cities have historically developed along coastlines around the planet. Take the example of Bangladesh, and think about the consequences of flooding there: what would be the impact for countries in neighbouring areas? Wouldn't flooding provoke massive migrations (both internal and international)? At the end of the day, if massive amounts of people are displaced, they will need to find a new place to stay, seeking higher and more fertile land to occupy.

All of these problems imply that either we leave it to power struggles or we manage the problem, in a more peaceful manner, as we move forward. The message I would like to communicate is fairly simple: a big transition is required in order to tame upcoming conflicts over scarce vital resources. I am going to focus on two of these problems and I will spend most of my time dealing with climate change.

Of the many issues we have briefly highlighted, climate change is by far the biggest problem. One of the main reasons for this is that taming climate change can only come through a global agreement. We might manage other problems locally but, because the atmosphere is a shared resource, we need a global agreement with all major parties on board in order to stop its deterioration. We need not only a solution that is sound scientifically, but also one that is capable of being accepted by all major nations. Climate change represents a paradigmatic case of a global challenge that can only be dealt with through a global consent on right remedial actions.

Here, let me introduce a brief detour: I still have said nothing about health and education. As the planet's resources are stretched, with growing populations within a globalized economic system, we have learnt that disease travels very fast. Take the example of avian flu, which first appeared in birds in 1995. The big fear, of course, is that H5N1 is a virus that no human being has previously been exposed to. We know what happened to the Hawaiian population when Christian missionaries arrived there bringing a flu virus that none of the Hawaiians had been exposed to. And, so the story goes, we are all at risk from H5N1 if it transforms itself from an avian flu virus to a human flu virus. That's precisely the worry. It's been around from 1995 to the present day and still avian flu hasn't reached the Americas. We know that the spread is largely connected to bird migration patterns.

But, human migration patterns are totally different. We move around in aeroplanes, go for holidays, travel for business, go to see our relatives, and so on. While I was in government, we modelled what would happen if a virus appeared somewhere on the planet, and how long it would take before it arrived in the British Isles. Well, it turns out that the model we built demonstrated that it would take three months for the virus to reach every country on earth. Even more disturbingly, much of this 'pandemic migration' would occur during the so-called 'silent spread period' of an epidemic. This is the period that epidemiologists fear the most because people are not yet showing symptoms and are therefore freely travelling about without restrictions or precautions. After this incubation period, the virus becomes infectious: just as it has reached the far corners of the earth, we start to realize its effects. The bottom line is that hundreds of millions of people would be put at risk with a (dangerous) disease being transported so efficiently by our global means of travel. All of this requires a new focus: more funding for research and more attention to planning coordinated solutions.

In the following, I would also like to go over the costs of food production. Firstly, let me point to the big hike in food prices that occurred in 2008. I believe this variation can be explained via two major causes. The first is an issue of unintended consequences (at least, I am going to be generous and suggest it was unintended) generated by the American policy of subsidizing grain farmers. Because of subsidies for bio-fuel generation from food grain, surplus food supplies that had previously been used as food aid to other parts of the world suddenly diminished very substantially. So using food as a resource for fuel has a direct effect locally (to contribute to US energy security), and yet a quite different one globally – namely the hike (or a big part of it) in world food prices.

Another cause of that hike, a significant part, is crop failures. Of course, we've had a couple of series of amazing green revolutions in India, in China, and in south-east Asia, where there has been a seven-fold increase in crop productivity and a steep upward trend in food productivity per hectare. These developments all came as a result of applying agricultural technology in a sensible way, which, in turn, has meant that those burgeoning populations have managed to feed their people more effectively than ever. But there is one particular form of crop destruction which has not been dealt with: every year, rice crops are lost through flooding. Now, a rice plant that is marketable can sustain itself under totally flooded conditions for about three days, maybe four, and after that the plant dies. We all know that rice needs a lot of water, and so the story continues – rice is always being planted in regions that are susceptible to flood risk. The very conditions that are required in order to have access to large amounts of water create a certain amount of risk when too much of the water that is needed comes along. This is exactly what happened in Asia in 2008, and so in that year there was a large loss of rice due to flooding.

Back in 1992, looking for flood-resistant rice was recognized to be an important issue. Seeking a solution, the International Rice Research Unit in the Philippines found that there was a variety of wild rice in India that can live right through flooding. In fact, it survives three or four weeks of total flooding. Now this is wild rice and it's not a commercial product that can be farmed simply. To be honest, it doesn't even taste very nice. But the key thing was to use genetic markers to find out which genes were responsible, in the wild rice, for creating the flood resistance. The gene is called FR (for flood resistant) 13A. So, having established this, using genetic markers, the scientists could then have snipped the gene from the wild rice into commercial varieties and generated flood-resistant marketable rice: something that could have been brought to the market in a couple of years. The gene was discovered in 1992, as we have said, but in the meantime there has been an opposition to GM crops, mainly generated in Europe. As a result, GM food crops have been banned in many developing countries, depriving local communities of many obvious benefits.

An alternative approach (and one that has been followed by the International Rice Research Institute) consists of going through the normal breeding process and, using genetic markers, picking out the products which carry the right genes. But normal genetic breeding follows growth cycles. To use a picturesque image, in order to select the right variety of rice, you literally have to get into the paddies up to your knees and your arms in mud. You are no longer in the laboratory snipping genes, you are doing something that is painfully slow and, in 2010, we now at last expect the flood-resistant commercial rice to hit the market.

We have the knowledge and technology to establish ourselves as a comfortable society (in western Europe at least) with plenty of food, and then we create scares about GM products. I have no reasonable explanation for such behaviour. Why shouldn't we genetically snip from a wild rice to a commercial rice product to shorten the development process? There is no known example of a human being suffering from consuming the products of such a process. So the solution could have been there long before 2010, and perhaps could have contributed to diminishing the effects of the hike in food prices we were considering.

As we move forward in time, however, what we need is not simply more flood-, drought-, saline- or disease-resistant crops, but more food per drop of water. On this topic, considerably more research needs to be done. Let's look at the question of water scarcity and where it's happening already. As you know by now, I am suggesting that by mid century we will have a global problem. But, once again, we are already finding areas where there is an absolute water scarcity, and areas where a relative water scarcity is rapidly moving toward becoming an absolute one. Water scarcity being caused by the combined effects of (a) population growth and (b) climate change, we have two factors driving its future.

In the following, I would like to address the issue of climate change in further detail. First, let me say at once that I think the nature of the climate change problem is now well understood scientifically, and I therefore just want to say that we need to take on board the nature of the challenge under the heading of 'climate change' that is now recognized at G8 level. When I was in government I was struggling to get some foothold on this problem. When we (the UK) held the presidency of the G8 in 2005, we managed to get the Prime Minister to put climate change on the agenda. This was a significant moment since the agenda only contained two issues: it was just climate change and African development. These are closely related problems, and, since then, successive governments holding the presidency have maintained climate change on the agenda of the G8 meetings. In 2008 in Japan, for the first time, we reached an important agreement which states that we now have a concrete target for emissions reduction: we are going to reduce our carbon dioxide emissions (globally) by 50 per cent by 2050.

Our media, misguidedly, picked up the latter agreement as some kind of further failure to decide and move forward. They pointed out that the starting point of the 50 per cent reduction wasn't stated (Was it 2000? Was it 2009?). They also pointed out there was no staging between now and 2050. They implied that the agreement was vague and without a clear road map, so to speak. But I believe that's carping, because managing to get from the heads of state an agreement halving our emissions by mid century was a tremendous step forward.

To picture how significant a step it has been, try to imagine what sort of effort it will take to decarbonize our economies. First of all recall that the 50 per cent reduction is a global target that does not take into account distributional differences in CO_2 emissions. This means, for the developed world, that a halving of emissions globally demands a considerably greater amount of reduction locally. For the UK, for example, an 80 per cent reduction would prove necessary. At this moment in time, we emit 11 tonnes of carbon dioxide per person per annum and, to take a convenient example from the developing world, in India that number is about 2 tonnes per person per annum; 80 per cent of 11 is 8.8, and 11 minus 8.8 makes 2.2 tonnes per person per annum. So, by mid century we need to be where India is today in terms of carbon dioxide emissions per person. That's the nature of the challenge. That is going to be the biggest transformation that our economic systems have witnessed since we had a global economy.

When I started talking about climate change in government eight years ago, I was able to show people data from paleoclimatology going back 250,000 years. The data were obtained from ice cores taken in the Antarctic. Imagine taking ice at the bottom of the ice core. You are looking at ice compacted from a snowfall that fell 250,000 years ago, and at the top of the ice core you've got last year's snowfall. Collected in the ice core are bubbles of air; you therefore have a sampling of what the atmosphere was like 250,000 years ago. From the water isotope ratio in the ice, you also have the temperature for the same period of time. Hence, through the analysis of ice, we can come to the knowledge of global temperatures and global atmospheric composition a long way back in time.

But we also possess data that go back much further than 250,000 years. The longest ice core that has been analysed is a 3 km section from the Antarctic, which goes back 852,000 years with a remarkable resolution. One can also compare data from ice cores with cores taken from the ocean sediment. The comparison in the 850,000-year cycle is remarkably good. To know what was happening further back in time, we need to concentrate on data obtained via sediment analysis. The latter tells us that the planet's temperature went through a maximum about 55 million years ago, the Eocene transition point. At that moment in time there was no ice left on the earth. The Antarctic was a sub-tropical forest with very large mammals. If you go just beyond the last bit of the ice core, you find the remnants of all these species there. The global temperature average was about 10 degrees higher than the recent pre-industrial period.

As we move forward in time, carbon dioxide levels come down. What the data tell us is that carbon dioxide concentration levels 55 million years ago were probably a couple of thousand parts per million (ppm). As carbon dioxide levels fall, the temperature falls and we come down to a temperature which we human beings (and large mammals in general) feel relatively comfortable with. This period comes about 2 million years ago. Over the period since then, the global temperature has been biphasic – in common parlance, passing through successive ice ages and the warm periods.

In each warm period, carbon dioxide levels are about 270 ppm. On the other hand, in each ice age carbon dioxide levels are about 200 ppm. There is, as the great mathematician Fourier has taught us, a coupling between global temperature and carbon dioxide concentration, although this is not a simple linear causal relationship.

As we come to the end of the last ice age, going from about 18,000 years ago to *circa* 12,000 years ago, we emerge into the present warm period (with remarkably stable temperatures). This latter development has been undoubtedly positive for human life on earth. The end of the ice age brought us warm and stable temperatures but also a strong rise in sea levels. These have gone up because the ice that's on land has melted and joined the ocean. The total sea-level rise has been estimated to be around 100 metres. In this context, as one can easily grasp, the world's map is strongly remodelled, and yet, since the end of the last ice age, developments are stable, and so is the new map of emerged and recently submerged land and continents. The coastlines have been, since then, so stable that we have been building our major cities on them, taking them for granted. We can go as far as stating that the stability in the climatic conditions of this period have created some of the basic features necessary to the development of human civilization as we know it.

The question that immediately comes to our mind is, of course, why is the present warm period longer than the others? That is a point of some live discussion at the moment. If one looks at the carbon dioxide signature, one can see that it's creeping up over this period whereas it should have started coming down (according to the analysis of previous trends). There is a discussion about whether this is the first anthropocene development in the earth's climatic history: that means, the first period in history in which human activity and the development of human settlements, through agriculture and the manmade destruction and degradation of forests in favour of cultivable land, have impacted the planet's ability to absorb CO_2. Put simply, taking trees out, taking forests out, entails removing material that captures carbon dioxide from the atmosphere. In this picture, maintaining the stability of the atmosphere in terms of carbon dioxide levels is a complex composite activity – a dynamic interplay – between green matter and us, and perhaps (as I have said the debate is lively on this point) the development of our human civilization started to affect such complex interplay as far back as 12,000 years ago.

Of course, the interplay with the ecosystem is a natural feature of any form of life. But humans are unique in how far they are capable of doing this. Here we have to leap forward to the 'wonderful' period of the Industrial Revolution. It is at this time in history that we started providing energy for our rapidly increasing requirements by going underground and finding naturally sequestered carbon in the form of coal, gas and oil. The net result of such endeavour is that we are now at CO_2 levels of 387 ppm, and rising at 2 ppm per annum. This compares with 265–70 ppm for all previous warm periods, and 200 ppm for ice ages.

So far, one could comment, the effects of these higher concentration levels are not, after all, so spectacular. The temperature has risen only 0.7 of a degree centigrade, and according to predictions it should have been higher. The main explanation for this discrepancy is presence of a large amount of inertia in the earth's climate system. This phenomenon is mainly caused by the oceans. The oceans take a long time to 'catch up': they take more time to register and absorb the temperature rise in the atmosphere. Because of this inertia we've got another thirty years of climate change ahead of us whatever we do, even if we stop at 387 ppm, which we're not going to.

Let me make just one further point. What would happen if we burnt all of our fossil fuels, in particular all of the coal? Can we get the temperature back up to where it was 55 million years ago? My research is basically theoretical and experimental but this is one experiment I'm going to suggest we don't try (because I believe we realistically could). I think there is enough coal on earth for us to produce a carbon dioxide level of about 1,500 ppm in 150 years or so. The future would be a pretty bleak one for a population of 9 billion, because managing the remaining habitable part of the planet is inconceivable. It is clear that this is a problem we have to manage, and whose consequences we will have to address as we move forward in time.

What we should ask ourselves now is, then, what is the likely rise in temperature as we move forward under different global agreements? What is the level of carbon dioxide we have to stay below to avoid a 2-degree temperature rise? I'm afraid the answer can only be given in terms of a probability distribution function. This represents the best state of current science today from around the world and it says that, for an ultimate carbon dioxide level of 450 ppm (this is a carbon dioxide equivalent, since I am including other greenhouse gases (GHGs) as well), the temperature peaks at 2.2 degrees. It is an asymmetric curve, and perhaps that's the most worrying feature.

Constant throughout our current analysis is the use of linear curves. Yet, as we were discussing earlier on, there seems to be the potential for important non-linear feedback processes that cannot be fully accounted for in linear models. For example, consider the (even potentially) sudden evolution of methane hydrates emissions from regions of the planet around the Arctic Circle. As the latter melts, and the gas trapped in the ice is progressively released into the atmosphere, the emissions levels for methane hydrates might increase rapidly. Methane is a very strong GHG, and its effects on climate change could be important. This point illustrates a common feature of scientists' mentality: their search for precision and accountability often turns into very conservative estimates of the phenomena they want to explain. If something cannot realistically (that is, according to a required standard of precision) be modelled, then it will simply be excluded from the model itself. And it is because of the very presence of such non-linear feedback processes that no scientist trusts the figures above a rise of about 3½ degrees on these curves. The effects excluded from modelling in such a scenario might simply turn out to be too great for the predictions of the model to be taken seriously.

What is the probability of exceeding 3½ degrees? The best answer we can give is that it is about 20 per cent, even in the best possible scenario in which we globally limit fossil fuel use on a short timescale. In other words this is a likely scenario even if we stay below 450 ppm. It will take 100 years for the temperature to rise to these levels. Nevertheless, as I said to the Prime Minister, if one gets on a plane and asks the pilot 'what are the chances of landing the plane safely?' and the pilot replies '80 per cent', I suggest one should immediately change flight. Unfortunately, we do not have that option collectively. The best available way forward for the planet at the moment is an 80 per cent chance of avoiding a rise in temperatures above 3½ degrees centigrade. It seems obvious, then, that we need a global agreement that keeps us on this, least dangerous, path. Of course the question is going to be whether we can deliver that: that is the big challenge daunting us.

Kyoto has produced virtually nothing except – and it is one great success – the European Emissions Trading Scheme (something I will explain in what follows). What we need now is a totally fresh view containing a better understanding of the science on the topic and a clearer vision of what we need to do. These are my 'de minimis' requirements for a decent global agreement. First, we need to agree on where we're going. Let's, for instance, decide that we absolutely need to stay below X ppm of GHGs as we move forward in time. I would like X to be a number even lower than 450, but, being politically realistic, we can keep this figure as a valid one. This objective also entails that we need to put forward a system of agreed national targets. If 450 ppm is our global target then we have to have national targets fixed in such a way that they can add up correctly to form that global figure, and we get to the point at which, by mid twenty-first century, we are all emitting about 2 tonnes per person per annum.

Once we've agreed national targets, we move on to the problem of how to manage the agreements already put in place. I am going to suggest that a system based on trading schemes is by far the most promising one. The main argument in favour of a trading scheme is that, once you have one in place, it's very difficult to stop it. To set up a trading scheme means to create a carbon dioxide market. If one looks at the European market for carbon dioxide, its worth oscillates around £55 billion. As one can easily predict, the creation of an analogous scheme on a global scale would increase the value of the carbon market place dramatically, and might bring it to a figure of about a trillion dollars. Put simply, a very large investment is already taking place in Europe to sustain the trading process and, as we move forward in time, and eventually the trading scheme goes global, the result will consist in the creation of a new global commodity. One can even go as far as picturing a future in which all major currencies will be valued against carbon dioxide as the major tradable commodity.

But we should be clear that carbon trading is not the end of the story. We need to move forward in order to deal with the demands of those parts of the planet where lifespan is not long. Africa has missed out on most of the developments of the twentieth century. The lifespan there is still forty to forty-five years, and, to put it bluntly, the African continent will simply not be able to adapt to the impacts of climate change. The UK, by contrast, has a clearly laid-out adaptation plan. I am proud of it because I helped to put it in place. The plan costs about £300–400 million a year and its associated investments will be ramped up as we move forward in time. But countries in Africa can't possibly afford anything like what the UK has put in place. We are in urgent need of an adaptation strategy for developing countries, and this will not come about through the very scarce resources they can mobilize but only through a massive technology transfer. We need to create a financial flow to back that up; one way to create the funds is to auction permits for carbon dioxide emissions. The Kyoto process includes a 'clean development mechanism', which has proved to be inadequate for this purpose.

Going back to one of our original concerns, what are the real implications of effectively managing – that is, taking seriously – climate change? Do we need to totally decarbonize our system of economic production and our ways of life? Perhaps things are not quite as dramatic as they seem. Our current energy systems are heavily biased toward fossil fuels. Why is this so? Quite simply because we didn't need to develop alternatives to carbon as an energy source. Coal was cheaply available and we were not inspired to generate alternative large-scale energy sources. But alternatives exist, and, even if not fully developed, they make perfect sense in terms of scale and potential to provide energy to the entire world. Take the example of solar power. How much sunlight arriving on the surface of the planet would we need to convert into usable energy to provide all the energy needed for 9 billion people? On average, we have about 10,000 times as much sunlight, or solar energy, reaching the planet as we would need, if we just converted it efficiently into energy.

The truth is that we have done very little when it comes to the development of credible alternatives to old and polluting ways of creating energy. Furthermore, even the private sector should refocus its efforts in this direction, in response to the incentive for rapid techno-logical change. I see a tremendous potential for great developments. So, for instance, I consider it to be very short-sighted to have solar panels which are made of silicon. This is a form of 'scientific laziness'. Semiconductors have been very successful in chip and microchip development, and most of these are silicon-based. Semiconductor physics, in short, is largely built around silicon. You then take the same group of scientists and ask them to develop photovoltaic energy, and they come up, again, with silicon. But silicon is not the only available alternative. We can imagine photovoltaics that are made of ceramics, plastics and paint so that architects and engineers can use them on the outside of every building. enabling all constructions to generate whatever energy they can from sunlight. Of course, you will then need a means of storing the generated energy, but even so, with real tech-nological advancement, these problems are solvable. And there are also different avenues to the resolution of our problems. For example, what about large-scale energy conversion? Desertified areas could be used, in Africa for instance, as sources of electricity which can be just piped back across the continent. In short, I believe that the necessity for technological change will drive through these new technologies to meet necessary changes imposed by our circumstances. Such changes will arrive, and effective solutions will emerge.

In order to meet these energy challenges, but also to meet the cur-rent financial crisis, we simply need new thinking. What comes out of our analysis is the need to be thinking very hard about how we globally interact to reach appropriate solutions. The first step toward real progress is to reform those global bodies that should provide the pillars of a global system of awareness. Unfortunately, at the moment, we are moving forward with somewhat dysfunctional global agencies. Here, I am suggesting that the UN institutions as currently constituted are not ready to meet the challenges we have been discussing. Unless we rethink these global bodies in light of the global problems we have to meet, we're going to struggle to go forward, because parochial national priorities and perceptions will dominate.

Global priorities need to be worked through and through in this multidimensional and multilateral way, with intelligent knowledge-based communities. At the end of the Second World War, we had an American President who saw the need to move on from the old League of Nations to a much stronger global body, the United Nations. Today, I think we are back into that position where leadership at the very top is needed. I believe it would be asking too much of an American leader, taken alone, to carry this vision forward. The current state of affairs requires developing countries' leaders, such as Hu Jintao and Manmohan Singh, to stand with the American President and with the

European Union and push for a stronger globalized system in which we can begin to move forward and meet the present challenges.

In what follows I am also going to suggest there are other issues that stand in our way and that we need to address. Economism – the idea that consumerism can drive all of our needs and their satisfaction through a completely free market process – is clearly something that we all understand has faults to it. A consumerism driven by creating funds out of the value of your house by remortgaging and then reusing the debt as finance for further spending is clearly not a wise economic attitude. What the current crisis has proved is that it might be the case that the money you were using was not really there after all. The consequences are that, nowadays, large amounts of that money and debt, trillions of dollars of bad finance, were generated in the system through this consumer-driven boom. As we emerge from the crisis (and the recovery process doesn't look placid) I hope we will see the latter as an opportunity to move forward into a system which manages the complexities of global capitalism, rather than one based on a blind trust in 'animal spirits'. We still need to rely on a market-based approach, and consumerism is a good idea, but we need strong regulatory systems in place in order to reap the benefits of the market system and minimize the risks of systemic market failures.

I want to make sure that these points do not entail some form of 'nostalgic Romanticism'. I am not advocating that we should look back to what we used to do in order to find optimal solutions to today's problems. I believe that the solutions lie with science, engineering technology, good economics, good behavioural sciences. Put bluntly, the solutions we are looking for are in the advanced knowledge base that we can create.

Eventually, and this is a challenge to scientific people, we need to re-gear science and technology (but I include economics as well) to meet the global challenges. I am going to suggest that we know a little bit more about landing a craft on Mars or the functions of a Higgs Boson, which is certainly topical, than we do about controlling malaria or treating HIV/AIDS, developing alternative technologies for low-carbon growth, and certainly about managing global economies. This means that we have put a lot more brain power into the first two topics than into the solution of more pressing issues. We need to re-gear global brain power to meet the real challenges accompanying the twenty-first century. What we need are brilliant people to come forward with very clever solutions at this point in time.

Let me put forward some final comments on the free market system. Let me first provide you with an anecdote. I was recently in South Africa giving a lecture. As I stood up and looked outside in the hot air of a Pretoria summer afternoon, I could see across to Johannesburg.

I could see on the skyline those amazing skyscrapers in that city in Africa. As a matter of fact all I could see were their tips. A clear vision of the city was hindered by a great pool of pollution below the tops of the buildings. I had two ministers in front of me and I have to say I took a bit of pleasure in then starting my lecture by saying that, until I stood up, I didn't realize that South Africa had not introduced car exhaust regulations. After the talk, a 'red-faced' minister asked how I knew about it. I simply replied that, as you travel into any city in the world, you instantly know whether it has car exhaust regulations or not: it's a policy package with health and 'visual' consequences.

There has been a massive clean-up of air through car exhaust regulations. These regulations were introduced back in the 1970s, beginning with California. In Europe we picked this up quite quickly. This is a progressive regulation. And progressive, in this context, indicates that, each time it is announced, it provides new minimum standards for the purchase of cars. We are now at a point in time where no new car can be purchased in Europe unless it meets extraordinarily strict regulatory requirements concerning NOx gases, carbon monoxide, particulate matter from diesel engines and so on. We are reaching such high standards that today, if we had, let's say, a BMW diesel engine car in this room with the car exhaust catalyst and trap system on the end of it, it would actually clean up the air in the room. That's what we've managed to obtain through a remarkable piece of technology in the back end of cars. And these developments did not come about by individuals saying 'I want to clean up the air as I drive my car!' They have been obtained by governments realizing this is a problem that can only be managed by regulatory systems.

I am labouring this point because I think that for decades the so-called 'Chicago School of Economists' has been pushing against any form of regulation. Let the market do its job and create the right forms of incentives and, automatically, good behaviour will emerge. But, to put it bluntly, good individual behaviour can't emerge to manage the problems we have been discussing so far, and this is so because good behaviour cannot solve the collective and complex nature of the problems we have analysed. Take a further example, the ozone hole. The basic mechanism consisted in the simple fact that hydrofluorocarbons, HFCs, started destroying the protective ozone layer in the earth's stratosphere. The solution came through a global agreement reached in Montreal. The ozone hole is going to take some time to repair itself but the good news is that, by mid century, we will have managed to repair the damages we had produced. So the mechanism at work has been fairly straightforward: scientists determined the nature and the cause of the problem, and we introduced regulatory systems and managed it successfully.

Regarding the car exhaust catalyst systems, it is striking how, each time a new announcement emerges from Europe, every car manufacturer complains. They say that compliance is impossible. And yet they have never failed to meet the new standards, all of them, each and every time that they were introduced. And this happened through a market-based system of incentives: knowing that competitors were likely to meet the regulatory requests, all companies considered it rational to invest in order to do the same. So, in this context, regulation was actually a driver for innovation. Now, by placing a high price on CO_2 emissions, and by ratcheting it upwards in time, we can use a similar approach to mitigate the effects of global warming.

2

The Climate for Science

Martin Manning

A rocky road between science and society

We often try to take advantage of new levels of scientific understanding quickly when these can become a basis for further economic development or a cosier lifestyle. But some aspects of new science can run into firm resistance.

Four hundred years ago Galileo Galilei was undertaking detailed studies of the solar system and using better telescopes than any others had before him. These showed that the Earth was not the centre of the universe. He published an account of this work in AD 1610 claiming that we were actually revolving around the Sun. That had been suggested about seventy years earlier by Nicolaus Copernicus, but Galileo could now produce hard evidence showing that it was right.

First of all Galileo won academic awards in Rome, but then some people decided that this was not what they really wanted to hear. What was wrong with thinking that the Earth was at the centre of all things – and surely scripture proved that was how it had been created by God anyway? Minor technical details could be scoffed at, and were not a part of most people's daily lives. So Galileo was denounced and when he subsequently produced his major published work, he was tried by the Inquisition and forced to stop saying things that some did not want to hear.

Fifty years ago, Charles Keeling, at the University of California San Diego, started new high-precision measurements which showed that we were steadily increasing the amount of CO_2 in the atmosphere. Again this confirmed ideas that had emerged in the previous century, this time started by Nobel Prize winner Svante Arrhenius, who had said that such increases would eventually happen and cause global warming. But Keeling found it was happening far more rapidly than Arrhenius had expected.[1] This led to more detailed scientific analyses of the role of CO_2 as well as other GHGs in the climate system, and opened the way for a far more detailed analysis of global warming.

In 2007, the Intergovernmental Panel on Climate Change (IPCC) won the Nobel Peace Prize after carrying out four careful assessments of climate change science. On the other hand criticism of the science had been growing steadily stronger, to the point where some people obviously do not want to hear what comes from scientific research. This time the Catholic Church is in quite a different position and Pope Benedict XVI criticized governments for their slow response to climate change at the United Nations Framework Convention on Climate Change (UNFCCC) meeting in December 2009. It seems that the 'religion' of today is now quite different, but the question is still whether we are seeing some sort of repeat of what happened 400 years ago.

The development of climate change science in recent decades has been closely linked to recognition of the greenhouse effect, which explains why the air gets colder as you go up in altitude, even though you are getting closer to the Sun where the energy is coming from. However, our climate is also strongly influenced by other things that control the energy balance, like cloud cover and the extent of ice sheets. So, while Arrhenius's original estimates of the amount of warming that would be caused by a doubling of atmospheric CO_2 are still consistent with the latest science, it has also been very important to develop much more detailed analyses of the processes that determine our global temperature.

By the 1980s, the range of processes that can be involved in global warming were becoming well recognized and extensive reviews of climate change science were carried out by agencies such as the US Department of Energy. Governments started to recognize that the global implications of climate change went well beyond the physical sciences because of the wide range of potential consequences for the environment, and the implications that arise because of our heavy dependence on fossil fuels.

A sense of growing urgency for a globally integrated approach to deal with these complex issues led to the formation of the IPCC in 1988 as a new way of conducting detailed communications between core science and government policymakers. Increasing concern was being expressed by world leaders such as UK Prime Minister Margaret Thatcher, who summarized the situation in an address to the United Nations in November 1989 as follows: 'We have all recently become aware of another insidious danger. It is as menacing in its way as those more accustomed perils with which international diplomacy has concerned itself for centuries. It is the prospect of irretrievable damage to the atmosphere, to the oceans, to earth itself.'[2] Then the IPCC produced its first summary of climate change science in 1990 and noted carefully that, while they were quite confident about some aspects of future climate change, this did not apply to all aspects.

Two years later, the United Nations Conference on Environment and Development reached international agreement on a 'precautionary principle' stating that: 'Where there are threats of serious or irreversible damage, lack of full scientific certainty should not be used as a reason for postponing cost-effective measures to prevent environmental degradation.' Around this time, the UNFCCC was formed, and established as its ultimate objective: 'stabilization of greenhouse gas concentrations in the atmosphere at a level that would prevent dangerous anthropogenic interference with the climate system'.

Well, it is now eighteen years later. Science has dug deeper into our understanding of climate change but not found any evidence that the key issues might have been exaggerated. In fact, the reverse applies in some respects. There are a few clearly focused government policies, led by Sweden and now the EU, for reducing greenhouse gas emissions, but there still seems to be a reticence to move quickly in many countries. It appears that we can change our planet faster than we can establish any well-integrated policy for managing it.

This inertia in addressing our growing effects on the climate system appears to run even deeper than the complexity of government policies and international equity. Once again there seems to be a rejection of science that says something people would rather not hear. For those of us who have been working on climate change for several decades, it is hard to understand the magnitude of the recent furore about a few mistakes in the last IPCC Assessment Report, and in some contentious emails. Clearly there is no excuse for such mistakes, and science must apply very high standards when addressing such a critical issue as climate change. But why do some now pretend that nearly all of the independently published science papers on climate change over the last fifty years must be wrong?

Let me summarize what the science is saying now about climate change and why I think that this will probably not lead to a repeat of what happened to Galileo. My analysis will be focused around the IPCC *Fourth Assessment Report* (AR4), completed in 2007, and will be limited to basic climate science rather than covering all the implications of climate change. To give some sense of the highly abbreviated nature of this summary I should point out that the Working Group I Assessment Report (WG1-AR4), covering the basic science, was based on results from about 5,000 scientific papers, the majority of which had been published in the previous five years.

The structure of my argument covers three key questions. Is the Earth warming, and if so is this occurring to an unusual extent? Can we be sure about the reason for such a warming? And where could it go in the future?

Is the Earth really warming?

Whether the Earth has a warming trend or not has to be considered in the context of natural cycles in the climate system which affect the global average temperature and in which a warming will be followed by a cooling. From a scientific perspective, the issue of global warming also goes much deeper than just surface temperatures because these are known to be linked to a complex energy budget for the whole planet. This brings in warming of the oceans, the amount of water evaporation, wind patterns and how they change, as well as other ways in which incoming energy from the Sun gets distributed.

Nevertheless, a clear focus on the Earth's surface temperatures is important and it is often what is being addressed by those who have contrary views to mainstream climate science. Global summaries of the data for surface temperatures are currently put together by three different groups. Some of the graphs presented in the IPCC WG1-AR4 were focused on the data from the Climatic Research Unit, University of East Anglia (UEA), which go back to 1850 and whose details have been covered in recent scientific papers. However, each of the other two groups has also produced analyses of slightly different sets of temperature records, all three have quantified their uncertainty ranges for the warming trends, and there is no significant disagreement.

The average global surface temperature fluctuates by several tenths of a degree from year to year, so identifying trends requires a focus on long-term averages. Prior to 1930, the ten-year running average was fluctuating slowly by about 0.3 °C. Then there was a sharper warming of about 0.2 °C from 1930 to 1940, followed by a fall of the same amount to 1950. Particularly in the southern hemisphere, the timing for this warm period links to the Second World War and there are still questions as to whether that caused some shifts in the pattern of data collection. However, since the 1970s a warming trend has emerged more clearly and this has averaged at about 0.15 °C per decade.

Cold weather in parts of North America and much of Europe during the 2009–10 winter probably made a lot of people think that global warming had completely reversed. But this shows the strong differences that can occur between some geographic regions and the rest of the planet because, while there were frigid conditions and adverse effects in Europe, it was unusually warm in the Arctic and elsewhere. Heavy snowfall in the cold areas can be linked to an air flow bringing in more water vapour from the warmer areas. Extremes in our weather are steadily becoming more common and are not always heat waves.

Some have argued that warming trends have occurred because the measurement sites became affected by local increases in population and growing energy use. However, the sites where this may be significant are generally being removed by the research groups. But, more significantly, a careful look at the data shows that increasing urbanization cannot be a significant factor in this measure of global warming because the greatest rates are occurring in areas that are remote from high population or energy use. Warming has been larger on the western side of the USA than on the more heavily populated eastern side; higher in the north of Canada than in the south where nearly all the people and industry are located; higher in the far north of China than around the major centres of development in that country. Even more clearly, the data show very high rates of warming in Greenland as well as a pattern of warming across the oceans that does not relate to shipping routes.

Another critique of the evidence for climate change comes from claims that warming stopped in the year 1998, which the UEA data still show as the warmest year on record. But that was a year in which a very strong El Niño event occurred and these are closely linked to shifts in the distribution of heat between the atmosphere and ocean that cause a temporary, and sometimes significant, warming over much of the Earth's surface. Ten years ago, climate science did not say that 1998 provided any new evidence for an increase in the long-term global warming trend because the science recognizes variability and does not focus on individual years. So why should the recovery from that anomalous spike in temperatures now be called evidence for global cooling? When the last twenty-five years were being used to define recent average warming trends in the WG1-AR4 some of us looked very carefully at the temperature records to make sure that these trend estimates were not significantly influenced by the choice of start and end years. They were not. But some critics of the science do not seem to apply the same standards.

As already mentioned, the scientific perspective on climate change is much broader than just considering the Earth's surface temperatures. Satellite measurements of atmospheric temperatures, several kilometres above the Earth's surface, have shown more variability, but with a closely comparable warming trend, since they started in 1979. There is also independent evidence that the amount of atmospheric water vapour is increasing to a degree that is consistent with the warming, and that oceans are now warming down to a depth of 3,000 metres. The amount of ice floating in the Arctic Ocean has been declining for twenty-five years, then it dropped very dramatically in 2007, after the WG1-AR4 was finished, and has not recovered to a longer-term average.

The major ice sheets on land in Greenland and Antarctica are melting at increasing rates, and mountain glaciers have been shrinking for decades, both of which can now be linked to an increase in the rate of sea-level rise in the last few decades. Those who argue that the planet is not warming are only taking a very limited view of small aspects of all this available information and have no way of explaining the remarkable pattern of consistency. That consistency from many independent sources led the IPCC assessment to conclude that the evidence for warming is now 'unequivocal'.

Can we be sure about the reason for warming?

This leads to the second key issue in climate science, which is objective consideration of what might be causing the changes. While, in some areas, people work with numeric trends in data, and then use statistical analyses as a basis for projecting what may happen next, that is not done in science. Climate change is an area where it is particularly important to diagnose the causes of recent changes in terms of basic physical properties. Attribution to causes requires a carefully balanced comparison of the options and a quantitative analysis of whether observations can be explained by one of the possible causes or by some combination of them.

A consistent framework for this uses the concept of radiative forcing which quantifies the extent to which changes in the atmosphere's composition, characteristics of the Earth's surface, or the incoming solar energy alter the rate of heating that occurs in the lower part of the atmosphere. Increases in greenhouse gases lead to more absorption of heat in the atmosphere's lower few kilometres which is then linked to a drop in the amount going into the stratosphere. Cooling of the stratosphere is well documented but this is mainly due to ozone depletion caused by chemical reactions with some specific gases, rather than just to an increasing greenhouse effect.

Aerosols are the very small particles formed from smoke or dust that tend to scatter incoming sunlight away and lead to a cooling effect in the lower atmosphere as well as to changes in cloud properties. Major volcanic eruptions can also cause changes in the stratosphere which lead to drops in surface temperatures but these recover over a year or two and there is no evidence for a long-term trend in the frequency of these eruptions.

The WG1-AR4 produced the first quantification of uncertainty ranges for all these key factors and so led to a new level of confidence for estimates of the total anthropogenic effects on radiative forcing. The central estimate was 1.6 watts per square metre and, to compare that with a possible warming caused more directly by human activities, it is about fifty times larger than the rate of energy production due to all our use of oil, natural gas, coal, nuclear power and hydroelectricity.

These anthropogenic effects in the atmosphere still have to be considered alongside changes in the incoming solar radiation and there is good evidence that past changes in the magnitude of solar radiation have led to global warming and cooling. However, the best estimate for changes in solar radiative forcing from 1750 to 2005 is that they added about 8 per cent more to the net warming due to greenhouse gases after including the cooling effect of aerosols. There is also a small eleven-year cycle in solar activity and the lack of any significant eleven-year cycle in global surface temperatures sets another constraint on the extent to which observed warming might have been driven by the Sun.

Despite this, some have argued that the recent global warming could be attributed to changes in solar radiation if these were actually much larger than we currently estimate them to be. While it is important to consider uncertainties in science, an objective approach must consider the full range of potential causes and not simply focus on the one we might prefer. Also to follow 'Occam's razor', the range of causes should not be extended beyond what is necessary for an explanation. So to argue that some unknown factors might be causing an amplification of the solar effects, while ignoring that the combined effects of greenhouse gases and aerosols already provide a good explanation for what is happening, is not a balanced approach.

Explanations of climate change then have to go into considering how the changes in radiative forcing affect our temperatures and other aspects of climate. While Arrhenius simply considered the effect of CO_2 on temperature, climate science is now based on much more detailed analyses of all the major processes influencing our climate. The only way of bringing these together is through the use of climate models that set up a quantitative way of combining the very large number of physical processes that are involved.

Some argue that the enormous complexity of climate models means that the results they produce can just be manipulated by those who build the programs and so cannot be trusted. However, scientific use of models is strongly based on determining whether a model correctly reproduces past changes before it is considered as a credible basis for making projections into the future, and so most of the supercomputer time is being spent checking the models against observations.

As more detailed internal structure was developed for the climate models, they started to reproduce more of the systematic details such as the variation in temperatures from equator to pole and from summer to winter. By the time of the last IPCC assessment, many peer-reviewed papers could now show that climate models were also able to cover patterns of change in water vapour, short-term variations such as the El Niño Southern Oscillation and the observed frequency of tropical cyclones.

Scientists will always see things that they want to improve, but there is already a very clear basis for using these models to consider how increases in radiative forcing can be expected to cause warming and other climate changes. The key result comes from comparing past temperatures over the last 100 years with climate model runs that can switch on or off the different potential causes of change. This has shown very clearly that, if the radiative forcing due to anthropogenic factors was not included, then we could not explain the warming that had occurred since 1970 – whereas when that forcing was included, most of the warming and the way it has changed over time were explained.

Another important advance coming from the WG1-AR4 was that this explanation of warming could be broken down into spatial detail showing that climate models correctly reproduce the warming rates being larger over land than over the oceans. Similarly, they reproduced changes at the continental scale in Africa and South America where the long-term trend is clearer because there is less inter-annual variability than in North America and Europe.

While a small number of climate scientists have argued that an increased greenhouse effect may not produce much change in surface temperatures due to compensating feedbacks, there is no clear physical basis for that. Science is based in identifying cause and effect and, because the patterns of warming are closely consistent with what can be explained by an increasing greenhouse effect, the WG1-AR4 went well beyond the previous IPCC assessment of climate change and concluded that 'Most of the observed increase in global average temperatures since the mid 20th century is *very likely*[3] due to the observed increase in anthropogenic greenhouse gas concentrations.'

More information on the attribution of climate changes to potential causes comes from paleoclimatic studies of what has happened in the past. These are important because they provide information on a wider range of changes than have been observed over the last 150 years. But, while that can be very valuable for our understanding, a careful treatment of the limits to what we know about the past is also important.

Much criticism of the mainstream climate science in this area has been focussed on a temperature record, produced by Mike Mann and colleagues in 1999, which introduced a new way of combining different sources of data that reflect past temperature changes, and the title of their paper was explicitly qualified by the words 'Inferences, uncertainties and limitations'. A key figure from that showed an inferred variation in northern hemisphere temperatures going back to AD 1000, with significant variations in the past but with the twentieth century clearly moving into a new type of warming trend. This was included in the IPCC *Third Assessment Report* (TAR) and, as one of those at the plenary meeting that finalized the 'Summary for Policymakers', I can say that the figure was placed there at the request of governments, not the authors.

While questions can be raised about combining many different indicators of temperature changes, the critics tend to overlook several things. The TAR also contained another figure showing a comparison of the Mann et al. estimate of long- term temperature changes with two other studies that had implied an even greater rate of warming over the last four centuries and that were based on simpler methods. A subsequent review by the US National Research Council did find reasons for using rather more conservative language to describe the results. But it also found no basis for rejecting them, and it summarized further new sources of data that also showed the second half of the twentieth century had become unusually warm.

In the WG1-AR4 we had, for the first time, a whole chapter devoted to an assessment of our understanding of the paleoclimate and this showed twelve different estimates of temperature changes over the last millennium, most of which still show a larger warming over the last four centuries than was given by Mann et al. and then so heavily criticized. While it is necessary to be careful with the amount of weight that is put on interpretations of the past, the growing consistency across many different studies provides reasonable confidence that global temperatures in the latter part of the twentieth century became warmer than for any multi-decadal period during the last 1,000 years. It is a field in which contrarian views are simply not covering the wide range of consistent information coming from many scientific studies.

Some have also challenged the interpretation of temperature changes over much longer time periods and the information that comes from the warm periods that occurred between ice ages over the last 1 million years. Ninety years ago, Milutin Milankovitch linked these big changes in past climate to changes in the Earth's orbit around the Sun, which slowly, over tens of thousands of years, moves from having large differences between summers and winters to having just moderate differences. But the temperature records, which are locked away in the fine details of ice cores retrieved from Greenland and Antarctica, show that much more rapid changes occurred in the Earth's temperature.

So, while some argue that, because past temperature changes precede CO_2 concentration changes, there cannot be a connection between them, this ignores the fact that changes in the amount of incoming solar energy are not large enough to explain the magnitude or the speed of the climate changes that occurred. The scientific explanation for ice ages and the intervening warm periods has to bring in links to the planet's internal structure and how these amplify the direct effects of a change in orbit around the Sun. The key feature learnt from the past interglacial periods is that this planet's response to some driving forces can involve major restructuring of our biogeochemistry and atmospheric composition which then feed into further change in climate. So changes in the major greenhouse gases, CO_2 and methane, are not expected to always precede the first temperature changes but they are still strongly linked to the magnitude of the changes that do occur.

Where can climate go in the future?

This leads me into the third aspect of the physical science of climate change which is about quantifying what can happen in the future. A key factor in this regard is 'climate sensitivity', which is defined as the amount of global warming that would result from a doubling of CO_2 in the atmosphere. For more than thirty years, climate science had only been able to put forward the range of 1.5–4.5 °C for this. But again we made significant progress in the WG1-AR4 by considering a wide combination of analyses of recent warming, as well as warming that occurred over longer timescales in the past. For the first time it was possible to provide a best estimate of 3 °C for climate sensitivity, together with the judgement that there was at least a 66 per cent probability that this fell within the range 2–4.5 °C.

This shows that climate science sometimes finds higher levels of concern for the future, because many of the studies that had taken place over the last two decades had been based on using 2.5 °C as a working estimate for climate sensitivity. That was derived as the logarithmic mean of the limits for the range that had been given earlier. Unfortunately, things seem to be turning out a bit worse than we had hoped.

A policy-relevant consideration of future climate change has to go beyond just determining climate sensitivity and use carefully tested climate models in conjunction with projections for the future emissions of greenhouse gases and aerosols, as well as land-use change. In this context it needs to be made clear that the difference between a projection and a prediction occurs because there is no scientific basis for predicting the amount of greenhouse gases that will be emitted every year during the rest of this century and beyond. Human behaviour falls outside the physical sciences.

The basis for considering future climate change is to examine a wide range of emission scenarios that cover a range of internally consistent future changes in population, technology and social development. There are many such scenarios and some have argued that we should use averages. However, because individual scenarios consider different alternatives for the development and uptake of energy technologies, the average involves a spread across many different options and so may not be economically sustainable. The range is more important than the average.

A set of forty scenarios for greenhouse gas emissions was developed in the late 1990s by several different groups and summarized in the IPCC's *Special Report on Emission Scenarios*. Six illustrative marker scenarios were established to span the wide range of options and these have, over the last ten years, been the basis for much of the climate modelling for the future. The lowest of these marker scenarios is broadly consistent with stabilizing climate change at the end of the twenty-first century, but in general these do not cover climate stabilization. New scenarios that do address stabilization have been developed more recently but these were not available in time for the detailed climate modelling that was covered in the WG1-AR4 report. Since then a growing emphasis on cross-disciplinary studies of climate stabilization has set up closer links between scenario construction and climate modelling which will be used in the next assessment.[4]

Presenting the results from climate models that cover a range of different scenarios has previously led to some misrepresentation of the science. In the TAR, results were shown as the merged range covering all available climate models, as well as all of the six marker scenarios. That led to later statements in 2006 in both *Time* magazine and *The Economist* saying that there was such a wide range of warming estimates coming from the science that it raised concerns about the urgency of addressing the issue. When we were putting the WG1-AR4 summary together, I persuaded my colleagues that we should not confuse uncertainties in climate science with the range of human choices about future emissions, so we kept the different scenarios quite separate, but unfortunately some other summaries of that report have mixed things up again.

The lowest emissions scenario used in the WG1-AR4 leads to a global average temperature trend comparable to or slightly above the current rate of warming but with a slowdown toward the end of this century and a net warming in the 2090s, relative to pre-industrial time, of 1.6 to 3.4 °C. For the highest of the emission scenarios, the rate of global warming is projected to have roughly doubled by the 2090s, with the net warming by then ranging from 2.9 to 6.9 °C. In all these cases global warming would continue into the next century.

However, a focus on global averages can be misleading. Much of the continental land area warms by about twice the global average, and the Arctic warms by even more. Both these features are already being reflected in recent surface temperature trends. Similarly, the effects of climate change on rainfall are not changes in the global average but rather in the intensity of contrasts between wet and dry regions, and climate models generally show that the wet areas get wetter and the dry ones get drier. This is also linked to increases in heavy rainfall events, as well as in the duration of droughts. In many respects it is the potential intensity of extreme events and a growing frequency for these that is the most serious implication of continuing climate change.

Confidence and uncertainties in science

Rather than go into more detail about the projections for future climate change or their implications, I would like to switch to a short summary of the emphasis that is placed on scientific confidence and uncertainties in the IPCC process. Why do we put terms like *very likely* in italics?

The 'Executive Summary' of the IPCC's *First Assessment Report* started with the words 'We are certain of the following'. This was then followed by sections headed up as 'We calculate with confidence that', and then 'Based on current model results we predict'. Clearly these assessments go beyond scientific reviews that appear in some of the top journals. Instead, the IPCC assessments are designed to have broad teams of experts go through the available scientific information very thoroughly and arrive at a careful consideration of the quality of information.

Some have mistakenly argued that the IPCC assessment process is designed to create consensus. However, while that is an underlying tendency in science, it is definitely not the purpose here, and Susan Solomon, the Working Group I Co-chair for the AR4, emphasized this to our authors more than once. In fact the word 'consensus' occurs only once in the entire definition of procedures for the authors, and as follows: 'Lead Authors are required to record in the Report views which cannot be reconciled with a consensus view but which are nonetheless scientifically or technically valid.'

So the instructions to authors state quite explicitly that the purpose is not to manufacture a consensus, or be limited to the range of a current consensus, but rather to cover the full range that can be seen as valid. This established the need for a clearer framework for covering uncertainties, rather than just guessing the best numbers.

As an aside to this, I was recently asked to present a summary of the last IPCC assessment to an annual meeting of judges from Australia and New Zealand. Being judges, they spent more time asking questions than listening to my summary and they were specifically interested in how the science dealt with uncertainties. One said that he preferred to have engineers giving expert evidence in his courts rather than scientists, because scientists always seemed to be arguing about the best number whereas engineers just stated a range and moved on to the implications. Fortunately, I was able to show that in the IPCC assessment process we do have a more comprehensive approach to uncertainties.

The IPCC's *Second Assessment Report* opened up the need for more detailed approaches to uncertainties in climate change and, as a prelude to the TAR, a group of scientists developed a clearer framework for consistent language for expressing different levels of confidence. However, in completing that assessment it was found there was some divergence in approach between WG1 and WG2, which reflects some structural differences across disciplines.

In preparing for the AR4, a senior French scientist, Michel Petit, and I ran a cross-disciplinary workshop on uncertainties and risk management. We had very pertinent contributions coming from the re-insurance industry and government planning groups who have to work with uncertainties and risks. The meeting was followed by discussions involving lead authors across all IPCC working groups, which took about a year and a half to produce a short four-page summary of consistent ways of addressing uncertainty, depending on the type of information that was being considered and its sources. This is raising new challenges because climate change is steadily moving us into circumstances for which there is little or no past experience and so we face growing difficulties in quantifying the risks.

A clear approach to uncertainty means that we need to distinguish between confidence in the depth of understanding of the underlying science and the ability to quantify the likelihood or probability for specific outcomes. While these are connected, there is a structural difference. For an issue like the impacts of climate change on future agricultural production, a large source of uncertainty arises from limited knowledge of the range of potential advances that can arise from ongoing research into food production. Whereas for an issue like future sea-level rise, we know all the basic causes but there is considerable difficulty in making quantitative projections for the amount that will be caused by loss of the major ice sheets.

New issues are emerging

Our research is becoming based on more extensive sets of data and deeper analysis but the climate is starting to change more rapidly as well. There is more than one example of new issues arising from this, but here I will comment briefly on rapid developments in our understanding of sea-level rise.

Large rises in sea level can have major effects on society because so much of our population, and so many centres of economic production, are located close to coastlines. For more than fifty years it has been recognized that global warming can cause a rise in sea level for two reasons. First, warming of the oceans causes the water to expand slightly; and second, melting of glaciers and ice sheets puts more water into the oceans.

Thermal expansion of the oceans can cause sea level to rise by more than a metre for even quite modest amounts of global warming, but there are uncertainties in quantifying how rapidly the additional heat goes into the ocean and how it is distributed between the surface and the deep ocean. Melting of mountain glaciers and snow fields can also make a significant contribution to sea-level rise, but it is the major ice sheets in Greenland and western Antarctica that are the largest potential cause and they have total volumes equivalent to a sea-level rise of about 6 metres and 3 metres, respectively.

Climate model analyses that were available for the WG1-AR4 were estimating that ocean thermal expansion would be responsible for about 65 per cent of sea-level rise this century with the remainder being due to the loss of glaciers and the Greenland ice sheet. These models also estimated that snow fall over the Antarctic would increase more quickly than melting at the edges of the ice sheets, thus leading to an accumulation of ice and so some reduction in the total amount of sea-level rise.

However, separate chapters covering current changes in snow, ice and frozen ground as well as the direct observations of current sea-level rise, were raising new questions. Coastal records of past sea-level rise, going back more than 100 years, were showing that the global average rate of rise was increasing and satellite measurements that started in 1993 were providing reliable global coverage of the oceans confirming this. In recent decades, the rate of sea-level rise has already been at the top end of the range being covered by models.

This led our 'Summary for Policymakers' to include the careful qualifier for the sea-level rise estimates that had been given: 'Larger values cannot be excluded, but understanding of these effects is too limited to assess their likelihood or provide a best estimate or an upper bound for sea level rise.'

Before summarizing the more recent information on sea level, I want to make a key point about the IPCC process, which is that in the WG1-AR4 we had to be careful not to insert subjective comments on sea-level rise, despite the fact that this was clearly becoming a major question. Our report was criticized by a few who wanted to emphasize sea-level rise and some of us then countered with a firm rebuttal,[5] pointing out that the assessment process had to be based on existing peer-reviewed literature and not on new ideas. Also, a simple statement that recent rates of sea-level rise were high, relative to the climate models, could not be justified at that stage because it was not clear whether all the sea-level rise was due to climate-related effects or whether there was some significant contribution from other causes such as slow continental drift and associated land movements.

However, in the last three years the science has advanced rapidly and a very large number of peer-reviewed scientific papers have now led to significant developments in our understanding. Extensive coverage of ice sheet changes in both Greenland and Antarctica are coming from several different satellite instruments and have provided strong evidence that both have had an accelerating rate of melting over the last two decades. In 2008, a new compilation of available data produced a carefully balanced budget for the different causes of sea-level rise over the period 1961 to 2003 which covered the increase in the rate and showed that glacier and ice sheet loss were already responsible for about 60 per cent of the rise.

It is clear that climate models now need to cover new levels of detail for ice sheet changes. But this also raises the broader issue of projections into the future because it is becoming increasingly clear that we are moving into a world that is being influenced by new processes for which there is not a lot of scientific data. Recent estimates of future sea-level rise have come from extrapolations of the past or by developing better analyses of the rates that occurred 125,000 years ago when the planet warmed by more than 2 °C due to natural causes. My compilation of estimates coming from many publications by different groups shows a median estimate for sea-level rise by 2100 now being just over 1 metre, but several estimates have ranges going up to 1.5 metres and more. This has also been reflected in government reviews carried out in the Netherlands and Australia that have each now set a planning level of 1.1 metres by 2100, and in California it is proposed to set that at 1.4 metres.

Why is this serious shift in our scientific understanding of the impacts of climate change not well covered in the news media, even though it is being accepted by some governments? What is it that makes the news media echo criticism of some minor parts of the last assessment, even though, for very serious issues, it is becoming increasingly obvious that the IPCC assessment process is conservative.

How is society responding to climate change?

The stealing of emails from the University of East Anglia and a rapid growth in criticisms of the IPCC AR4 started in late 2009 and appear to be linked to the timetable for the UNFCCC meeting in December that had been intended to set up a clearer framework for planning the reduction of greenhouse gas emissions. These events probably did not make much difference to government positions as they had been established many months earlier. But the media coverage became intensive.

The WG2-AR4 chapter covering the effects of climate change in Asia made the statement that global warming could lead to the Himalayan glaciers 'disappearing by the year 2035'. This has been heavily criticized and it is now hard to understand why the statement was ever made. Some have argued that it is a misprint and should have said 'by the year 2350', others have said that the very short paragraph is confusing and the statement was extreme, and then some have implied that this means everything on the other 975 pages of the report is wrong also.

At this stage I suspect that it is no longer possible to discover why the statement was made. However, it opens up issues about the review process for the IPCC reports because very similar wording survived two rounds of open review by both experts and governments. All the review comments and author responses are a matter of public record and they show that, while the Japanese government did question the authors' confidence in this particular statement, no reviewer was saying it was wrong. In retrospect it seems clear that these reports do require a higher standard of review. For the WG1-AR4, our co-Chair Susan Solomon had initiated that approach herself by ensuring that a range of experts had agreed to review each chapter so as to be sure that the 'open review' process was thorough.

But one also has to ask why those who are now putting the WG2-AR4 through this intense scrutiny did not do so when those drafts were available for open review? So the other side of this story is that some seem to want to find any reason to discredit the report after it comes out rather than ensuring that it comes out correctly in the first place.

The spate of criticism of the WG2-AR4, which featured strongly in the news media, raised other issues of poor wording or misleading references. Some criticized the IPCC authors for citing a report by the World Wildlife Fund but a good news reporter would have dug into that and seen that those statements were based on peer- reviewed science literature in major journals. The IPCC authors should have cited the original sources, but there is no reason for saying that their statement was wrong. In some cases the media are now retracting positions that they took earlier this year, so perhaps it is being seen as something of a storm in a teacup.

The United Nations request for the InterAcademy Council to conduct a review of the IPCC process can definitely lead to some improvements in the process. Given the seriousness of climate change, there may also be a good case for conducting such reviews more often. But this then raises the question of how the quality of public comments on the science by some in the media and by organizations promoting contrarian views could also be improved.

This leads me back to the analogy with how Galileo's discovery of the solar system was treated. In that context, some who hold a contrarian view on climate change science are actually claiming that they are playing the role that Galileo did 400 years ago. I cannot agree with that as it could only make sense if their views had a strong basis in scientific observations which would then be appearing in peer-reviewed papers in the science literature. The open structure of scientific journals and their lack of ties to any particular research outcomes does establish a clear difference from the world that Galileo lived in.

A divide between science and society could still get wider, because the quality of our understanding of climate change can only really be assessed within the science community, and so the question becomes whether or not scientists will be trusted. The public perspective is harder to define objectively and I think the findings of many of the opinion polls are just confusing. Clearly some vested interests are opposed to reductions in greenhouse gas emissions, and then there are others who hold strong personal viewpoints which are being propagated through a multitude of web pages. This can resonate with those in the media who are always looking for controversy.

However, there are now layers of our social structure that are neither tied to basic science nor driven by erratic media and which are steadily adapting to a world with climate change. A recent example comes from this year's US *Quadrennial Defense Review Report* which identified climate change as now having 'significant geopolitical impacts around the world contributing to poverty, environmental degradation, and the further weakening of fragile governments'. That major military report identified climate change as now being a serious issue to be considered when planning future national defence. From a totally different perspective, some shipping companies are now planning to exploit the loss of Arctic ice sheets by opening up more efficient avenues for transport than continuing to use the Suez or Panama canals.

The UNFCCC seems to be making slow progress, but the recently appointed Executive Secretary, Christiana Figueres, has explicitly noted that the international politics was moving more slowly than the climate. This means that the quality of scientific projections is probably going to be tested even though that is not what most of us would want. Recognition of the need to manage future impacts is becoming more widespread at international, national and local levels. This is also propagating into the private sector as shown by growing concern in the re-insurance industry that climate change may be reducing the size of their market as risks become less predictable.

About ten years ago some social scientists started to point out that the key issues arising from climate change were no longer to do with our understanding of the physics that controls the Earth's temperature. Rather, it had become a matter of how society can respond to a growing need for rapid structural change. The issues go beyond traditional politics and economics because they have growing implications for our grandchildren. Climate change is now primarily a matter of social psychology.

Notes

1. Rodhe and Charlson (1998).
2. Some argue that Margaret Thatcher later reversed her position on climate change science, but this point is made to simply reflect on process rather than individual opinions.
3. The probability for this is assessed as being more than 90 per cent.
4. Moss, Edmonds, Hibbard et al. (2010).
5. Solomon, Alley, Gregory et al. (2008).

Bibliography

Moss, R., Edmonds, J., Hibbard, K. et al. (2010) 'The Next Generation of Scenarios for Climate Change Research and Assessment', *Nature*, 463.

Rodhe, H. and Charlson, R. (eds.) (1998) *The Legacy of Svante Arrhenius – Understanding the Greenhouse Effect*, Stockholm: Royal Swedish Academy of Sciences, Stockholm University.

Solomon, S., Alley, R., Gregory, J., Lemke, P. and Manning, M. (2008) 'A Closer Look at the IPCC Report', *Science*, 319.

3

Global Shocks, Global Solutions: Meeting 21st-Century Challenges

Ian Goldin

My aim is to provide some perspectives on the future and to stimulate a conversation which will help us to think about how we begin to understand systemic shocks. The future is always unpredictable and anyone who thinks they are able to foresee the future is certainly wrong. Many will be aware that the financial analysts, and institutions such as the IMF, were unable to foresee what was happening prior to the recent financial crisis. If finance, which has been a long-standing preoccupation of global governance, was overwhelmed, how much more will climate change require a new institutional capacity and focus?

I will explain some of the reasons why we are not able to see the future. This problem is getting worse but it's not a new problem, as shown by a quote from the US Patent Office, which in 1899 wrote that 'innovation had ended'. We have repeatedly seen similar statements from very smart people who are on top of their game. The leaders in technology, in insurance, in government and in economics have repeatedly got it dramatically wrong. So too did Downing Street when it commented just three years before Nelson Mandela was released that there was no chance of this happening.

It is not because people aren't smart and it's not because they don't have the best available information systems that they get the future wrong. It is because of the complexity of change, the pace of change, the way that change always surprises. What we can do is begin to understand how these surprises are likely to manifest themselves and how we can prepare ourselves for them. How can we best prepare to seize the opportunities and meet the challenges of the future?

Let me begin by taking a long look back. Before we look forward, the important thing to stress, particularly for young people today, is that this is a most remarkable time in history – a time unlike any other in terms of the pace, depth and global reach of change. There is more opportunity, there is more integration than was imaginable

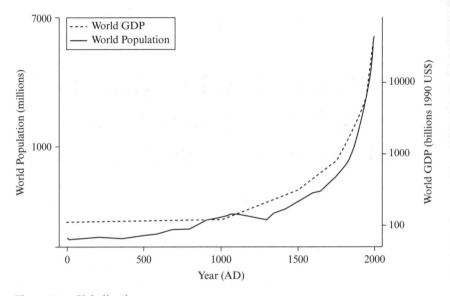

Figure 3.1   Globalization

Source: A. Johansen and D. Sornette (2001)

even thirty years ago. A 2,000-year sweep of GDP and population shows another remarkable trend.

Note that these are exponential growth rates on the Y-axis on the right, so this is a period of exponential change in income. There has only been one other period in the past 2,000 years when income growth exceeded population growth and that was about 1,000 years ago. That was also a period of great innovation, of great migration, of integration, a period when the East came to the West, when the inventions of Islam and China were brought into Western civilization, and vice versa. There was an explosion of what the economists now call endogenous growth arising from innovation, through creation, through new ideas, by people sharing their past experiences and all of their past histories of innovation.

There have also been great setbacks in globalization, not least during the World Wars. This is not the place for a history lecture, but the last thirty years or so have seen another remarkable leap forward, when income growth has exceeded population growth despite the fact that population growth has been extraordinarily rapid. This is a phenomenon which is unprecedented in history. As is evident in figure 3.1, if one takes a long-term perspective on human development, one can see this period as a very, very unusual time in the earth's history: a period of most remarkable development and opportunity.

In the last thirty to forty years, life expectancy at birth has grown on average, in developing countries, by about twenty years. It previously

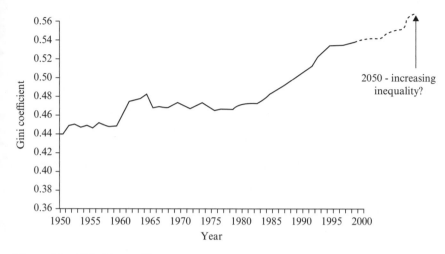

Figure 3.2　Global inequality

Source:　Milanovic (2007)

took around 1,000 years for that sort of improvement to happen – indeed, even longer in many regions. In this same period, illiteracy has halved on earth. The number of poor people living on less than a dollar a day has gone down by about 300 million, despite the world's population increasing by about 2 billion over this period. So these are remarkable times.

If you don't like these measures – and I certainly have great reservations with all of them, crude as they are – do look at other measures. Whichever measure you find – if you go, for example, to the United Nations Development Programme's Human Development Indices and look at connectivity to water, or look at other measures that matter to you – you'll find similar rapid change over these years. But don't be blinded by averages because for individuals what matters is their personal experience. The devil is in the detail for many people. It has been a period of expanding inequality as well. So while we have these massive leaps forward, a great number of people, including what is termed 'the bottom billion', stagnated behind, living in ways that have not changed or improved (Collier 2007). This has led to widening inequality. The Gini coefficient, which measures inequality, has gone up very rapidly. Vast disparities have arisen in virtually every country. There is widening disparity between the achievements of those who have access to the benefits of globalization and those who have not. Although the average is a remarkably positive story, inequality means that the distribution is very skewed (see figure 3.2). While too many people have not shared in the benefits, the majority have enjoyed unprecedented development.

The question, looking forward, is where are we going? Is this going to continue? Is there to be a period of continuing leaps in opportunity

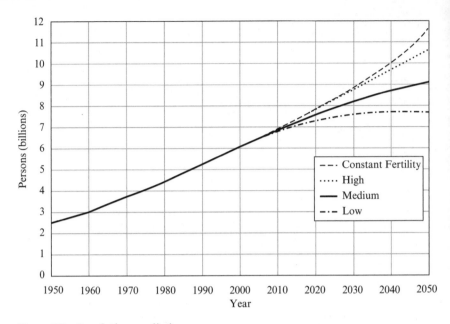

Figure 3.3   Population predictions

Source: UN Population data 2004

in the coming years or are we going to revert to the long-term trend? Is growing inequality going to mean instability and an inability to manage? What are the constraints? The remarkable thing about looking forward, as you'll see from the UN projections in figures 3.3 and 3.4, is the uncertainty even in areas that we used to think were rather measurable.

Social scientists used to think that it was possible to project populations. This is clearly no longer the case. There are currently just under 7 billion people on earth, but it's unclear, by 2050 – only forty years away – whether there's going to be close to 12 billion people or under 8 billion people, a range of over 4 billion, almost two-thirds of the current population of the earth. This range of uncertainty has massive implications for resource use, for economic growth, and, of course, for climate change and environmental degradation, and many other areas.

Why is there so much uncertainty? When we disaggregate by region you begin to get a feel for what's driving it. The dotted lines are projections from current trends; the shaded areas are the range that we expect, with the dark line being the midpoint. You'll see that, particularly in Latin America and Africa, you have very wide ranges. But what's underlying this uncertainty is the two key drivers of demographics, the one being fertility and the other being life expectancy. These together underlie demographic change.

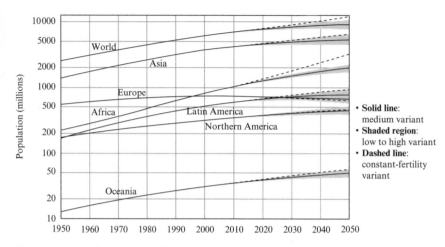

Figure 3.4 Predicted population growth

Source: United Nations Population Division (2007)

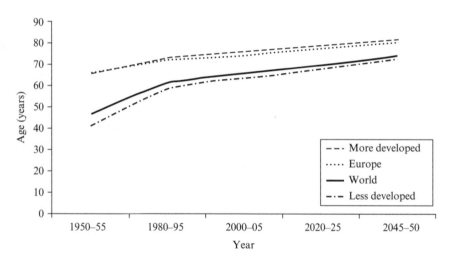

Figure 3.5 Projected life expectancy

Source: Oxford Institute of Ageing (2008)

First, looking at life expectancy (figure 3.5 is from the Institute of Ageing, which is part of the Oxford Martin School of the University of Oxford), what you see is a projection of a very steady increase in life expectancy at birth over all regions, plus a convergence between the different regions over this period. This is an average increase in life expectancy of over two months per year. Anyone born next year, on average, may expect to live for two months longer than someone born this year. That's an increase of around two years per decade. These are, of course, averages again, which mask great discrepancies. In some

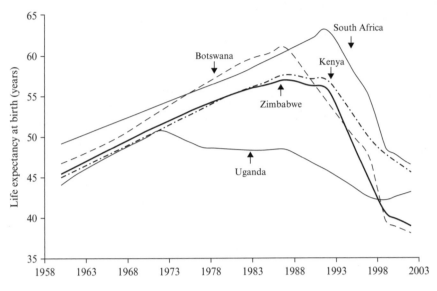

Figure 3.6 Life expectancy

Source: World Bank (2004)

countries like Botswana, life expectancy at birth has gone down from sixty-seven to under forty years over this period because of HIV and AIDS (see figure 3.6). Despite these exceptions, the overall trend is one of massive improvement. How likely are these projections? I think they are rather conservative. I think we will see a more rapid acceleration of life expectancy on average over this time due to the medical changes that are happening. There are those who talk of the current generation being the lucky generation that enjoys the benefits of leaps ahead in public health. It is a very complicated story, but for those who think that how long you live is an important determinant of wellbeing, it is a very positive story. Of course the quality of life is important too and we'll come back to that.

The other key driver of demographic change is fertility and this is where the most unexpected and rapid changes are happening. Many people still tend to think the world's biggest problem will be overpopulation. However, for many countries a future challenge could rather be a lack of workers and a lack of skills. The elderly are particularly vulnerable, as there is likely to be a shortage of workers who pay for pensions and take care, financially and in other ways, of the elderly. Dramatic declines in fertility are projected over the period to 2050, not least in the emerging markets (see figure 3.7). All countries are converging to fertility rates of under 2, which is below replacement level. This may even be on the high side as fertility rates are falling more rapidly than expected. And you see this in one generation. In Taiwan, for example, fertility rates have gone from 7 to under 2 in one generation.

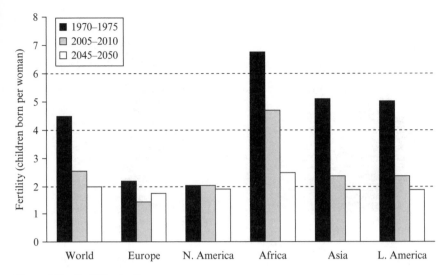

Figure 3.7   Fertility decline

Source: UN Population Division (2007)

In Hong Kong, life expectancy at birth is approaching 100 and fertility is around 0.9. This is dramatic, and in many countries will pose severe social and economic challenges.

We're beginning to understand what lies behind this rapid decline in fertility. It is women's education, it's urbanization, and it's jobs. When women get an opportunity to do a decent day's work, they have fewer children. When society allows women to participate, there is a dramatic decline in fertility. This can be very uneven. In certain provinces of China, because of selection at birth – which is a problem arising from gender discrimination – there are 1.3 males to every female. This will lead to an even more rapid decline in fertility over time, and to too few women in these provinces. These are dramatic but unstable trends. They are the reason why the population projections are so uncertain. They also have powerful implications for labour markets, for pensions, for housing stocks and so on. In the future, inverted pyramids, or skyscrapers, will replace the population pyramids, which people imagine characterize population dynamics. China by 2050 will have a skyscraper, with virtually the same share of people at each decile of the population with a little peaked cap as people in their nineties die (see figure 3.8).

As fewer people support retirees in terms of pension contributions and taxes, as well as services provided in the labour market, the concept of retirement and entitlements will change. It may well be that societies will be worrying more about underpopulation than overpopulation in the future.

Could migration solve this problem? Perhaps in certain localities at

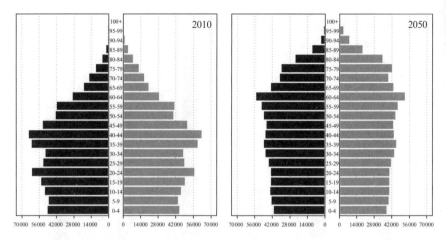

Figure 3.8   China's population 2010 and 2050

Source: US Census Bureau (2009) http://www.census.gov/ipc/www/idb/informationGateway.php

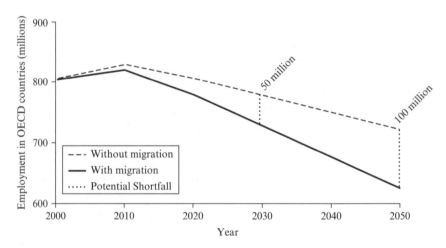

Figure 3.9   Migration potential

Source: Institute of International Migration (2007)

certain times, but not in aggregate terms because the scale of possible migration is simply too small in relation to the scale of the future deficits in the labour markets. In rich countries the number of workers will go down from approximately 800 million to 650 million people in 2050 (see figure 3.9). An influx of 100 million migrants would be four to five times current levels. The other part of the question is: where will the migrants come from? Their societies will also be demanding many more workers. So the ability, or the desire, of people to migrate will be changing dramatically over this time. Indeed we've already seen this with the net emigration of Poles from the UK. I personally believe that

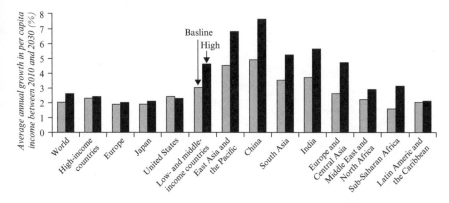

Figure 3.10   Economic growth

migration is absolutely vital, particularly for endogenous growth and innovation, which is key for a dynamic economy and society.

Looking east to India and China, over the long term this is predicted to be an area of continued, wonderful opportunity and growth. These are the World Bank projections, actually produced when I was there, so they're out of date, but the projections are rather robust. Between 2010 and 2030 growth rates for base and high case projections are around 5–8 per cent for India and China. Will the current crisis affect this dramatically? I don't think so. These are long-term projections. I don't think the crisis will change the long-term trends in a very significant way. The remarkable thing about the graph in figure 3.10, looking forward to 2030, is that it looks rather like the past. The last twenty years would not look very different from this. Based on comparative advantage, technological change, demographics and productivity growth, the next twenty years, in terms of the relationship between emerging markets and the rich countries, will look broadly similar to the past twenty years. Emerging countries will be pulling the world economy along, they will be the stabilizing force; that's where the growth is going to be, not in the mature markets.

This is in part due to the transformative experience of the past two decades, with the collapse of the Berlin Wall, with the opening up of China, with containerization, with fibre optics. A whole range of political and technological changes has come together to create a super-charged globalization phenomenon. This supercharged globalization is reflected on multiple dimensions. One can look at many indicators to see this. One can see it in people moving, telecommunications, goods and services traffic, and in the flows of foreign direct investments (FDIs), remittances, equity and capital markets (see figure 3.11). When you unpack this global trend you begin to get a much more nuanced story.

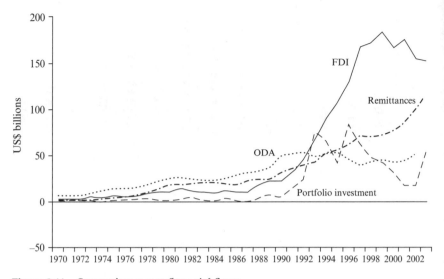

Figure 3.11   Comparing recent financial flows

ODA = Overseas Development Assistance

Source: World Bank (2003)

Many flows are concentrated in China, India and a few other markets. The structural jump in the trends of the financial flows is remarkable.

We now turn to a long view of market indices. This is on many people's minds at the moment. What's happening with the stock markets? When will they come back to equilibrium? Where does it go from here? The extraordinary thing about the equity markets is that they display strong growth over the long term. Composites of the whole world, over 200 years, show a steep upwards trend. If you're planning to live to 100, put your money in equities. The instability behind the trend can lead to sharp setbacks. The overall process is not unlike it was in 1997. When you look at the long view, equity markets are growing. This is associated with population and GDP growth as well as accelerating technological change in certain areas.

So, where is this technology going and what's driving technological change? Is it likely to continue? Change is accelerating. It offers extraordinary opportunities. It also raises major questions.

Looking at computing power, by price, which tells us what average people can buy, figure 3.12 illustrates the exponential growth. This is a continuing trend upwards in available computing power, which has continued for fifty years. Gordon Moore famously predicted in the 1960s that the power of computers would double about every two years. Yet he also said this would run out of steam after about three generations of computers. He was right on the 'power' issue, and we call that result Moore's Law: the ability to double the capacity of computers every few

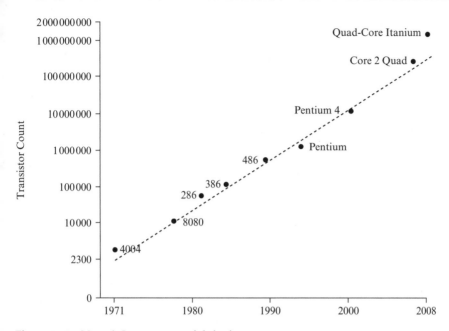

Figure 3.12   Moore's Law: exponential rise in processor power

Source: compiled from various sources by James Martin 21st Century School, University of Oxford

years. But he was wrong on it running out of steam. In fact, leading computer experts will tell you that they don't see any hard barrier to the continued extension of Moore's Law. This is so because, as we begin to reach binding constraints in about ten years' time, when the ability to etch will be defined by constraints of molecular size, other options will be developing, including parallel processing, and then later we may well have quantum computing. So this is unlikely to be constrained and we may approach what Ray Kurzweil (he calls it 'the Singularity') and others see as a turning point in computing history. They argue that exponential growth in technological developments will go on and will overtake our capacity to manage it. The same people also think that, at some point before the mid twenty-first century, computers will become smarter than humans. Now, it is important to realize that exponential growth means that things happen extremely quickly. For instance, the new iPhone has many times the capacity of Apollo spacecraft computers for a tiny fraction of the price. The PlayStation 3 has capacity equivalent to the most powerful computer in the world in 1997, for a fraction of the price. The trend is clear: our technologies become increasingly faster, cheaper, and available almost ubiquitously. Every twenty years, price per power becomes more or less a million times lower. The question is: what do you do with that power? The question is realistic and worth asking.

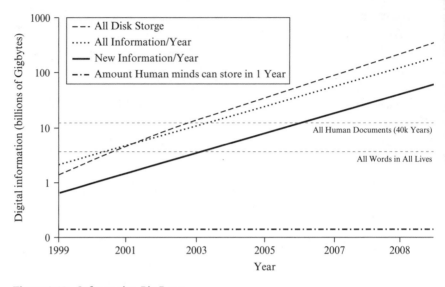

Figure 3.13   Information Big Bang

Sources: Lesk, Berkeley SIMS, Landauer, EMC

One option for using so much technological power is to run data: every day there are 20 billion Google downloads. This is one possible, and indeed interesting, representation of it: our ability to store, harness and capture information in ways that exceed anything imagined before (see figure 3.13). Every year more information is being produced than in the whole history of mankind before. Clearly this is one of the uses of increased technological and computing power. Every couple of months we produce more documents than we have produced in more than 40,000 years of human history. These are billions of gigabytes, and way in excess of what we can have in our minds. So the question is: what do you do with it? How do you interact with it? How do you begin to use it in ways that are useful not only for you, but for society? What is the implication of this when information becomes so widely dispersed and so available? Is it going to be constrained by disk storage as some have argued?

The rate of growth of disk storage is even bigger than the rate of growth of information flows. Nowadays you can buy an 80-gigabyte memory stick for a tiny fraction of what you would pay for a 1-gigabyte stick only a few years ago. Trends in storage capacity are also similar in terms of expansion and this means that for the foreseeable future we will be able to continue to rapidly expand the information from networks and computers. But the main questions remain unaltered: what use is this to people? Will this enable us to be more productive? Will it enable us to become more effective? Will it enable us to communicate more, and will this communication lead to greater or smaller divisions among people in the world? These trends have made possible new ways to create communities of all sorts, and also re-established some that were broken by historical and political circumstances. For example an Armenian living in Chicago can now, through Facebook, become part of a global Armenian community, which was unimaginable only five years ago. We are witnessing new processes of identification, new ways of coming together. This changes politics, as we've seen in a number of countries. People communicating by mobile phone or via the internet are more difficult to control and repress. The state can no longer claim, even when it wishes to do so, effective control over information flows. This has dramatic implications for democracy; for knowledge; for who controls what you think, when you think it, why you think it. We are entering a totally different information era and the differences will tend to become starker as the technology unfolds.

A different perspective on how to look at the development of this wide-ranging technological revolution is, of course, the nano-perspective. We still need some time before we can say exactly what this will mean for us, but its developments are being researched in many academic and non-academic institutions and laboratories. In order to get a grasp of what we are dealing with, one has to realize that 'nano' means less than a hundredth of the width of a human hair, or, more precisely, a billionth of a metre. It is a technology invisible to the human eye. This is not science fiction. We're building these things in Oxford.

One of the major issues around nano is its consequences for people. These are tiny, tiny molecular structures, which are very sharp and small, and one of the things the Oxford Martin School is trying to work out, before they become widely available, is their appropriate regulatory environment. First of all, do you really need one? Do you need to control nano, or shall we just let industry do whatever they want with it? That's an extremely important question to ask, because we really don't understand what the consequences would be. What we know instead is that these machines will be things, which we will be able to control. We will be able to have nano machines that run invisibly around our bodies or in the air. Nano sensors could tell where a toxic material is and enable acute sensing of our environment.

A further crucial development is stem cell research. Stem cell research will make it possible one day to create virtually any part of the body from scratch, from a single cell. Recently I saw, for the first time in my, life a throbbing heart cell and a nerve cell created from stem cells. It was one of the most moving moments of my life. If you know anyone who, for example, has a spinal cord injury, you begin to get a sense of what this development can potentially achieve: it could quite simply revolutionize therapy.

We need to understand the determinants of future inequality. Increasingly this will have to do with differential access to new technology. New inequality will put before our eyes – say, in 2050 – a world in which the richest people may be able to overcome spinal cord injuries but poorer people may not be able to afford to pay for the new technologies. As we increase our understanding of stem cells, almost anything will become possible in terms of replacing parts of human bodies. Of course there are major questions which still need to be resolved, including rejection questions. This is only one direction in which medical technology is evolving. The field of medical genetics is similarly exciting.

Tremendous possibilities are developing, via genetic engineering, to identify pre-natal DNA problems that might severely impede healthy lives. The ethical question of course is: how far and where will these developments take us? Are we heading for a new eugenics? As these technologies become more widely available, it will become increasingly possible to create human beings with intentionally predetermined characteristics. We will be able to create our children to be closer to what we find 'perfect' or wish to replicate. But this clearly will not be something which everyone will be able to afford, at least not for the next thirty or forty years. This will be, once again, something which only the privileged – maybe the Swiss, maybe people in Hampstead, but not people in the poorer suburbs of Glasgow, let alone Africa – will be able to afford. The UK's National Health Service (NHS) is unlikely to offer this type of treatment, or at least not in the short term, and if that's true of the NHS, it's even more true of health services in poor countries with a less-developed system of social security.

Society needs to be thinking about how and where these technologies are growing. This is needed because we know that, at least in the early stages of development, such technologies are not likely to be widely available. The latter point raises very difficult questions, because, if the UK, for example, decides that we don't want to do it because it's not equitable to spread the gains of progress so unevenly, this will not automatically imply that our competitors or neighbours will follow us. What if they decide that, after all, they do not have a problem with the ethical or other concerns that led us to stop our path to innovation? What happens to us, relative to them? And this applies not only to medical technologies in a strict sense of the term. These advances will also concern our ability not only to cure people, but more broadly to manipulate and cognitively enhance their performances. So the potential, for example, to sprinkle something on your workers' canteen food to increase their alertness and productivity by 10 per cent will be with us in the not-too-distant future. If you were a CEO, would you do it? And if you don't and your competitor does, what will you do? And if you were the CEO of a truck-driving company and you knew that a high share of your accidents were caused by people falling asleep at the wheel, what would you do then? Wouldn't you see it as a social good? These are very difficult questions, questions that need to be asked, questions that need to be understood as we go forward; the significance of bio-ethical issues of this kind cannot be overestimated.

All the issues I have touched upon have the potential to develop into serious risks. The problem with risk is that it's impossible to measure except with hindsight. But the development of technologies whose consequences we cannot fully appreciate works against our ability to capture risk. We have the risks that we already partially understand, but now coupled with those which we don't really grasp. Although risk is often associated with the idea that we can actually assess a situation from the point of view of its possible consequences, we will face an even more radical type of risk, where the lack of information constitutes a more systemic problem.

Globalization has led to an explosion of growth and wellbeing on earth. However, we now also face risks and vulnerabilities on a scale we have never witnessed before. This is so because we're much more integrated than ever before. This also means that we are much more interdependent than we used to be. Whenever something happens in one part of these new thicker structures, its consequences are greater, because they affect more agents. They also are more unpredictable since the structure is more complex. Take the example of the recent financial crisis. We rightly worry about its consequences for the real economy and what it means and will mean in the future for people's welfare. But it is also worth noting that the speed at which the crisis spread was astonishing. The sub-prime crisis went around the world in little time: almost instantaneously a meltdown in one part of the structure caused other meltdowns or threatened to cause them.

Let me now turn from systemic to catastrophic risk. What's the probability of this existential risk – in other words, the probability of civilization not surviving into the future? This doesn't mean *Homo sapiens* biologically disappearing – there might be outposts of *Homo sapiens* surviving. Rather, what existential risk means is that civilization as we know it may not survive. Lord Rees, President of the Royal Society, puts a 50 per cent probability on civilization not surviving the twenty-first century. Others disagree with him and have put forward different probabilities and rankings. I don't know who has the correct or best answer in this debate, but just for a moment let's assume the risk we face is something like 5 per cent. I believe that would be enough for all of us to make this our Project Manhattan and make sure that we manage this existential risk going forward.

The first question that comes to mind is: where can this existential risk come from? First, it could come from a natural cause, like an asteroid hitting the Earth. A similar event is what many think has led to the virtual extinctions of species in the past. But second, the existential risk could be anthropogenic – in other words, we create the risk ourselves. We could initiate a nuclear war on a planetary scale, or perhaps a manmade climate change disaster. Whatever the possible causes of the extinction of human civilization are, we need to address them. Handling such issues is difficult. The data we have about them are often contradictory, and they change all the time. The evidence that we need to gather to assess existential risk resembles that of a physics phenomenon, with changing states and tipping points which are unpredictable. In attempts to predict hurricane developments and directions of movement, our complex modelling attempts constantly remind us of our very limited abilities: we systematically get it wrong. The hurricane prediction system in the US uses the latest technologies and includes brilliant people: the best of both that you can possibly get. Still, its efforts are frustrated: it often gets it wrong. No matter which centre of prediction you listen to (there are three of them), and how much you readjust their models, on average they are almost always wrong. They cannot predict, a day before a hurricane hits the US coast – as was seen with Katrina – when it's going to hit, how it's going to hit, what's going to happen, let alone predict something much more complex like the global weather system or anything with more global characteristics.

Modelling has its limitations. There are other ways to think about risk. A further option we have is to ask people directly. The private sector uses this practice extensively via risk surveys which try to assess where the greatest risks are to be found. Predictably, they tend to get it wrong too. Sometimes such risk assessments do in fact include some of the things that will eventually turn out to be true. But it is the very nature of such exercises, providing long lists of potential factors or elements of risk, that makes it more likely that part of the answer is indeed correct. The longer the list is, the more it is probable that some of its parts will happen. A long list of potential risks cannot be easily translated into policy options or prescriptions.

Risk commentators tend to be informed by hindsight – in other words, risk isn't really risk, it's yesterday's news. So, if there's a terrorist strike and you ask people what's going to happen, they'll say there's going to be another terrorist strike. Yet we know this is not the correct way to go about it. We understand that future risks simply cannot be informed by past news, yet it seems that the very nature of risk, its being assessed according to the availability of information on a given subject, biases our judgements when we want to address risk in the future.

Pandemics are one major risk. Historically, pandemics have been the biggest risk facing humanity. People often forget that in 1918, just as the First World War was destroying Europe, the Spanish 'flu was killing ten times more victims. At the time, we didn't have information systems analysing the consequences and the impact of the 'flu. Perhaps this explains our inability to learn from the past when it comes to pandemics. And although people seem to have become very complacent about the threat from a global pandemic, this has been, historically, the biggest systemic risk we have faced. What we know is that, from the Plague to global influenzas, risks associated with such forms of illnesses are high. But what we fail to realize, or perhaps to conceptualize, is that it is the very nature of the new global, and complex, system of interdependences that tells us that the risks of new pandemics have greatly increased. Old types of risks recreate themselves in a new, and more integrated, system of human relations, making our assessment of their magnitude challenging and, at the same time, even more urgent.

How should this kind of problem best be managed? One can try to engage in an exercise of very complex modelling to try to work out how to limit the phenomena in one way or another. But how exactly can you construct an effective and responsive drug distribution programme? Do you give it to the nurses, to the young, to the old, to the vulnerable, or do you distribute all over the country? The most sensible answer from our modelling seems to be to distribute the necessary drugs to everybody you can as quickly as possible. Selection processes will cost lives, since they will exclude some and get to others when it is already too late. The only certainty that we can bear in mind is that we clearly face a duty to engage with such issues and to increase our level of awareness and preparedness.

Another major risk is bio-terrorism. The scary thing about this issue is that its associated risk seems to be growing exponentially. Biochemists can now sequence DNA – that is, the DNA of a very complex biological being – or are getting to the point where they can begin to sequence DNA. Why would they want to do that? There are many good reasons, which will advance human wellbeing and the prevention of crushing diseases. However, there is a danger that a small number of mavericks will abuse this extraordinary power.

They could create bio-pathogens that kill many millions of people by recreating smallpox, ebola or another terrible threat. Society urgently needs to understand and manage better these looming new threats.

Climate change clearly is a major risk. I think that most projections are conservative, and this clearly represents a very serious challenge for many people, especially poor people and poor countries. Those who live in places like Bangladesh or the Maldives are clearly more

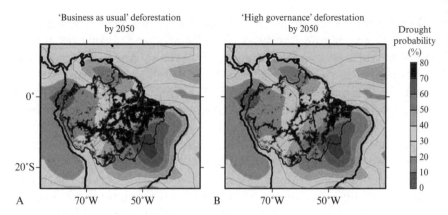

Figure 3.14   Environmental governance

Source: Malhi et al. (2008)

vulnerable to sea-level rises, while people living in the Sahel and many other arid zones are highly vulnerable to rising food insecurity as a result of climate change. Climate change is a risk for humanity of a proportion that will likely lead to many hundreds of thousands of deaths and immense and widespread economic costs. How do we begin to manage this? Is it possible to govern these risks?

The Tropical Forest Group in Oxford has provided figure 3.14, which shows – if you do nothing – how much the forest in the Amazon is going to be destroyed. This is a business as usual, carry on as you are scenario. If a governance structure to control that is put in place, it makes a major difference to managing the risk. There are lots of other ways, of course, to manage the climate change risk. This is just illustrative, but the important thing is to act quickly. Do it now. It requires global, national, local action.

In the previous passages I mentioned some of the vulnerabilities that are associated with current global risks. All of them call for a much deeper global and ethical conversation. Yet the point is not that all these domains of enquiry face us exclusively with negative circumstances. All the technologies that we have (albeit briefly) touched upon have an upside potential which is the counterpart of the hazards they could pose.

The fundamental question is: 'Where do we go from here?' Are we going to be able to use the technologies, including those I have mentioned, and become more effective at managing them? Are we going to address the ethical and social risks associated with them? When you look at structures of governance in these multiple areas, you can understand that there are major problems and many of the global institutions are out of date. We have become much more interdependent. Globalization has led to massive improvements in the quality of life. There are also major concerns because of the implicit inequalities of access associated with these developments. There are also a number of benefits, as well as problems, caused by the fact that many of the global processes we have outlined tend to happen outside state control.

The main point with all of these issues is strikingly similar: there has been an extraordinary growth in integrated challenges to which no one country or community can be the sole solution. These challenges call for processes of global decision-making – from bio-ethical challenges up to the broader ones of climate change, nuclear proliferation, biological weapons. All demand internationally coordinated responses.

We need a global conversation and an ability, at the global level, to manage the planet in a way we simply don't yet have. We have a series of institutions (many of which are already under pressure), at least fifty years old, formed after the Second World War, which are simply unfit for the purpose at hand. The problems we face are structurally different. They add to the pressing issues we face, such as global poverty and inequality. The problems we need to address are urgent, integrated and complex. They require rapid decision-making, and greater amounts of legitimacy, because their solutions need to be applied more widely. Put bluntly, the biggest challenge facing us all is to ensure that the global governance system of the twenty-first century is up to these global challenges. Whether we can meet this governance challenge will determine which way we go from there – whether this will be our best century ever, or our worst. The responsibility on all of us is to ensure a positive outcome. The choices are ours.

Bibliography

Collier, P. (2007) *The Bottom Billion: Why the Poorest Countries are Failing and What Can Be Done about It*. Oxford: Oxford University Press.

Johansen, A. and Sornett, D. (2001) 'Finite-time Singularity in the Dynamics of the World Population and Economic Indices', *Physica A*, 294 (3–4) (15 May).

Malhi, Y. et al. (2008) 'Climate Change, Deforestation, and the Fate of the Amazon', *Science*.

Milanovic, B. (2007) *Worlds Apart: Measuring International and Global Inequality*. Princeton: Princeton University Press.

UN Population Division (2007) *World Population Prospects: The 2006 Revision*, New York: UNESA.

World Bank (2004) *World Development Indicators*, World Bank.

4

The Economics of Climate Change

Alex Bowen and James Rydge[1]

Introduction

Of all the challenges the world will face over the coming century, managing climate change is one of the most urgent and significant. Without strong and decisive action soon to reduce greenhouse gas emissions, the risk of catastrophic changes to the physical geography of the planet is high. Such changes would have major impacts on where and how people can live their lives, and the prospects and security for future generations would be severely undermined. Thus society faces critical decisions over the coming decade that will profoundly shape our future.

Economics has an important role to play in analysing climate change and informing policy. This chapter examines some of the key elements of the economics of climate change. It begins with a brief description of how the scale of the potential impacts of climate change and the risks around them shape the economic analysis. It then examines the core economic issues: the greenhouse gas 'externality'; the important market failures that allow greenhouse gas emissions to grow; and the three core policy instruments that aim to encourage emission reductions.

The world is already committed to a certain amount of climate change from past emissions. Therefore adapting to a changing climate is also a crucial part of societies' response. While rich countries have more resources to adapt – at a cost – poor countries have less capacity to respond and will be hit earliest and hardest. This inequality in climate change consequences places a great responsibility on rich countries, which account for the majority of past emissions, to support developing- country adaptation efforts.

The nature of the relevant science, economics and ethical considerations points to the need for a global deal to tackle climate change. A global deal must be effective, efficient and equitable if it is to succeed.

With strong action and commitment from developed countries, progress can be made toward securing a stronger political deal than was possible in Copenhagen in December 2009.

The scale and risks of climate change

There are several links in the chain of causality from human actions to the impacts of climate change on societies and economies. Each link involves significant risk and uncertainty, so policy on climate change is largely about the management of risk.

People, through their production and consumption decisions, encourage production processes that emit flows of greenhouse gases (emissions). The current level of annual emissions is significantly more than the planet can absorb via the carbon cycle.[2] Thus concentrations or stocks of greenhouse gases in the atmosphere are continuing to rise. Concentrations have increased from around 285 parts per million (ppm) CO_2 equivalent (CO_2e) in the 1800s to over 435 ppm CO_2e today.

If there is no action to reduce emissions, so that the world continues on a business-as-usual (BAU) path, concentrations are likely to increase by 3 ppm per year or more over the coming decades, largely because of the rapid industrialization of developing countries. That would push up concentrations to around 750 ppm CO_2e by the end of this century. There are more than enough stocks of oil, natural gas and coal, capable of extraction at costs similar to today's energy prices, to fuel such increases. In addition, if there is feedback from changes in the carbon cycle induced by climate change, concentrations at the end of the century could be much higher and harder to control. Potential feedbacks include reduced absorptive capacity of the oceans, the retreat of the Amazon rain forest and release of methane from melting permafrost. Although the global slowdown will have tended to lower BAU trajectories of emissions, this is likely to be outweighed by the higher-than-expected growth rates of China and India, which proved remarkably resilient in the face of the world economic crisis.

There is considerable uncertainty about the sensitivity of the climate system to such large increases in concentrations. For example, for stabilization at 750 ppm CO_2e, figure 4.1 indicates around a 50–50 chance of an eventual global mean temperature rise of more than 5 °C compared to pre-industrial levels, with significant risks of a rise much more than 5 °C. Such high temperatures are outside the range of human experience. The planet last experienced such temperatures more than 30 million years ago.

What our climate would look like with such high temperatures and what impact this would have on our ability to live our lives are very

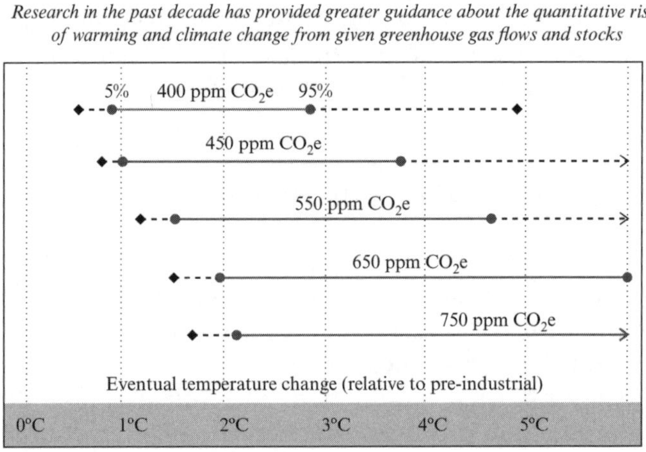

Research in the past decade has provided greater guidance about the quantitative risk of warming and climate change from given greenhouse gas flows and stocks

Figure 4.1   From concentrations to global warming

Source: Stern (2007), table 1.1, Crown Copyright

uncertain, but the mounting scientific evidence discussed elsewhere in this book suggests that major changes to the physical geography of the planet would take place. As a result, where people could live and how they could live their lives would be transformed, probably leading to the forced migration of many millions of people. Given the history of human movement on a large scale, that would be likely to cause instability, poverty and extended conflict.

From the point of view of economic analysis, the key points are that potentially heavy environmental, social and economic costs would ultimately be incurred even for the central estimates of climate sensitivity, and that there is a long upper tail in the frequency distribution of temperature increases. In other words, there is not a small risk of dangerous climate change but a large risk of profound changes to the planet and human life if emissions are allowed to grow unhindered, with some not insignificant upside risk of catastrophic changes.

In response to these risks, many policymakers, informed by their scientific advisors, have agreed to try to limit average global temperature rises to 2 °C above nineteenth-century levels. In particular, the Copenhagen Accord, the product of the United Nations Framework Convention on Climate Change Conference of Parties (COP-15) in Copenhagen in December 2009, agrees that actions should be taken to hold the increase in global temperature to below 2 °C.[3] The 2 °C ceiling has the great merit of having been discussed widely and reflecting a broader range of considerations than usually considered in economists' cost–benefit analysis of small-scale investment projects. However, some economists argue that there should have been more comparison with the costs and benefits of adopting alternative

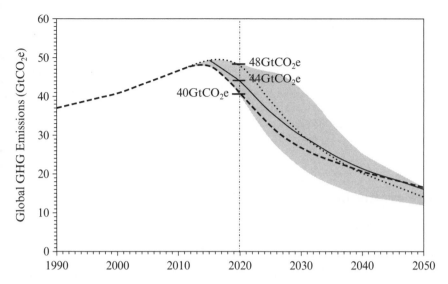

Figure 4.2   Paths for annual global emissions consistent with a 2 °C path

Source: Bowen and Ranger (2009)

stabilization targets, and more attention paid to the costs of reducing emissions at different speeds.

Recent analysis (e.g. Bowen and Ranger 2009) has sketched out global emissions paths over time that would give a reasonable chance (around 50–50) of staying below a 2 °C increase. Figure 4.2 illustrates the range of admissible emissions paths and highlights three. The middle path in figure 4.2 requires annual emissions to peak before 2020 and then to fall, from around 47 gigatonnes (Gt) of CO_2e in 2010 to around 44 Gt in 2020, under 35 Gt in 2030 and well under 20 Gt in 2050 (around 50 per cent of 1990 levels). Other emissions paths consistent with a 2 °C path are possible, and two of these are illustrated within the shaded range. However, less action to reduce emissions now will require faster cuts in the future at rates of reduction that may be very costly and disruptive because of the structural changes entailed, the rise in investment required and the adverse impact on productivity growth, especially if there is continuing investment in traditional carbon-intensive machinery and buildings in the interim.

Cutting emissions on this scale will require strong action across all sectors of the economy, with a focus on energy efficiency, new low-carbon technologies (especially in electricity production and transport) and the reversal of deforestation.

This brief discussion of the risks, scale of the problem and actions required highlights that any economic analysis must be about risk and uncertainty, it must be global in its scope and it must consider long time horizons. Failure to see the problem in these terms is likely to result in poor policy choices that do not adequately reflect the seriousness of the threat. While traditional economic techniques such as project cost–benefit analysis and other marginal analysis techniques are useful as a guide, the primary analysis must consider how to bring about large changes in our economic structures, in particular a transition away from high-carbon to low-carbon growth, while always maintaining the flexibility to accommodate changes in our understanding of the science, economics and ethics of climate change.

The economics of climate change

Market failure

Why are greenhouse gases an economic problem? A thorough answer to this question requires an understanding of efficient markets and market failure. The first fundamental theorem of welfare economics is that, under certain conditions, markets are efficient, in the sense that they generate an allocation of resources such that no-one can be made better-off without someone else being made worse-off. Some of the most important of the conditions are that there are well-defined, exclusive, transferable, secure and enforceable property rights; there are no transaction costs; there is perfect information; there is perfect competition; and there are no externalities. In the real world, some or all of these conditions are violated some or all of the time. When one or more of these conditions is not satisfied, there is an inefficiency and economists refer to this as a market failure. It is then the role of collective action, for example through government policy, to correct the market failure. This will make everyone better-off without making anyone worse-off, a so-called 'Pareto improvement'.

Greenhouse gases are an economic problem as they impose an externality. Therefore they are associated with a market failure. An externality occurs when the benefits or costs of an economic agent's actions fall on other economic agents, and these benefits or costs are not accounted for by the agent responsible. Greenhouse gases represent a 'negative' externality; people, through their production and consumption decisions, impose costs on and disrupt other people's activities, and the emitter does not have to pay for these costs and disruptions.[4] Markets therefore fail, in the sense that they generate prices that do not reflect the true cost to society of our economic activities; these prices do not give the correct signals about where to devote resources. Greenhouse gases entail a unique externality for several reasons: they are global in scope and impacts; they involve significant uncertainty and risk in the scientific chain of causation; they are long-term and governed by a stock-flow process (flows of emissions in excess of the absorptive capacity of the climate system add to stocks of greenhouse gases in the atmosphere); and the effects are potentially huge and irreversible. Stern (2008) describes greenhouse gases as the biggest market failure the world has ever seen.

Economists have a number of standard tools for correcting market failures, with the nature of the failure influencing the appropriate policy choice. Given the particular characteristics of the greenhouse gas externality, a price on greenhouse gases is required. There is general consensus across the economics profession that a price on greenhouse gases is an essential part of the policy response (see Krugman 2010). In addition, the science and the economics suggest that, because a tonne of carbon dioxide does the same damage wherever it is emitted, this price should be the same everywhere (as long as there are appropriate transfers to compensate those who would otherwise suffer).

Policy instruments to price greenhouse gases

A broad and flexible policy instrument is required to price greenhouse gases. Taxes, tradable quotas (cap-and-trade schemes) and regulations are the three policy instruments commonly proposed, or currently used, to price greenhouse gases. Each has different advantages and disadvantages, and in practice a combination of all three policies is likely.

A tax imposes a fixed price on greenhouse gases and provides an incentive to reduce emissions to the point where the tax is equal to the marginal cost of emissions reductions. An advantage of a tax is that it provides price certainty, which is valued by economic agents.

At what level should the tax be set? Standard economic theory suggests that prices should reflect the marginal social cost (MSC) of greenhouse gases – the cost to society of emitting one extra unit of emissions.[5] The level of the tax should be set where the marginal abatement cost (MAC) and the MSC are equal. The MAC is defined as the cost of reducing emissions by one extra unit.[6] However, estimating MACs and MSCs in the real world is very difficult. Estimating MACs requires, amongst other things, assumptions about future technologies and their development. This is very difficult, partly because technological innovation is dependent on how effectively market failures are addressed in this area, and partly because it is impossible to predict the pace of technological innovation. It also requires governments, who set taxes, to have good information about MACs across the economy.[7] Estimating MSCs is even more challenging. They depend on future economic growth, whether policies to halt climate change are in place, the value placed on future generations' wellbeing, assumptions about risk and uncertainty, the strength of the carbon cycle, valuations of non-market and social impacts, climate sensitivity and a range of other factors. There is considerable debate in the economics profession over many of these factors, especially concerning how to take into account different ethical positions about the distributional and intertemporal impacts of climate change and climate policies.[8]

Discounting is central to the valuation of intertemporal impacts as the costs of action are generally front-loaded in time, while the benefits of action will largely accrue to future generations. Discounting has caused much discussion in the economics profession, with differences in moral and ethical judgements about the weight to be given to future generations driving much of the variation across estimates.

One approach to discounting adopts an explicit ethical or moral position, such as the idea that future generations should not be valued less than current generations simply because they are in the future, or they may be more wealthy. This moral assumption results in a low time preference discount rate and leads to a much higher social cost of carbon, increasing the case for strong climate action. A different approach advocates the use of observed or historical market interest rates, arguing that they reveal individual preferences and intergenerational values, and that this avoids the need to make explicit moral judgements. However, a current market interest rate (or historical rate) reflects the current economic growth path and the returns required by investors on existing marketable assets within well-defined risk classes. As climate change policy involves choosing from very different future growth paths, investments in very different assets, and consideration of very different risks from those faced now, using market rates may be misleading. In addition, current market rates apply over relatively short time periods. Climate change will affect future generations 100 or more years in the future, and there are no liquid markets that cover such long periods. Discount rates also differ across time, between people and by the types of goods being valued. Hence it has been argued, for example, that irreversible losses of environmental amenities should be subjected to a lower discount rate than losses to marketed production. In principle, discount rates are endogenously determined, with each different potential growth path having its own unique set of discount factors and rates (Hepburn and Stern 2009). Debate surrounding the calculation of discount rates will no doubt continue.[9]

Given this non-exhaustive explanation of issues and challenges in estimating MSCs, it is not surprising that estimates vary widely. Pearce (2003) surveyed the literature and found that MSC estimates for emissions in a world of BAU ranged from around $3 per tonne to around $100 per tonne. Such a wide range of estimates has led to a wide range of positions on the need for action on climate change, with higher estimates implying greater action is warranted now.[10] In our view, many economists' estimates of the social costs imposed by emissions have failed to reflect either the risks of very bad outcomes or non-market impacts adequately.[11] They have also failed to understand the arguments around discounting and have assumed growth rates that would see future generations significantly better-off than current generations. That may not be the case, particularly in countries that are poor today, if future generations inherit severely degraded environmental assets and a hostile climate.

In a world of risk, uncertainty, imperfect information and different values, it will be impossible to find agreement about precisely what is the 'correct' tax rate. However, best estimates can be made and the assumptions debated, and policymakers can adjust the tax rate as new information arrives and uncertainty is reduced.

An alternative instrument to price greenhouse gases is to use tradable quotas (cap-and-trade). An advantage of a tradable quota system is quantity certainty.[12] A fixed quantity of permits is allocated to firms participating in the scheme (with, say, one permit representing the right to emit one tonne of greenhouse gases). These permits can then be traded on a secondary market with the price of permits or emissions being determined by supply and demand.[13] The price of tradable quotas in the market, like a tax, will provide an incentive to reduce emissions to the point where the marginal cost of emissions reductions is just equal to the permit price. If the firm wishes to emit more than its allocation, it must purchase at the market price permits equal to its extra emissions.

Critical to the effectiveness of a tradable quota scheme is its design. One important design feature is permit allocation. In practice, free or partial allocation of permits on implementation of the scheme may be required to increase its political acceptability. However, less than full auctioning of permits, for example free allocation based on historical emissions, can reduce the effectiveness of the scheme by creating perverse incentives. For example, firms may overstate past emissions to receive excess permits during the allocation process. They then sell these excess permits on the market for a windfall profit. This creates an excess supply of permits, depresses the carbon price and weakens the price incentive. Free allocation also leads to the transfer of an asset to the shareholders of certain firms, rather than to governments, who could use the revenue to support the transition to low-carbon growth and reduce other distortionary taxes. Hence full auctioning of permits should be the ultimate aim when designing a tradable quota scheme.

The experience of the European Union Emissions Trading Scheme (EU ETS), the world's first large-scale tradable quota system, has taught policymakers something about good design. During its first phase

(2005–7), prices were extremely volatile as there was a lack of transparency: the market was unaware of the total allocation of quotas. When market participants became aware of the true situation, prices crashed. The total allocation of permits and the cuts in emissions that they imply must be completely transparent. In the second phase (2008–12), allowance allocations were more transparent and supply was limited. As a result, carbon prices were initially much higher than during the first phase. However, the economic downturn has had a significant impact on prices. As industrial output has fallen, firms have sold many allowances they no longer require to raise cash. Consistently low prices have led some to argue that a price floor (or ceiling) may be appropriate to reduce price volatility and maintain a consistent and sufficient incentive for firms to cut emissions. The EU continues to learn from its experience with the Emissions Trading Scheme; tough quotas, deep and liquid markets, transparency, auctioning of allowances and price limits (floors and ceilings) may help to increase the effectiveness of such schemes. Despite these design issues, the European Environment Agency predicts that the EU-15,[14] with a collective target of an 8 per cent cut in emissions below 1990 levels over the 2008–12 period, will achieve at least an 11 per cent cut.[15] The figure may be higher when the impact of the recession is fully factored in.[16]

The third policy instrument to price carbon is regulation. Regulations, such as emissions standards, are used frequently to deal with specific environmental problems and establish an implicit price.[17] While regulations avoid uncertainty for investors, they are not necessarily efficient. Under imposition of a standard, for example, each firm is told the emissions level they must achieve. However, that ignores firms' individual MACs. Firm A may have a modern production process and be able to meet the standard at a low cost, while Firm B may use an older or less flexible process and face significant costs to achieve the same standard. It may have been possible to achieve the same emissions reductions at much lower cost overall by Firm A doing more and Firm B doing less. Despite this problem, direct regulation has been the most widely adopted form of environmental policy and applied across a wide range of areas from dumping waste in rivers to vehicle exhaust standards.

In practice, all three of the policy instruments to price greenhouse gases are likely to be used over the coming decades. For example, in Europe the EU ETS applies to emissions from large industry, and there are regulations on cars and buildings and taxes on petrol. One important question for policy makers is whether all the instruments are being adjusted with the same target carbon price (or quantity) in mind or whether there is a danger of inconsistency in instrument settings, which may reduce their effectiveness.

Other market failures, policy design and interaction

The greenhouse gas externality is not the only market failure relevant to the climate change problem. A number of other market failures must also be corrected if climate change is to be managed success-fully. For example, policy is required to correct market failures in low-carbon technological innovation and low-carbon investment, which is crucial if emissions are to be reduced at reasonable cost and a new era of low-carbon growth established. These failures range from knowledge 'spill-overs' where innovators are unable to appropriate the full benefits of their R&D (the social returns to R&D appear to exceed the private returns on average by a factor of around four[18]) to financial market imperfections that restrict the supply of 'green' investment capital – problems of risk management in the financial system, exacerbated by current uncertainty about the future path of climate change policies, are holding back funds for low-carbon invest-ment. Other market failures involving asymmetric information are preventing builders and property developers from adopting energy efficiency measures and other low-carbon innovations. And network externalities are inhibiting the establishment of improved electricity grids, new fuel delivery systems and low-carbon urban infrastructures.

There are many policy instruments available to correct these vari-ous market failures. Examples include research subsidies and feed-in tariffs to promote research, development, demonstration and deploy-ment of new technologies; risk reduction through government loan guarantees; building construction regulations; and whole-house street-by-street insulation schemes to promote energy efficiency. A sharp increase in public funding for R&D of low-carbon technologies is required and the establishment of more stable policy regimes is cru-cial to encourage private sector innovation. So also is a new approach to intellectual property rights to ensure that bright ideas are put to use quickly throughout the world.

There are public policy failures to contend with as well, such as fossil-fuel subsidies. These policy failures help to entrench old tech-nologies and slow the pace of the low-carbon transition.

This analysis suggests that multiple policy instruments will be required to correct the multiple market failures; a price on green-house gases on its own will not be sufficient to achieve the cuts in emissions required and drive the transition to a new period of low-carbon growth.[19] Correcting these market failures and reforming public policy, where it exacerbates the problem, should be a primary focus of policymakers.

It is also very important for policymakers to consider how these vari-ous instruments interact. For example, renewables targets may reduce emissions in the energy sector, reducing the demand for allowances in a tradable permit scheme and lowering the carbon price. In addition, poor coordination and/or poor policy design – 'government failure' – may significantly slow the pace of innovation and change. Policy must also be able to adapt and respond to what is learnt about the science, economics and social consequences of climate change.

Promoting a shared understanding of responsible behaviour is also important. The power of behavioural change should not be disregarded in the field of public policy. If households and firms understand the scale and risks of climate change and the actions required, they will shift their preferences away from high-carbon goods and be more willing to recycle, drive less and fly less. That will reduce the power of vested interests and the required intensity of policy.

Costs of action

A wide range of economic models have been used to provide estimates of costs of achieving climate goals, such as stabilizing concentrations of greenhouse gases in the atmosphere at certain levels. 'Bottom-up' models estimate the costs of individual emissions reduction options across sectors (quantities of reductions and costs) and aggregate these, taking the pattern of production as given. 'Top-down' models of costs, in contrast, pay more attention to macroeconomic responses to policies (such as induced changes in relative prices) but tend to have less sectoral detail; some incorporate simple climate models and attempt to estimate the benefits of climate policies as well as the costs.[20]

Within both categories, estimates of the costs of strong climate policies have differed, although not as widely as estimates of the costs of unrestrained climate change.[21] The Stern Review (chapters 9 and 10) used both top-down and bottom-up models, concluding that it would cost around 1 per cent of GDP a year by 2050 (within a range of -1 to +3 per cent) for stabilization of greenhouse gases at 500–50 ppm CO_2e. Scientific evidence since the Stern Review was released suggests that the risks of dangerous climate change are higher than previously estimated (see King in this volume). Hence Stern (2009) recommends initial stabilization at 450–500 ppm CO_2e, with subsequent further reductions (this is roughly consistent with a 2 °C path), and suggests that this is likely to cost around 2 per cent of GDP. Recent research by the International Energy Agency (IEA) (e.g., Enkvist, Nauclér and Rosander 2007; IEA 2009; Edenhofer, Knopf, Barker et al. 2010) estimates around the same level, and several model comparison exercises have suggested that the 2 °C path is achievable at a cost of a few per cent of GDP.[22]

Others are more sceptical about the technologies that will be available at scale and reasonable cost, the degree of substitutability in production and consumption in economies, the speed at which the capital stock can be decarbonized and the capacity of governments to implement cost-effective policies.[23] Other factors that could raise costs include unexpectedly high growth in GDP (and hence emissions), initially easy and cheap energy efficiency improvements that mask the need ultimately to change to low-carbon production methods, and rebound effects whereby energy efficiency improvements that reduce costs and energy prices lead to greater energy use. Recent research has shown the rebound effect may be significant, especially in developing countries (see UK Energy Research Centre 2007).

We interpret these disagreements as implying that rapid decarbonization and the 2 °C target are economically feasible but require an unprecedented effort to make sure that policies are well designed, cost-effective and credible over the long term.

The energy industry must be centrally involved in emissions cuts in the coming decades, given that this sector, broadly defined, is responsible for over 60 per cent of global emissions. Recent research by the IEA estimates the total *incremental* investment required in low-carbon technologies and energy efficiency, to meet a 450 ppm greenhouse gas concentration goal, is US$ 2.4 trillion over the period 2010–20, and US$ 8.1 trillion for 2021–30. This represents around 0.5 per cent of global GDP in 2020 and 1.1 per cent in 2030 (IEA 2009). These levels of investment are significant and ways must be found to attract the necessary finance. Also, other investment may have to grow less rapidly. After all, if the current generation is to leave future generations a better environment and a lower risk of extreme climate damages, it would not be unreasonable for the current generation to bequeath less manufactured capital to them.

While it is important to consider the costs of emissions cuts, an alternative way of framing them is to see these costs as investments in a transition to a more sustainable low-carbon development path. There will be many significant opportunities in the transition for firms, households and governments, and for private investors, including long-term investment funds. Climate change is a 'wake-up call' to pull down the barriers that impede innovation and direct it away from the support of sustainable growth. This transition to low-carbon growth has the potential to be one of the most dynamic and innovative periods in history with investment, technological change and new discoveries transforming our economies and our way of life. The benefits will be significant if the opportunity is embraced.[24] And when low-carbon growth is achieved, there will be significant co-benefits, from the protection of biodiversity in the oceans and forests, to cleaner air due to the shift away from dirty fossil-fuel-based energy sources.

Positive perspectives on this issue are key to motivating constructive action. While the policy challenge is substantial and there are many possible pitfalls along the way, the potential for technological innovation and the role of human ingenuity are vast and must be actively encouraged.

Adaptation

Climate change will affect the entire world over the coming decades, the result of past emissions and current concentrations of greenhouse gases. Societies will have to adapt to the effects of a changing climate. While rich countries can adapt at minimal cost and with relative ease, for example by simply purchasing air-conditioning systems for their homes, offices, cars, buses and trains, developing countries are in a much more difficult position as they have the least capacity to respond. There is also a fundamental inequality that must be addressed: the climate change that will affect developing communities over the coming decades is not of their making (it is largely the result of past rich-country actions), but it will hit them first and hardest and threaten to derail their development efforts. Changing weather patterns, rising sea levels, increased frequency and intensity of droughts and floods, and loss of biodiversity will make life much harder for millions, especially in the developing countries of Africa and Asia.[25]

Given these future challenges, adaptation and development must be intertwined; development plans and adaptation plans must be integrated across the economy. Development that is resilient to climate change will create stronger and more flexible economies. Many international institutions are recognizing this and incorporating climate change adaptation into their development work. For example, the Network on Environment and Development Co-operation (ENVIRONET), part of the OECD Development Assistance Committee (DAC), promotes progress toward meeting the Millennium Development Goals (MDGs) by creating a shift to low-carbon growth and integrating adaptation into development planning. In addition, given the inequality, rich countries have a responsibility to contribute to the additional costs of climate-resilient development in developing countries. There are a number of cost estimates. One of the most widely cited is that from the United Nations Development Programme (UNDP). They estimate an additional US$ 86 billion a year by 2015 will be required to reach the MDGs (UNDP 2007). This estimate is based on a temperature increase of 0.8°C from nineteenth-century levels; higher temperature increases would significantly raise it.

A global deal

The science, economics and ethics point to the need for a global agreement to manage climate change. A global deal must satisfy three fundamental criteria or principles or it will not be sustainable. It must be effective, efficient and equitable.

Effectiveness

A global deal must lead to the cuts in emissions of greenhouse gases necessary to keep temperature increases below 2 °C, given the widespread consensus that such a target balances costs and benefits appropriately. Table 4.1 presents estimates from Stern and Taylor (2010) of individual country commitments as submitted to the Appendix of the Copenhagen Accord. These commitments, in aggregate, are approaching those required for a 2 °C path – around 44 Gt of CO_2e by 2020 – but more ambition is required, especially from developed countries. Recent discussion about increasing the EU emissions target from 20 to 30 per cent reductions on 1990 levels is encouraging. This higher EU target is represented in the estimates in table 4.1, column 3. However, even at the higher level of ambition, the science suggests that current commitments of around 48 Gt CO_2e remain too high (see figure 4.2).

Efficiency

A global deal must be implemented in a cost-effective way, with mitigation focused when and where it is cheapest. If any significant sector, country or technology to reduce GHG emissions is left out,

Table 4.1 Estimate of global emissions based on Accord Appendix targets and actions (billions of tonnes CO_2e)		
	2020 total – low intentions	2020 total – high intentions
Developed country total	16.7	15.7
Developing countries total	29.7	29.7
International aviation and maritime	1.3	1.3
Global total (excluding peat)	**47.7**	**46.7**
Estimate for peat emissions	1.5	1.5
Global total (including peat)	**49.2**	**48.2**

The developing countries total of 29.7 billion tonnes excludes 0.9 billion tonnes of peat emissions in Indonesia. Peat emissions for the rest of the world are assumed to be 0.6 billion tonnes. Therefore the estimate for peat emissions is assumed to be 1.5 billion tonnes.

Source: Stern and Taylor (2010)

costs will rise. In principle, efficiency requires that the marginal cost of reducing emissions is the same everywhere. This is often cited as an advantage of a tradable permit scheme. Such schemes could in principle be linked to create a global marginal price for carbon. While country-based action is likely in the short run because of political and institutional constraints on implementing global policies, global policy instruments and a global price of carbon should be the aim.

Reducing deforestation is also key here as it is a low-cost way of reducing emissions and results in significant co-benefits such as protecting biodiversity. The Copenhagen Accord established the Oslo–Paris process to encourage global action on Reducing Emissions from Deforestation and Forest Degradation (REDD+). To date, developed countries have committed over US$ 4 billion to combat deforestation in developing countries. Other interesting initiatives are also emerging. For example, Norway recently agreed to pay Indonesia US$ 1 billion for a two-year moratorium on new logging concessions, and has a similar agreement with Brazil.

Equity

Achieving participation across all countries, both developed and developing, is challenging because of the fundamental inequality in the impacts of climate change: rich countries very largely caused the climate-change problem, while developing countries will feel the effects first and have less capacity to adapt. In addition, while rich countries prospered on high-carbon growth, developing countries are being told they must find an alternative low-carbon development path, a path which they perceive to be uncertain, costly and a threat to their development and poverty-alleviation goals.

This inequality is inextricably linked to both effectiveness and efficiency. Without strong action in developing countries, especially in India and China, their emissions are likely to grow strongly over the coming decades and account for increasing shares of the global total. Therefore, without developing-country participation in a global deal, the world will not be able to achieve emissions reductions on the scale and at the speed required, and costs of action will rise.

As a result, if the world is to have any chance of securing a global deal that is effective and efficient, it must first address the fundamental injustice in climate change. Rich-country finance for mitigation and adaptation in developing countries, sharing of technology and strong rich-country emissions cuts (to demonstrate low-carbon growth is attractive and feasible) are crucial to restore trust and encourage developing-country participation in ongoing global negotiations.

Given the responsibility of rich countries and the pressing need for adaptation and mitigation funding, the Copenhagen Accord set out a new High-Level Advisory Group on Climate Change Financing (AGF). Its role is to examine ways of raising US$ 100 billion per year by 2020 to finance adaptation and the transition to a low-carbon economy in developing countries. Key to climate financing will be the establishment of institutional arrangements for record keeping, reporting and accountability. In time, given the likely complexity of the instruments required to deliver loans and transfers on this scale, a new institution such as a World Environmental Organization may be required. Initially, existing models of developed/developing-country interaction such as the IMF Article IV Consultations, the OECD DAC or the World Trade Organization Trade Policy Reviews may provide helpful models, and delivery of funds could be channelled through existing institutions such as the African Development Bank. The AGF final report was released on 5 November 2010.

Technology transfer and Measurement, Reporting and Verification (MRV) of emissions are also key areas where progress must be accelerated. Progress is now in the hands of rich countries. They have a unique opportunity to address the inequality in climate change, restore the trust of developing countries and drive a strong deal forward.[26]

Conclusion

The challenge of climate change is immense but it is a challenge that must be met with urgency. The alternative of weak or delayed action would let the risks of dangerous climate change rise to threatening levels, increasing the chances that the current generation will pass on an ever more hostile planet to their children and grandchildren. A solution to the challenge will not emerge out of competitive markets left to their own devices, because of the plentiful supplies of fossil fuels and the multiple market failures (and some policy failures) associated with greenhouse gas emissions.

Well-designed policy frameworks that reflect the size of the risks, span the world and involve the long term are urgently required to cut emissions at reasonable cost and to push forward the transition to a low-carbon economy. This represents nothing short of large-scale changes in the structure of economies.

Economic analysis, when it goes beyond the more typical consideration of marginal changes, makes clear the elements of good policy design that will bring about these changes. First, introducing a price on greenhouse gases, preferably a common global price, is the core policy response. Policy on this front needs to win public credibility – firms and households need to be convinced that pricing will persist into the long term and that the price will not be excessively volatile. One option is to build on the experience of cap-and-trade systems, especially the EU ETS. Another is to introduce carbon taxes more widely. The two approaches have different implications for how the stringency of climate change policies reacts to unexpected macroeconomic developments, with unexpected recessions, for example, leading to less abatement under cap-and-trade than under carbon taxation. They also have different distributional implications, especially if quotas under cap-and-trade are distributed to firms for free. But governments need to avoid introducing a plethora of pricing measures and regulations that lead to a wide variation in the implicit price of carbon across countries and sectors, and firms being exposed to several overlapping carbon prices. And fossil fuel subsidies should be withdrawn.

Second, the market failures standing in the way of technological innovation need to be tackled. That will entail increased government support for low-carbon energy R&D and the development of new energy distribution networks. All these problems need to be addressed by policymakers at a time of fiscal austerity in much of the developed world. That will give rise to new challenges of public finance, accountability and governance. But the good news is that a new approach to innovation in the round has tremendous potential to stimulate long-run growth while pointing it in a more sustainable direction.

Third, adaptation to climate change is also important. The world is committed to a certain amount of climate change over the coming fifty years or so, the result of past emissions, and rich countries have an ethical obligation to support the adaptation needs of developing countries.

Fourth, more attention needs to be given to the distributional consequences of both climate change impacts and efforts to mitigate them. That is important for clarifying the ethical issues involved and for winning political support for the key elements of climate change policies. Some economists are prone to forgetting that, even using a strictly utilitarian calculus, the correction of market failures is only unambiguously welfare-improving if appropriate side payments are made.

Fifth, more needs to be known about the risks from climate change and the potential costs and benefits of policies to combat them. More research is vital. Civil society should be engaged with these questions, as many of the ethical and social questions to which they give rise are not amenable to resolution by experts alone.

Finally, a global response to climate change is crucial. A global deal must be effective, efficient and equitable – *effective* as total *global* emissions must be reduced sharply if dangerous climate risks are to be minimized, *efficient* as a global price on carbon allows emissions reductions to occur where they are cheapest, and *equitable* as global policy action can foster participation by developing countries and compensate them for a problem not of their making.

The world has a limited period to resolve its differences, come together and start to implement strong action. Annual global emissions need to peak and start to fall this decade, with a reduction to at least 50 per cent of their 1990 level by mid century being a sensible target given our current state of knowledge. Leadership at all levels of society is required. There is much for international negotiators and governments to do, but there are some encouraging signs. A strong global deal, comprising the key elements of good economic policy, would push forward the transition to a low-carbon future and significantly reduce the risk of dangerous climate change.

Notes

1. This chapter draws on, among other material, our colleague Nicholas Stern's Collège de France lecture series in 2010, available at: www.college-de-france.fr/default/EN/all/ni_ste/index.htm. Rydge contributed extensively to the research for and drafting of these lectures.
2. Recent projections for 2010 suggest that annual global emissions will be around 47 billion tonnes of the greenhouse gases covered by the Kyoto Protocol (e.g. Bowen and Ranger 2009).
3. See http://unfccc.int/resource/docs/2009/cop15/eng/l07.pdf.
4. There are both positive and negative externalities. An example of a 'positive' externality is the inability to appropriate the full benefits of R&D: benefits of R&D often accrue to others. This reduces the incentive to invest in R&D and represents a market failure. This R&D market failure is very important to climate change as R&D of new low-carbon technologies is essential to lower the costs of emission reductions.
5. Plotting the cost of each additional unit of pollution produces an MSC curve. As concentrations of greenhouse gases increase, the costs or damage to society from an additional unit of emissions are likely to rise, so the MSC curve may be relatively flat in the short run but rise steeply in the long run.
6. Plotting the cost of each additional unit of emissions reduction produces an MAC curve (this can be estimated at the firm, country or global level). In the short run, MACs are often low initially and then rise as more expensive abatement or emissions reductions are undertaken. The intuition behind this is that initial emissions reductions may require only a relatively inexpensive change in process, while further reductions may require significant investment in new plant and equipment. The slope in the long run will depend on the level of technological innovation.
7. Recent research by McKinsey&Company has produced estimates of MACs across a number of industries, economies and at a global level. But there is controversy over how robust the estimates are to changes in assumptions about the economy-wide feedbacks from climate policies and over the reliability of engineering estimates of the real-world potential for energy efficiency improvements.

8. For example, one of the most distinguished climate economists, Nordhaus, argues for a more gradual ramping up of policies and higher discount rates than does Stern – but still advocates immediate imposition of a carbon tax as widely as possible (Nordhaus 2008).

9. More complete discussions of discounting, ethics and values can be found in Dasgupta (2008), Stern (2008), Stern (2009) and Dietz, Hepburn and Stern (2008).

10. In a world with strong climate policies, the future stock of greenhouse gases in the atmosphere would be a lot lower than under BAU, so that the MSC would be lower. Ideally, climate policies should be just strong enough to bring the MSC into equality with the MAC (which rises with the policy's severity).

11. Non-market impacts include most damages to ecosystems and the direct effects of climate change on human societies that are not transmitted via impacts on marketed output and productivity. Environmental economists are investigating how to assess such impacts.

12. If the BAU MSC curve is steep in the long run, as the evidence suggests it is, setting an incorrect tax rate and maintaining it through time risks excess emissions and large damage costs (see Weitzman 1974). Therefore, given the nature of the uncertainty, a quantity target is preferable in the long run. But setting a quota in the short run risks imposing very high costs on firms if governments misjudge its size, because the short-run MAC is likely to be much steeper than in the long run (when firms can alter their capital stock and technologies). Hence there is an argument for banking and borrowing to be allowed in quota schemes to enable firms to smooth abatement costs over time.

13. This can be compared with the range of MSC estimates to check prices are within the range.

14. The EU-15 consists of Austria, Belgium, Denmark, Finland, France, Germany, Greece, Ireland, Italy, Luxembourg, the Netherlands, Portugal, Spain, Sweden and the United Kingdom.

15. http://themes.eea.europa.eu/.

16. Under an emissions tax regime, firms would have been under greater pressure to continue seeking ways to reduce emissions as the global slowdown took hold.

17. Calculated as the additional cost of compliance with the regulation divided by the quantity of emissions/pollution reduced.

18. See Popp (2006).

19. A price by itself will also have to be higher if not used in concert with other instruments. In Fischer and Newell (2008), for example, the policy portfolio comprises an emissions price, an R&D subsidy and a renewable generation subsidy. Applying their model to the US electricity industry, they find that the use of their renewable energy support policies allows the CO_2 emissions price to be 36 per cent lower than it would have to be if hitting the chosen emissions target relied on the emissions price alone.

20. Such Integrated Assessment Models have produced a range of results, some sensible and some implausible. For example, Nordhaus's DICE model indicates a loss of global GDP (relative to future levels of GDP much higher than today's) of only around 50 per cent from an 18 °C temperature increase (Ackerman, Stanton and Bueno 2009). This suggests that close scrutiny of the assumptions in these models is warranted.

21. Cost estimates and the influences upon them are discussed further in Bowen and Ranger (2009).

22. See, for example, the ADAM project (Knopf, Edenhofer, Flachsland et al. 2010) and the RECIPE project (Edenhofer, Carraro, Hourcade et al. 2009).
23. See, for example, papers in the December 2009 Special Issue of *Energy Economics* (vol. 31, supplement 2).
24. Perez (2002) provides a historical perspective of major economic transformations. She argues that there are common themes that apply to each wave of technological innovation and major change – a breakthrough in a technology or range of technologies sets off a transformative, dynamic and innovative period of industrial and social change with accompanying benefits and opportunities, and decline and resistance from 'old' industries that are left behind.
25. Many of these factors are already a major issue for people in developing countries.
26. For further discussion of a global deal on climate change, see Aldy and Stavins (2008) and Stern (2009).

Bibliography

Ackerman, F., Stanton, E. and Bueno, R. (2009) *Fat Tails, Exponents, and Extreme Uncertainty: Simulating Catastrophe in DICE*, Stockholm Environment Institute, Working paper.

Aldy, J., and Stavins, R. (2008) *Architectures for Agreement: Addressing Global Climate Change in the Post-Kyoto World*, Cambridge: Cambridge University Press.

Bowen, A. and Ranger, N. (2009) *Mitigating Climate Change through Reductions in Greenhouse Gas Emissions: The Science and Economics of Future Paths for Global Annual Emissions*, Policy Brief, December: Centre for Climate Change Economics and Policy and Grantham Research Institute on Climate Change and the Environment.

Dasgupta, P. (2008) 'Discounting Climate Change', *Journal of Risk and Uncertainty*, 37.

Dietz, S., Hepburn, C. and Stern, N. (2008) 'Economics, Ethics and Climate Change', in K. Basu and R. Kanbur (eds.), *Arguments for a Better World: Essays in Honour of Amartya Sen*, vol. II: *Society, Institutions and Development*, Oxford: Oxford University Press.

Edenhofer, O., Carraro, C., Hourcade, J. C. et al. (2009) *The Economics of Decarbonization: Report of the RECIPE project*, Potsdam: Potsdam Institute for Climate Impact Research.

Edenhofer, O., Knopf, B., Barker, T. et al. (2010) 'The Economics of Low Stabilisation: Model Comparison and Mitigation Strategies and Cost', *The Energy Journal*, 31.

Enkvist, P.-A., Nauclér, T. and Rosander, J. (2007) 'A Cost Curve for Greenhouse Gas Reduction', *The McKinsey Quarterly*, 1.

Fischer, C., and Newell, R. G. (2008) 'Environmental and Technology Policies for Climate Mitigation', *Journal of Environmental Economics and Management*, 55.

Hepburn, C. and Stern, N. (2009) 'The Global Deal on Climate Change', in D. Helm and C. Hepburn (eds.), *The Economics and Politics of Climate Change*, Oxford: Oxford University Press.

International Energy Agency (2009) *World Energy Outlook 2009, Part B: Post-2012 Climate Policy Framework*, Paris: IEA

Knopf, B., Edenhofer, O., Barker, T. et al. (2009) 'The Economics of Low Stabilisation: Implications for Technological Change and Policy', in M. Hulme and H. Neufeldt (eds.), *Making Climate Change Work for Us – ADAM Synthesis Book*, Cambridge: Cambridge University Press.

Knopf, B., Edenhofer, O., Flachsland, C., et al. (2010) 'Managing the Low-Carbon Transition – from Model Results to Policies', *The Energy Journal*, 0 (Special Issue).

Krugman, P. (2010), 'Building a Green Economy', *The New York Times*, 5 April.

Nordhaus, W. (2008) *A Question of Balance: Weighing the Options on Global Warming Policies*, New Haven, CT: Yale University Press.

Pearce, D. (2003) 'The Social Cost of Carbon and Its Policy Implications', *Oxford Review of Economic Policy*, 19 (3).

Perez, C. (2002) *Technological Revolutions and Financial Capital: The Dynamics of Bubbles and Golden Ages*, London: Edward Elgar.

Popp, D. (2006) 'R&D Subsidies and Climate Policy: Is There a "Free Lunch"?' *Climatic Change*, 77.

Stern, N. (2007) *The Economics of Climate Change: The Stern Review*, Cambridge: Cambridge University Press.

Stern, N. (2008) 'The Economics of Climate Change', *American Economic Review*, 98 (2).

Stern, N. (2009) *A Blueprint for a Safer Planet: How to Manage Climate Change and Create a New Era of Progress and Prosperity*, London: The Bodley Head.

Stern, N. and Taylor, C. (2010) *What Do the Appendices to the Copenhagen Accord Tell Us about Global Greenhouse Gas Emissions and the Prospects for Keeping the Increase in Global Temperature below 2 °C?* Policy Paper, March: Centre for Climate Change Economics and Policy and Grantham Research Institute on Climate Change and the Environment in collaboration with staff from the United Nations Environment Programme (UNEP).

UK Energy Research Centre (2007) *The Rebound Effect: An Assessment of the Evidence for Economy-wide Energy Savings from Improved Energy Efficiency*, London: UKERC.

United Nations Development Programme (2007) *Human Development Report 2007/2008: Fighting Climate Change – Human Solidarity in a Divided World*, New York: Palgrave Macmillan.

Weitzman, M. (1974) 'Prices vs. Quantities', *The Review of Economic Studies*, 41.

5

Democracy, Climate Change and Global Governance: Democratic Agency and the Policy Menu Ahead

David Held and Angus Hervey

This chapter examines the role of democracy in meeting the urgent challenge of climate change. The challenge is multifaceted and multi-layered, involving many actors and agencies, and demanding effective policy at the level of both the nation-state and global governance. Moreover, it is difficult to address because it requires long-term policy commitments, and solutions that depend on complex scientific and technical developments. It is also difficult to solve because it involves great costs and effort, and because of the complicated distributive implications involved at every turn.

In order to unpack the issues at stake, this chapter is structured in five parts. The first section examines the relationship between democracy and climate change at the level of the nation-state, briefly reviewing existing literature and examining evidence for and against the claim that democracies are unable to address the problem. The second section focuses on the same issues in relation to global governance, concentrating on the enormous collective action problem that climate change poses to an international community of distinct nation-states, and the problem of multiple actors, organizational overlap, and representation and accountability in international environmental institutions. The third section examines the policy debates about climate change, asking about the range of options available to nation-states and, in particular, liberal democracies. The fourth section focuses on the political elements of a democratic global deal on climate change, while the final section draws together the various arguments presented around the theme of democracy and the policy menu ahead.

Democracy: the democratic nation-state and climate change

At the most basic level, it can be argued that modern liberal democracies suffer from a number of structural characteristics that prevent them from tackling global collective action problems in general, and climate change in particular. These are as follows.

Short-termism

The electoral cycle tends to focus policy debate on short-term political gains and satisfying the median voter. The short duration of electoral cycles ensures that politicians are concerned with their own re-election, which may compromise hard policy decisions that require a great deal of political capital. It is extremely difficult for governments to impose large-scale changes on an electorate whose votes they depend on, in order to tackle a problem whose impact will only be felt by future generations.

Self-referring decision-making

Democratic theory and politics builds on a notion of accountability linked to home-based constituencies. It assumes a symmetry and congruence between decision-makers and decision-takers within the boundaries of the nation-state. Any breakdown of equivalence between these parties, i.e. between decision-makers and stakeholders, or between the inputs and outputs of the decision-making process, tends not to be heavily weighed. Democratic 'princes' and 'princesses' owe their support to that most virtuous source of power: their people. The externalities or border spill-over effects of decisions they take are not their primary concern.

Interest group concentration

In democracies, greater interest group pluralism reduces the provision of public goods because politicians are forced to adopt policies that cater to the narrow interests of small groups (Olson 1982). The democratic process rewards small, well-organized interest groups and results in their proliferation. Also, strong competition among such groups leads to gridlock in public decision-making, delaying both the implementation and effectiveness of public goods provision (Midlarsky 1998).

Weak multilateralism

Governments accountable to democratic publics often seek to avoid compliance with binding multilateral decisions if this weakens their relationship to their electorate. There is a notable exception; it occurs when strong democratic governments can control the multilateral game.

These concerns have generated scepticism about the compatibility of democratic forms of governance with the need for the drastic and urgent changes in policy required to combat climate change. The implication is that they are unable to meet the scale of the challenge posed by climate change, and that more coercive forms of government may be necessary. Such thinking finds its historical precedent in the work of the 'eco-authoritarians' of the 1970s, who argued that it might be difficult in democracies to constrain economic activity and population growth that results in pressures on the environment. They suggested that some aspects of democratic rule would have to be sacrificed to achieve sustainable future outcomes, since authoritarian regimes are not required to pay as much attention to citizens' rights in order to establish effective policy in key areas (Hardin 1968; Heilbroner 1974; Ophuls 1977).

Such thinking has, however, been undermined by a body of theory arguing that there are a number of reasons why democracies are more likely than authoritarian regimes to protect environmental quality (Holden 2002). Democracies have better access to information, with fewer restrictions on media and sources of knowledge, and greater transparency in decision-making procedures (Payne 1995). They also encourage scientific research and the exchange and dissemination of new evidence, which are responsible for our awareness about different forms of environmental threat in the first place (Giddens 2008: 74). Concerned citizens can in turn influence political outcomes not only through the ballot box, but through pressure groups, social movements and the free media – channels that are closed in autocracies (Payne 1995). Finally, there are many examples of cases where environmental interest groups have been able to overwhelm business interests pursuing environmentally damaging practices, and of cases where they have changed the public agenda (Falkner 2007; Bernauer and Caduff 2004). At the same time, authoritarian regimes have fewer incentives to adopt or stick to sustainable policies. Environmental concerns are often trumped by economic development plans and external security (Porritt 1984), and those in power control a substantial fraction of society's resources, encouraging payoffs to a relatively small elite (Bueno de Mesquita, Smith, Siverson et al. 2003). Given their insecurity of tenure in office, dictators can be expected to have high discount rates which favour the allocation of present resources at the expense of future resources. Leaders are also unaccountable to the public, giving them even less incentive to enact long-term policy (Congleton 1992). In democratic countries, there are structures and institutions such as the executive, legislature, judiciary and free press which curtail the extent of these myopic behaviours. These kinds of checks and balances either do not exist in autocratic countries, or, where they do, are usually ineffective (Didia 1997).

It would not be unreasonable then, to expect a strong correlation between democracy and environmental quality. Indeed, on one of the most important indicators of environmental quality – carbon emissions – the countries that have the best records among the forty highest emitters (cumulatively responsible for 91 per cent of total world emissions) are all democracies.[1]

However, upon closer examination, the record is less compelling, and detailed empirical evidence is inconclusive. Environmental quality is not just measured by a broad-based commitment to addressing emissions of carbon and other greenhouse gases (GHGs). While some studies have shown that authoritarian regimes have worse records than democracies on environmental protection,[2] others find no evidence to suggest that this is the case.[3] Indeed across a range of measures and geographical areas, numerous studies prove that outcomes are varied.[4]

On balance, the link between democratic rule and environmental sustainability is not as strong as we might expect. Why is this the case? Part of the reason might be attributed to the different types of transmission mechanisms that translate policy commitment into policy outcomes. Bättig and Bernauer (2009), for example, find that while the effect of democracy on political commitment to climate change is positive, the effect on policy outcomes, measured in terms of emissions and trends, is ambiguous. They observe that the causal chain from environmental risks to public perceptions of such risks, to public demand for risk mitigation, and to policy output is shorter than the one leading from risk via policy output to policy outcome. Because of that, outcomes are influenced by a range of other factors, such as the properties of the resource in question, mitigation costs and the efficiency of implementing agencies. Politicians might easily declare a set of public policy commitments to climate change mitigation, but the outcome of such efforts is affected by factors that are often outside of their control. The result is that policymakers respond quite well to public demands for more environmental protection, but tend to discount implementation problems, hoping that voters will not be able to identify these within a short enough time period to use their votes as a punishment for any failure to deliver.

Table 5.1 World carbon emissions, by country (measured in millions of metric tonnes of CO_2)

Rank	Country	2000	2006	per capita (tonnes), 2006	% change since 2000
1	China	2966.52	6017.69	4.58	103
2	United States	5860.38	5902.75	19.78	1
3	Russia	1582.37	1704.36	12.00	8
4	India	1012.34	1293.17	1.16	28
5	Japan	1203.71	1246.76	9.78	4
6	Germany	856.92	857.60	10.40	0
7	Canada	565.22	614.33	18.81	9
8	United Kingdom	561.23	585.71	9.66	4
9	South Korea	445.81	514.53	10.53	15
10	Iran	320.69	471.48	7.25	47
11	Italy	448.43	468.19	8.05	4
12	South Africa	391.67	443.58	10.04	13
13	Mexico	383.44	435.60	4.05	14
14	Saudi Arabia	290.54	424.08	15.70	46
15	France	402.27	417.75	6.60	4
16	Australia	359.80	417.06	20.58	16
17	Brazil	344.91	377.24	2.01	9
18	Spain	326.92	372.62	9.22	14
19	Ukraine	326.83	328.72	7.05	1
20	Poland	295.00	303.42	7.87	3
21	Taiwan	252.15	300.38	13.19	19
22	Indonesia	273.93	280.36	1.21	2
23	Netherlands	251.73	260.45	15.79	3
24	Thailand	161.86	245.04	3.79	51
25	Turkey	202.38	235.70	3.35	16
26	Kazakhstan	143.45	213.50	14.02	49
27	Malaysia	112.14	163.53	6.70	46
28	Argentina	138.42	162.19	4.06	17
29	Venezuela	134.46	151.97	5.93	13
30	Egypt	119.32	151.62	1.92	27
31	United Arab Emirates	115.72	149.52	35.05	29
32	Belgium	148.57	147.58	14.22	-1
33	Singapore	107.64	141.10	31.41	31
34	Pakistan	109.11	125.59	0.78	15
35	Uzbekistan	106.35	120.84	4.43	14
36	Czech Republic	113.45	116.30	11.36	3
37	Greece	101.27	107.07	10.02	6
38	Nigeria	80.75	101.07	0.77	25
39	Iraq	73.58	98.95	3.69	34
40	Romania	93.33	98.64	4.42	6

Source: EIA (2006)

An additional concern is that political commitment to tackling climate change is critical, yet may require political leaders to adhere to a particular course of action that is potentially unpopular, and hence contrary to structural democratic pressures. The actual implementation of policies that reduce global warming may infringe on the democratic preferences of citizens. In such a context, political leaders can be caught between a desire for recognition and esteem in the international community – recognition that comes from peer admiration for leadership – and the need to ensure accountability to domestic electorates (Keohane and Raustiala 2008). However, good democratic leadership is not confined to policymaking alone – it also involves educating constituents about pressing issues that may not be obvious to them. In this sense, the fact that democratic publics do not always have fully formed preferences is an advantage as well as a risk. Citizens can significantly shift their preferences, faced with new information and evidence about pressing issues. The democratic citizen who is capable of being 'fact-regarding, future-regarding and other-regarding' is not simply a myth (Offe and Preuss 1991: 156–7, in Held 2006a: 232).

Such an approach to democratic 'will formation' can be found within the tradition of what is known as deliberative democracy, broadly defined as 'any one of a family of views according to which the public deliberation of free and equal citizens is the core of legitimate political decision-making and self-governance' (Bohman 1998: 401). Deliberative democrats advocate that democracy moves away from any notion of fixed and given preferences, to be replaced with a view that democracy should become a learning process in and through which people come to terms with the range of issues they need to understand in order to hold defensible positions. They argue that no set of values or particular perspectives can lay claim to being correct and valid by themselves, but rather are valid only in so far as they are capable of public justification (Offe and Preuss 1991: 168). Individual points of view need to be tested in and through social encounters which take into account the point of view of others. Ultimately, the key objective is the transformation of private preferences via a process of deliberation into positions that can withstand public scrutiny and test. Empirical findings show that citizens can and do alter their preferences when they engage with new information, fresh evidence and debate (Held 2006a: 247–55). These can lead to new and innovative ideas about public policy and about how democracy might function and work.

Deliberative democracy can, in principle, increase the quality, legitimacy and therefore the sustainability of environmental policy decisions. This is partly due to the uncertainty associated with environmental issues, which demands a wide range of experience, expertise and consultation. The complexity of climate change problems also requires integrated solutions that have been vetted by multiple actors and that cut across the narrow confines of expert knowledge and the responsibilities of established institutions and organizations. And the concerns of environmental justice require the political process to be as inclusive as possible, giving voice to the under-represented, including future generations. Effective and just action on climate change depends upon the continuing involvement of citizens in the making and delivery of policy; conventional representative democracy alone is a poor way to achieve this. To remodel environmental politics around deliberative democracy is thus to create an opening for a change in the way democracies address environmental management in general, and climate change in particular.

In shifting from policy commitments to real and binding action, democracies have all too often been unable to override the problems of short-termism, collective action and other factors that cut against emissions reduction efforts. This is not to say that democracies are incapable of tackling climate change (certainly the alternative, in the form of authoritarian regimes, seems to be far worse). Rather, certain aspects of democracies typically fall short. The questions now are whether democratic systems can be evolved to handle the problem better, and how this may be achieved.

Democracy: global governance and climate change

Complex global processes, from the ecological to the financial, connect the fates of communities to each other across the world, yet the problem-solving capacity of the global system is in many areas not effective, accountable or fast enough to resolve current global challenges. What has been called the paradox of our times refers to the fact that the collective issues we must grapple with are of growing cross-border extensity and intensity, but the means for addressing these are state-based, weak and incomplete (Held 2006b). While there are a variety of reasons for the existence of these problems, at the most basic level the persistence of the paradox remains a problem of governance. The abilities of states to address critical issues at the regional and global level are handicapped by a number of structural difficulties, domestic and international, which compound the problems of generating and implementing urgent policies with respect to global goods and bads.

One significant problem is that a growing number of issues span both the domestic and the international domains. The institutional fragmentation and competition between states can lead to these issues being addressed in an ad hoc and dissonant manner. A second problem is that, even when the global dimension of a problem is acknowledged, there is often no clear division of labour among the myriad of international institutions that seek to address it: their functions frequently overlap, their mandates conflict and their objectives often become blurred. A third problem is that the existing system of global governance suffers from significant deficits of accountability and inclusion, which can result in less economically powerful states –and, hence, their entire populations – being marginalized or excluded from decision-making.

Today, there is a newfound recognition that global problems cannot be solved by any one nation-state acting alone, nor by states just fighting their corner in regional blocs. What is required is collective and collaborative action, something that the nations of the world have not been good at, and which they need to be much better at if the most pressing issues are to be adequately tackled. The failure to generate a sound and effective framework for managing global climate change is one of the most serious indications of the challenges facing the multilateral order. The former British chief scientist Sir David King has warned that the threat posed by climate change is more serious than that of terrorism (2004: 177), and Sir Nicholas Stern has referred to it as 'the greatest market failure the world has ever seen' (2004: xviii). In the broad view of the scientific community, climate change has the capacity to wreak havoc on the world's diverse species, bio-systems and socioeconomic fabric, and the process has clearly begun.

Anarchic inefficiency

The number of actors and variety of organizations involved in both agenda setting and policymaking at the level of global environmental governance has increased substantially over the past decade. In addition to private, public and civil society actors, new types of actors have emerged such as transnational activist networks (Keck and Sikkink 1998), private rule-making organizations (Prakash and Potoski 2006), government agencies and public–private partnerships (Börzel and Risse 2005). Moreover, established organizations have adopted new roles and responsibilities. For example, many intergovernmental organizations have acquired a higher degree of autonomy from the governments that have established them, and many non-government organizations (NGOs) now engage in agenda setting, policy formulation and the establishment of rules and regulations (Betsill and Corell 2001). However, the increased engagement of diverse actors does not necessarily guarantee either effectiveness or equal access to diverse voices. In fact, it often leads to double representation of the West and

North through both powerful states and NGOs (Kahler 2005; Biermann and Pattberg 2008).

At the institutional level, while many international environmental agreements exist and possess some admirable characteristics, they are often both poorly coordinated and weakly enforced. Furthermore, they are supported by a plethora of different international organizations fulfilling various functions. The current constellation of over 200 international environmental agreements suffers from a problem of what might be called 'anarchic inefficiency', featuring a diverse set of players whose roles are largely uncoordinated between each other. The most prominent are as follows.[5]

The UN system, including the *United Nations Framework Convention on Climate Change (UNFCCC)*, the *Environmental Management Group (EMG)* and the *Centre for Sustainable Development (CSD)*

While international action on climate change relies overwhelmingly on the evidence presented by the UNFCCC (including the Kyoto Protocol), the UN system overall has so far been ineffective in reducing GHG emissions, and is hampered by major divisions between North and South. The internal UN system is also still arguably uncoordinated on climate change, although there are plans to change this (UN System Chief Executives Board for Coordination 2008). The EMG, chaired by the United Nations Environmental Programme (UNEP), is a key vehicle for this cooperation, but it remains too early to judge its progress. The CSD has engaged with NGOs in a constructive manner, and has an important agenda-setting role, but is also relatively ineffective.

Global Environment Facility (GEF)

The GEF has a climate change remit, including serving as the main financial mechanism for the UNFCCC. However, it has suffered legitimacy problems: developing countries have opposed GEF control of the Kyoto Adaptation Fund, perceiving a voting bias in favour of richer countries and control by the World Bank. The current governance structure of the Adaptation Fund is regarded as an interim solution until this can be resolved. Elsewhere, the GEF has delivered important grants for climate change mitigation and adaptation, but has a tendency to support smaller technical or pilot projects that are not mainstreamed in countries or economic sectors.

The Organization for Economic Co-operation and Development (OECD) Environmental Directorate

While this division of the OECD is technically proficient (having conducted agenda-setting work, for example, on environmental indicators and economic modelling of carbon markets), it is globally unrepresentative. It also regards climate change as amenable to technical, pro-growth economic solutions, contrary to the views held by many of the key actors in the debate.

The World Trade Organization (WTO) Committee on Trade and Environment

Collaboration between the UNEP and the WTO was proposed in 2006, yet the Committee has not even been able to agree to a limited environmental package within the Doha Round. There is little appetite to recognize climate change damage as grounds for unilateral member state exceptions (GATT/WTO Article XX) to world trade rules. Collaboration is, therefore, largely symbolic – the WTO is seeking more environmental legitimacy, while the UNEP wants access to WTO deliberations.

Environmental Chamber of the International Court for Justice (ICJ)

The ICJ has thus far played an insignificant role, with no cases since its formation in 1993. It has been hampered by limited rules of standing and divided opinion over the need for a separate International Court for the Environment (Stephens 2009).

Representation and the responsibility of the wealthy

Problems with representation at the level of global governance are high on the list of obstacles to addressing climate change.[6] Multilateral bodies need to be inclusive; unless both developed and less developed states come on board, the net reduction of GHG emissions becomes a much harder task, if it can be achieved at all. Ensuring effective representation is not a question of just providing a seat at the negotiating table in a major intergovernmental organization or at a major conference. For, even if there is parity of formal representation (a condition typically lacking), it is generally the case that developed countries have large delegations equipped with extensive negotiating and technical expertise, while poorer developing countries frequently depend on one-person delegations, or have even to rely on the sharing of a delegate, and lack the negotiating strength to participate fully in discussions (Chasek and Rajamani 2003). This is indicative not only of the problem of unequal access to decision-making, but of inequality of all types of resource. Many developing countries do not readily command the public funds, capacity or technology to come into compliance with agreed regulations designed to reduce emissions. As a result, any future agreement cannot simply build on the traditional burden-sharing approach of dealing with a problem inherent in the global commons; given the scale of transformation that is required for a sustainable future, wealthy industrialized states will have to bear a significant part of the cost of the transformation in developing countries.

The policy debate: squaring the circle?

The greatest differences in the debate about the politics of climate change tend be revealed in issues of how to square the circle of participation, effectiveness and compliance. Or, to put the point more broadly – is it possible to combine coherently democracy, markets and universal standards (Held 2004: ch. 9)? The answer is far from straightforward. If international rules become stricter, we can expect reluctant states to become even more reluctant to be bound by them, while if participation increases, agreement may only become possible via lax rules (Keohane and Raustiala 2008).

A critical component of a global deal will be the way in which market incentives are structured. In terms of targeting GHG emissions, two principal market-based instruments exist: cap-and-trade and taxation. Supporters of the former include Stern (2009) who points out a number of disadvantages with taxes. They do not allow certainty over how big future GHG reductions will be, since estimates are imprecise and there is a long lag time between policy output and actual outcomes. They are hard to coordinate internationally, and developing countries are unlikely to agree to such arrangements, which impose economic burdens on industries without offering the offsetting gain of being able to sell emissions permits. Moreover, electorates in general are mistrustful of governments' use of tax resources, potentially opposing them in the belief they provide an excuse for 'stealth taxation'. A better approach is to set targets, and then seek out the cheapest method (via the price mechanism) of reaching them.

The cap-and-trade system

According to its supporters, cap-and-trade makes the most sense, of the options available, because it allows for greater certainty about eventual emissions levels and provides better incentives for producers.[7] At this point, it also appears to be the approach most likely to be adopted at the global level, with a European Union Emission Trading System (EU ETS) already in place, and a successful precedent in the form of markets for sulphur in the United States. However, global markets in carbon and other GHGs are likely to be far larger and more complex than any previous emissions trading schemes, with a commensurate increase in levels of risk, opportunity for leakage and distributional consequences. Negotiating a comprehensive global accord and meshing national systems so that they operate coherently will be a highly fraught and difficult process, if it can be achieved at all.

Indeed, while cap-and-trade seems to be an ideal solution on the surface, it is in fact an odd way to do business. Politicians like it because it is market-based, does not require the imposition of unpopular taxes, and can be worked out with special-interest groups in back-room negotiations. Indeed, with regular auctions to sell off emitting rights, and the lack of a long-term or stable price, cap-and-trade is a lobbyist's and trader's dream (Helm 2008). Yet, putting the dangers of rent seeking aside, it is not even clear that cap-and-trade will lead to required emissions reductions. As Sachs (2009: 2) observes:

> a cap-and-trade system can be more easily manipulated to allow additional emissions; if the permits become too pricey, regulators would likely sell or distribute more permits to keep the price 'reasonable.' Since the long-term signals from cap-and-trade are less powerful than a multi-year carbon tax, the behavioural changes (e.g. choice of the type of power plant) brought about by cap-and-trade could well turn out to be far fewer, as well.

Such concerns are borne out by the existing record on carbon emissions trading. The global market grew to £126 billion last year, up from £63 billion in 2007 and nearly twelve times the value in 2005. This represented the value of a total of 4.8 billion tonnes of carbon dioxide, up 61 per cent from the 3 billion tonnes traded in 2007. However, the actual emissions cuts made and sold by United Nations-registered clean energy projects in developing countries fell by 30 per cent in 2008 to 389 million tonnes (Chestney and Szabo 2009).

A tax on carbon

Contrary to the claims of cap-and-trade advocates, it can be countered that taxes are less likely to result in policy failure. Economic efficiency demands that those who create emissions should pay the costs, and taxes are the simplest way of forcing them to do so. Their advantages are many. They offer a broader scope for emissions reductions, as opposed to trading systems which can only be implemented among private firms or countries, and not among households and individual consumers. In this sense, they are the more democratic option, since they create greater coverage and are less susceptible to strategic lobbying for exceptions by firms or NGOs. Their universal guiding principle is distributive, since they simultaneously discriminate against polluters while allocating priority to the most vital cases of environmental need. They involve fewer administrative costs, are less complicated and more familiar to policymakers, and provide new avenues of generating revenue to tackle climate change for governments that are increasingly unwilling to incur political costs by expanding general taxation. Finally, they place a clear price on emissions for many years ahead, allowing for better long-term policy planning. Of course, there remains the substantial challenge of shifting taxation structures away from their primary focus on work and production toward a greater emphasis on pollution, externalities and consumption. It goes without saying that this will require a great effort, marked by short-term and long-term objectives, which could be weakened by new election results, changing coalitions and so on.

A new policy mix

In reality, the policy mix is likely to contain multiple policy instruments. The prospect of large revenues from permit auctions has established significant political and economic interest in the creation and maintenance of markets for GHGs. Cap-and-trade also offers the potential for far greater levels of private sector funding than is the case for government-financed funds and schemes, and will create significant private sector flows from developed to developing countries, an absolute necessity for reaching a global deal. However, if policymakers are serious about putting a true price on carbon and other GHGs – essential if markets are to sort out efficient supply- and demand-side responses – then taxation will have to form a key element of policy as well, in order to ensure predictability of outcome, and the generation of new resources for the provision of urgent environmental goods.

Even then, putting a price on all GHG emissions (whether through tradable permits or taxes) is not enough on its own to deliver the needed reductions. Existing market-based schemes, such as the EU ETS, or carbon taxation by individual European countries and US states, have so far failed to generate large-scale research into the development of breakthrough technologies. Such schemes might eventually result in a levelling-off or even a slight reduction of emissions, but will only stimulate a marginal diversification into alternative forms of energy such as solar and wind power. This is because private sector firms under-invest in research and development if they fear they will not be able to earn a decent profit on resulting product development. What is ultimately required is a fundamental overhaul of energy systems through transformative technologies that require a combination of factors to succeed – not only market incentives, but also applied scientific research, early high-cost investments, regulatory changes (e.g. building codes and practices), infrastructural development, information instruments (e.g. eco-labelling of energy appliances) and public acceptance.

To ensure flexibility and encourage innovation, regulations should be based on achieving particular results, rather than simply specifying the methods or technologies to be used to achieve those outcomes (Organization for Economic Co-operation and Development 2007). Care needs to be taken in choosing instruments in a policy mix to ensure that they are complementary and avoid unnecessary overlap, and that they are cost-effective. By setting too high a price or too tight a cap, policy will result in excess costs, while choosing policies that are too lenient will forgo the potential benefits of added, cost-effective mitigation measures and risk the failure of meeting required targets.

The political elements of a democratic global deal

Climate change is a problem with global causes and consequences. A coordinated international effort is therefore required to achieve cost-effective and successful mitigation policies. However, the nature of the problem also means that international agreements will be difficult to reach. Countries and regions have very different interests in achieving a solution, implying a highly contested distribution of costs and benefits. In addition, developing countries, given their relatively small contribution to historical emissions, object to having their development impeded by restrictions. Finally, the challenges associated with enforcing a global solution may make some nations reluctant to participate, adding a source of uncertainty about how cost-effective the policies will be (Congressional Budget Office of the United States 2005). However, despite the vigorous debate surrounding the type of policies required to combat climate change and how they should or should not be implemented, there is considerable overlap on what the political elements of a global deal might look like. At the most general level, most commentators agree that it should be broadly inclusive, multifaceted, state-centric and sustainable.

Participation

The key requirement is participation from all countries, and, most importantly, participation by the most powerful democracy in the world, the United States. The integration of less developed states is also crucial, as already noted. Even if the developed states of the world were to cut their emissions to zero by 2050, without significant cuts in the rest of the world the overall goal of keeping a global rise in temperatures to under 2 °C would be missed. Developing countries need to be convinced that they can simultaneously reduce their emissions and increase their growth rate by increasing their energy efficiency.

They need, for instance, to eliminate distortions in their energy markets, such as large oil subsidies. But for most developing countries, the cheapest form of energy is coal (or other high-emission energy sources), and in those cases, there is a real trade-off. Money spent to reduce GHG emissions is money that could be spent to provide education, better health and clean water, or to grow faster. In such cases, developed countries, it can be argued, should pay for the incremental costs. However, as Victor, Granger Morgan, Apt et al. (2009) have pointed out, this is unlikely to happen – it is simply unrealistic to expect industrialized nations to deliver the hundreds of billions of dollars needed for mitigation and adaptation when official development assistance (including for wars in Iraq and Afghanistan) currently stands at around $100 billion for all purposes. The fact that these amounts have been pledged does not amount to the same thing as payment. Moreover, the countries that would get the most compensation, such as China and India, are fast becoming the West's economic competitors.

Offset schemes and financial incentives

The alternative is some form of offset scheme that allows industrialized nations to fund emissions reductions in developing nations, and to count those reductions toward their own legal commitments. The idea is that this would require industrialized nations to pay a majority of the costs while also laying a foundation for the creation of a global emissions trading market. This was the aim behind the creation of the Clean Development Mechanism (CDM). However, although the CDM has, after a difficult start, been successful in creating a global market for GHGs, its design is fundamentally flawed, and it has done very little to actually cut emissions or to assist host countries in achieving sustainable development (Pearson 2007; Olsen 2007; Muller 2007).

Another important requirement will be the prevention of deforestation, which contributes roughly one-fifth of total global carbon emissions, almost twice as much as transport (International Panel on Climate Change 2007). Developing countries' tropical forests are an important source of carbon sequestration, yet they are not provided with any compensation for these environmental services. Providing financial incentives will help reduce emissions while at the same time helping them to invest in low-carbon paths to sustainable development. In this regard, encouraging steps have been made in the implementation of the United Nations Fund for Reducing Emissions from Deforestation and Forest Degradation (REDD+). However, the establishment of a final framework for the transfer of funds is still some years away, with a conclusive agreement only likely to come into effect after 2012. Moreover, there are serious concerns about the appropriate geographical scale of accounting and incentive mechanisms, monitoring, land tenure, elite capture of funds and the potential for fraud (Karousakis and Corfee-Morlot 2007; Olander, Boyd, Lawlor et al. 2009).

Participation and deliberation on a global scale are necessary, yet, in their current forms, existing instruments of global environmental governance are ill equipped to achieve results. What is required are representative institutions armed with the capacity and legitimacy required to translate policy commitments into real-world outcomes. If a global deal is going to work it must have an answer to the problem of governance, and embody an institutional structure that shapes and determines decisions which reflect the whole world in an even-handed way. Recourse to inclusive and broadly representative global decision-making channels is the most appropriate and effective way of doing this, and strengthening mechanisms of global governance will be key to constructing a global democratic response to the issue.

Democracy and the policy menu ahead

The challenge of tackling climate change will require the development of considerable additional institutional capacity and policy innovation. The goal of achieving this capacity, and the means to get there will be undermined if countries of all stages of development are not directly involved in the shaping of solutions. Current policy development demonstrates this concern. The short-term path to effective environmental governance is to integrate a broader set of interests into existing multilateral governance capacity. The existing mandate of the GEF could be broadened in order to help coordinate and fund international environmental agreements and reflect developing-country priorities. Complementary to this, the UNEP could increase its status and responsibilities by becoming a specialized UN agency, with all the compulsory UN funding that this entails. The central challenge in the years ahead of compliance monitoring and enforcement could be facilitated through a formal international mechanism for settling environmental disputes through mediation and arbitration, potentially similar to the World Bank's investment dispute body (Mabey 2007). Enhancing the capacities and responsibilities of the GEF and the UNEP in this way would be a step toward the more consolidated and formal institutional capacity of a World Environmental Organization as a longer-term goal, driven perhaps by the G2 + 1 (the USA, China and the EU), but accountable to the G195.

The key role of the state

In all of these challenges, states remain the key actors, as they hold the key to both domestic and international policymaking. The implementation of international agreements will be up to individual states; emissions trading and carbon pricing will require domestic legislation; and technological advance will need state support to get off the ground (Giddens 2008). However, state strategies at the domestic level should involve the creation of incentives, not overly tight regulation. Governments have an important role in 'editing' choice, but not in a way that precludes it altogether. This approach is represented in the form of what Giddens (2008) calls 'the ensuring state', whose primary role is to help energize a diversity of groups to reach solutions to collective action problems. The state, so conceived, acts as a facilitator and an enabler, rather than as a top-down agency. An ensuring state is one that has the capacity to produce definite outcomes. The principle goes even further: it also means a state that is responsible for monitoring public goals and for trying to make sure they are realized in a visible and legitimate fashion.

This will require a return to planning – not in the old sense of top-down hierarchies of control, but in a new sense of flexible regulation. This will require finding ways to introduce regulation without undermining the entrepreneurialism and innovation upon which successful responses will depend. It will not be a straightforward process, because planning must be reconciled with democratic freedoms. There will be push and pull between the political centre, regions and localities, which can only be resolved through deliberation and consultation. Most importantly, states will require a long-term vision that transcends the normal push and pull of partisan politics. This will not be easy to achieve.

All this takes place in the context of a changing world order. The power structure on which the 1945 multilateral settlement was based is no longer intact, and the relative decline of the West and the rise of Asia raise fundamental questions about the premises of the 1945 multilateral order. Democracy and the international community now face a critical test. However, addressing the issue of climate change successfully holds out the prospect of reforging a rule-based politics, from the nation-state to the global level. Table 5.2 highlights what we consider are the necessary steps to be taken along this road. By contrast, failure to meet the challenge could have deep and profound consequences, both for what people make of modern democratic politics and for the idea of rule-governed international politics. Under these conditions, the structural flaws of democracy could be said to have tragically trumped democratic agency and deliberative capacity.

Table 5.2 Summary of governance and policy recommendations

Guiding principles

Inclusiveness, political equality, deliberation, environmental sustainability and economic effectiveness

	Governance	Policy
Nation-state	• Broadening and deepening of the deliberative process	• Taxation of carbon and other GHGs
	• Transformation of private preferences via a process of deliberation into positions that can withstand public scrutiny and test	• Just and equitable markets for carbon and other GHGs
		• Applied scientific research
	• Continued involvement of citizens and civil society in the making and delivery of policy	• Early high-cost investments
		• Regulatory changes
		• Infrastructural development
	• Leadership that confronts narrow interests, and sets out acompelling scientific and economic case for action	• Information instruments
Global	• Promotion of inclusive and broadly representative global decision-making channels	• Develop effective offset schemes that allow industrialized nations to fund emissions reductions in developing nations
	• Assistance for developing countries to access necessary resources, capacity and technology for mitigation and adaptation	• Establishment of a formal international mechanism for settling environmental disputes through mediation and arbitration
	• Broaden the existing mandate of the GEF	• Development of formal institutional capacity for a World Environmental Organization
	• Increase the status and responsibility of the UNEP by upgrading to a specialized UN agency	

Notes

1. The authors acknowledge that table 5.1 does not control for level of development and other variables. Nonetheless, we think it is a useful approximate indicator of emission levels during the period when the politics of climate change has become increasingly acute.
2. See Jancar-Webster (1993) and Desai (1998).
3. Cf. Grafton and Knowles (2004).
4. Midlarsky (1998) finds that democracies have a good record on land area protection, but not on deforestation, CO_2 emissions and soil erosion, while Didia (1997) holds that democratic countries in the tropics have lower deforestation rates, and Bhattarai and Hammig (2001) claim a similar result in Latin America and Africa. Li and Reuveny (2006) show a positive effect for democracy on emissions, deforestation, land degradation, and water pollution, but Barrett and Graddy (2000) find that while political and civil freedoms mostly impact positively on air pollution, results for water pollution are mixed, and Torras and Boyce (1998) maintain that democracy is statistically insignificant for dissolved oxygen, fecal coliform and particulates emissions. Neumayer (2002)

demonstrates that democracies sign more multilateral environmental treaties and comply more fully with international obligations, while Ward (2008) claims that liberal democracies generally promote sustainability in fossil fuel emissions, but only very weakly.

5. We would like to thank Michael Mason for his guidance through this maze of agents and agencies.
6. For a more detailed overview of problems of accountability and representation in the transnational governance of environmental harm, see Mason (2008).
7. As Stern (2009: 104) points out, greater certainty about emissions levels comes with less certainty about prices. Unfortunately, there is always trade-off – it is impossible to achieve both price and quantity certainty in an uncertain world. In this case, he suggests that price uncertainty is the lesser of the two evils.

Bibliography

Baber, W. and Bartlet, R. (2009) *Global Democracy and Sustainable Jurisprudence*, Cambridge, MA: MIT Press.

Barrett, S. and Graddy, K. (2000) 'Freedom, Growth, and the Environment', *Environment and Development Economics*, 5.

Bättig, M. and Bernauer, T. (2009) 'National Institutions and Global Public Goods: Are Democracies More Cooperative in Climate Change Policy?' *International Organisation*, 63 (2).

Bernauer, T. and Caduff, L. (2004) 'In Whose Interest? Pressure Group Politics, Economic Competition and Environmental Regulation', *Journal of Public Policy*, 24 (1).

Betsill, M. and Corell, E. (2001) 'NGO Influence in International Environmental Negotiations: A Framework for Analysis', *Global Environmental Politics*, 1 (4).

Bhattarai , M. and Hammig, M. (2001) 'Institutions and the Environmental Kuznets Curve for Deforestation: A Cross-country Analysis for Latin America, Africa and Asia', *World Development*, 29 (6).

Biermann, F. and Pattberg, P. (2008) 'Global Environmental Governance: Taking Stock, Moving Forward', *Annual Review of Environment and Resources*, 33.

Bohman, J. (1998) 'The Coming of Age of Deliberative Democracy', *The Journal of Political Philosophy*, 6 (4).

Börzel, T. and Risse, T. (2005) 'Public Private Partnerships: Effective and Legitimate Tools for Transnational Governance?' in E. Grande and L. Pauly (eds.), *Complex Sovereignty: Reconstituting Political Authority in the Twenty First Century*, Toronto: University of Toronto Press.

Bueno de Mesquita, B., Smith, A., Siverson, R. and Morrow, J. (2003) *The Logic of Political Survival*, Cambridge, MA: MIT Press.

Chasek, P. and Rajamani, L. (2003) 'Steps toward Enhanced Parity: Negotiating Capacity and Strategies of Developing Countries', in I. Kaul, P. Conceicão, K. Le Goulven and R. Mendoza (eds.), *Providing Global Public Goods: Managing Globalisation*, New York: Oxford University Press.

Chestney, N. and Szabo, M. (2009) 'Global Carbon Market Doubled in 2008, Cut Less CO_2', *Reuters*, 27 May.

Congleton, R. (1992) 'Political Institutions and Pollution Control', *Review of Economics and Statistics*, 74.

Congressional Budget Office of the United States (2005) *Uncertainty in Analyzing*

Climate Change: Policy Implications, Report for the Congressional Budget Office of the United States, Washington, DC: CBO.

Desai, U. (1998) 'Environment, Economic Growth, and Government', in U. Desai (ed.), *Ecological Policy and Politics in Developing Countries*, Albany: State University of New York Press.

Didia, D. (1997) 'Democracies, Political Instability and Tropical Deforestation', *Global Environmental Change*, 7 (1).

EIA (2006) *International Energy Annual 2006*, Washington, DC: United States Energy Information Administration.

Falkner, R. (2007) *Business Power and Conflict in International Environmental Politics*, Basingstoke: Palgrave Macmillan.

Giddens, T. (2008) *The Politics of Climate Change*, Cambridge: Polity Press.

Grafton, Q. and Knowles, S. (2004) 'Social Capital and National Environmental Performance: A Cross-sectional Analysis', *Journal of Environment and Development*, 13 (4).

Hardin, G. (1968) 'The Tragedy of the Commons', *Science*, 162.

Heilbroner, R. (1974) *Inquiry into the Human Prospect*, New York: Norton.

Held, D. (2004) *Global Covenant: The Social Democratic Alternative to the Washington Consensus*, Cambridge: Polity Press.

Held, D. (2006a) *Models of Democracy*, Cambridge: Polity Press.

Held, D. (2006b) 'Reframing Global Governance: Apocalypse Soon or Reform!' *New Political Economy*, 11 (2).

Held, D. and McGrew, A. (2007) *Globalisation/Anti-Globalisation: Beyond the Great Divide*, Cambridge: Polity Press.

Helm, D. (2008), 'Climate-change Policy: Why Has So Little Been Achieved?' *Oxford Review of Economic Policy*, 24 (2).

Holden, B. (2002) *Democracy and Global Warming*, London and New York: Continuum.

International Panel on Climate Change (2007) *Synthesis Report of the IPCC's Fourth Assessment Report*, Geneva: IPCC; available at: http://www.sciencedirect.com/.

Jancar-Webster, B. (1993) 'Eastern Europe and the Former Soviet Union', in S. Kamieniecki (ed.), *Environmental Politics in the International Arena: Movements, Parties, Organisations and Policy*, Albany: State University of New York Press.

Kahler, M. (2005) 'Defining Accountability Up: The Global Economic Multilaterals', in D. Held and M. Koenig-Archibugi (eds.), *Global Governance and Public Accountability*, Oxford: Blackwell

Karousakis, K. and Corfee-Morlot, J. (2007) *Financing Mechanisms to Reduce Emissions from Deforestation: Issues in Design and Implementation*, OECD/IEA information paper, Annex I Expert Group on the UNFCCC, Paris: OECD.

Keck, M. and Sikkink, K. (1998) *Activists beyond Borders: Advocacy Networks in International Politics*, Ithaca: Cornell University Press

Keohane, R. (2003) 'Global Governance and Democratic Accountability', in D. Held and M. Koenig-Archibugi (eds.), *Taming Globalisation: Frontiers of Governance*, Cambridge: Polity Press.

Keohane, R. and Raustiala, K. (2008) *Toward a Post-Kyoto Climate Change Architecture: A Political Analysis*, UCLA School of Law, Law and Economics Research Paper Series, Research Paper No. 08-14.

King, Sir D. (2004) 'Climate Change Science: Adapt, Mitigate, or Ignore?' *Science*, 303.

Li, Q. and Reuveny, R. (2006) 'Democracy and Environmental Degradation', *International Studies Quarterly*, 50 (4).

Mabey, N. (2007) 'Sustainability and Foreign Policy', in D. Held and D. Mepham (eds.), *Progressive Foreign Policy: New Directions for the UK*, Cambridge: Polity Press.

Mason, M. (2008) 'The Governance of Transnational Environmental Harm: Addressing New Modes of Accountability/Responsibility', *Global Environmental Politics*, 8.

Midlarsky, M. (1998) 'Democracy and the Environment: An Empirical Assessment', *Journal of Peace Research*, 35 (3).

Muller, A. (2007) 'How to make the Clean Development Mechanism Sustainable –The Potential of Rent Extraction', *Energy Policy*, 35 (3).

Munton, R. (2003) 'Deliberative Democracy and Environmental Decision-making', in F. Berkhout, M. Leach and I. Scoones (eds.), *Negotiating Environmental Change: New Perspectives from Social Science*, Cheltenham: Edward Elgar.

Neumayer, E. (2002) 'Do Democracies Exhibit Stronger International Environmental Commitment? A Cross-country Analysis', *Journal of Peace Research*, 39 (2).

Organization for Economic Co-operation and Development (2007) *Climate Change Policies*, OECD Policy Brief, August 2007, Paris: OECD.

Offe, C. and Preuss, U. (1991) 'Democratic Institutions and Moral Resources', in D. Held (ed.), *Political Theory Today*, Cambridge: Polity Press.

Olander, L., Boyd, W., Lawlor, K., Myers Madeira, E. and Niles, J. (2009) *International Forest Carbon and the Climate Change Challenge: Issues and Options*, Nicholas Institute for Environmental Policy Solutions Report, Report No. 09-05.

Olsen, K. (2007) 'The Clean Development Mechanism's Contribution to Sustainable Development: A Review of the Literature', *Climatic Change*, 84.

Olson, M. (1982) *The Rise and Decline of Nations*, New Haven, CT: Yale University Press.

Ophuls, W. (1977) *Ecology and the Politics of Scarcity*, San Francisco: Freeman.

Payne, R. (1995) 'Freedom and the Environment', *Journal of Democracy*, 6 (3).

Pearson, B. (2007) 'Market Failure: Why the Clean Development Mechanism Won't Promote Clean Development', *Journal of Cleaner Production*, 15.

Porritt, J. (1984) *Seeing Green: The Politics of Ecology Explained*, Oxford and New York: Basil Blackwell.

Prakash, A. and Potoski, M. (2006) *The Voluntary Environmentalists: Green Clubs, ISO 14001, and Voluntary Environmental Regulations*, Cambridge: Cambridge University Press.

Sachs, J. (2008) 'Keys to Climate Protection', *Scientific American Magazine*, April.

Sachs, J. (2009) 'Putting a Price on Carbon: An Emissions Cap or A Tax?' *Yale Global*, 360 (9 May).

Schumpeter, J. (1942) *Capitalism, Socialism, and Democracy*, New York: Harper.

Stephens, T. (2009) *International Courts and Environmental Protection*, Cambridge: Cambridge University Press.

Stern, N. (2004) *The Stern Review on the Economics of Climate Change*, London: HM Treasury, Government of the United Kingdom.

Stern, N. (2009) *A Blueprint For a Safer Planet: How to Manage Climate Change and Create a New Era of Progress and Prosperity*, London: The Bodley Head.

Stiglitz, J. (2007) *Making Globalization Work*, London: Penguin.

Stiglitz, J. and Stern, N. (2009) 'Obama's Chance to Lead a Green Recovery', *Financial Times*, 2 March.

Torras, M. and Boyce, J. (1998) 'Income, Inequality, and Pollution: An Assessment of the Environmental Kuznets Curve', *Ecological Economics*, 25.

UN System Chief Executives Board for Coordination (2008), *Acting on Climate Change: The UN System Delivering as One*, New York: United Nations.

Victor, D., Granger Morgan, M., Apt, J., Steinbruner, J. and Ricke, K. (2009) 'The Geoengineering Option: A Last Resort Against Global Warming?' *Foreign Affairs*, March/April.

Ward, H. (2008) 'Liberal Democracy and Sustainability', *Environmental Politics*, 17 (3).

6

'Until the Last Ton of Fossil Fuel Has Burnt to Ashes': Climate Change, Global Inequalities and the Dilemma of Green Politics

Ulrich Beck and Joost van Loon

Introduction: some historical remarks on the sociology of climate change

Our title – Max Weber's famous quotation,'until the last ton of fossil fuel has burnt to ashes'[1] – is more than a metaphor. In Weber's view, industrial capitalism generates an insatiable appetite for natural resources, which undermines its own material prerequisites. There is an 'ecological subtext' waiting to be discovered in Weber's writings, a Max Weber for the twenty-first century and the era of climate change – or, to put it another way, an early theory of reflexive modernization: the victories of modern capitalism produce, unseen and unwanted, the global crises of climate change, its combined natural–social, unequally distributed catastrophic consequences for all of humanity.

This early example of ecological enlightenment teaches us three things. First, there are indeed inspiring insights and conceptual ideas for a sociology of climate change to be found in the writings of sociology's classic authors, not only in Max Weber, but, of course, also in Karl Marx, John Dewey, Herbert Mead, Emile Durkheim, Georg Simmel and many others. Like Weber, Dewey spoke of American capitalism's 'waste' and possible 'exhaustion' of natural resources (see, e.g., Dewey 1988 [1954]). This demonstrates that the founders of sociology did have an idea of an unintended dynamics of capitalist modernization which changes and threatens its own foundations and its frame of reference: they had an idea of non-linear, discontinuous change, a change of change, of the 'uncertain times' meaning 'meta-change'.

Second, this horizon of a highly ambivalent process of modernization got lost in the post-World War II generation of classical sociologists.

Daniel Bell's *The Coming of Post-Industrial Society*, for example, dismissed 'limits to growth' and the 'apocalyptic hysteria of the ecological movement' (Bell 1999: 487). He and Talcott Parsons asserted that modern society 'lives more and more outside nature', i.e. our environments are technologically and scientifically mediated, and so resource problems will be managed by technological innovations and economic trade-offs (see Rostow 1959; Parsons 1965).

Third, in the 1970s (and 1980s and 1990s) in the face of recession, stagflation, oil price rises and other economic problems, and of an increasing awareness of ecological disasters and perspectives, a growing number of social theorists began to re-appropriate and refine the ideas that post-war modernization theorists had declared dead.[2] For example, they argue that by enormously increasing capitalism's speed, reach and growth rate, neoliberal globalization also greatly accelerates the speed and the volume of its throughput of natural resources, of the creation of waste and of catastrophic risks. Carrying forward programmes of modernization that are in part responsible for our problems doesn't make sense. If the post-war modernization narrative presupposes the separation of 'natural' and 'societal' forces (with the latter taken as what have to be tackled in order to prevent a catastrophe), climate change actually demonstrates and enforces exactly the opposite: an ongoing extension and deepening of combinations, confusions and 'mixtures' of nature and society; it makes a mockery of the premise that society and nature are separate and mutually exclusive (Adam 1998; Latour 1993).

Effectively, globalization offers us a choice which is no choice at all: to be for or against a process we cannot control, when the response to global issues should rather be one of correcting a situation we have helped to create. Climate change and nuclear proliferation require coordinated policy responses; so do poverty, disease and terror. These are 'global issues', but they can be addressed through both aggregated and collective changes in behaviour. Waste recycling by individuals and investment in alternative energy research by governments are both useful, but also in sum totally inadequate. There is a hidden convergence between globalizing and national thinking, because both divert attention from global issues. This is reflected institutionally by Western governments, where finance ministries promote globalization and competitive advantages. Professional networks tend to reinforce these tendencies. It is global issues, however, that render the foreign–domestic divide obsolete (Albrow 2007).

In this chapter, we want to outline in five steps the argument for a sociology of climate change:

(1) in order to mark the difference between the perspectives of climate science and sociology, we distinguish between the future of a catastrophic climate to come (science perspective) and the present anticipation of a catastrophic future (social science perspective);
(2) we ask: how did the global construction of the 'undisputable fact' of climate change become possible?
(3) and: does climate change radicalize global inequalities?
(4) we discuss 'the cosmopolitan moment' of climate change, or the ruse of history;
(5) we look at the dilemma of Green politics, or how to modernize modernity.

The present anticipation and the future of the catastrophic future

In 2007 the joint award of the Nobel Peace prize to the UN Intergovernmental Panel on Climate Change (IPCC) and to Al Gore put the challenge of climate change squarely on the global stage. Carefully balancing claims and uncertainty, the IPCC report asserted that the evidence for manmade climate change was 'unequivocal', and hence certain.[3] Despite the seeming certainty asserted by a coalition of climate scientists and politicians, warning of approaching catastrophic 'tipping points' and 'points of no return', sociologists have to make an important distinction, which both characterizes and distinguishes the sociological perspective from that of the climate scientist. The social and political meaning of 'climate catastrophes' changes dramatically depending on whether we use the term to refer to the *future* of catastrophic climate change to come (the perspective of the climate scientist) or to the *present anticipation* of a catastrophic future (the perspective of the sociologist). This is because the anticipated future of climate change opens up completely unexpected and, more importantly, *unforeseeable* opportunities for radical transformations of the conditions that are considered likely to cause the expected catastrophe in the first place. This present anticipation of future catastrophes and of their social and political impacts can be studied empirically. And, from this, it follows that uncertainty does not necessarily mean that things can only get worse.

In this chapter, we seek to argue that one modality through which uncertainty has a radical impact not only on the future but already on the *here and now* is the very ambivalence of climate change. Climate change is *pure ambivalence*. For example, it is not unthinkable that it is the politicization of climate change that will function as a lever for the emergence of a 'cosmopolitan realism' (Beck 2006), enabling the narrow-minded framing of environmental politics by the nation-state to be overcome. This is not a form of idealistic wishful thinking since such cosmopolitan realism can function to serve the interests of nation-states. More than that, it can renew their sovereignty in the era of global warming and global interconnectedness. The pure ambivalence of climate change can only be revealed if we abandon the linear paradigm of forecasting based on models that do not factor in the complexities of time (see also Adam 1998; Urry 2003). It is from this perspective that sociology has something useful to add: whereas the dominant discourse of climate change refers to a (still) non-existent catastrophic future, a *sociology* of climate change concentrates on the presently anticipated catastrophic future and its social and political implications. The future of climate change in the present, however, is a still largely uncomprehended/unconsidered key variable of a fundamental transformation of modern societies.

This transformation has remained unconsidered, because in a naively realist way we imagine it as a natural catastrophe (and likewise its societal consequences), and not as the socially constructed anticipation of natural catastrophes. Climate change does not only mean rising sea levels, geographical/physical shifts of rain zones and rapidly advancing desertification. These important matters of concern should be *supplemented* by what one might call the 'social implications', such as struggles over scarce resources, market fluctuations, war and migration. That is – and this is, of course, not news to ecologists and natural scientists – there are neither 'purely natural' nor 'purely social' phenomena.[4]

We should take into account the social and political consequences of this anticipation in the present. The 'catastrophic' aspect of climate change is not, for example, the drying up of the Aral Sea or Lake Chad or the drought in Australia, it is the proof that these must be ascribed to *human interventions* and that they alter or destroy the foundations of (the) societal order. The credibility of the catastrophic, however, creates in the present the counter-forces of its prevention – perhaps. Just as human actions are considered/deemed to be causally responsible for climate change and are thus part of the problem, they can also be part of the solution (that the forecast catastrophe does not come to pass in the end does not necessarily prove the forecast false, and can also be proof of its correctness, in the sense that it has had the effect in the present of a *self-refuting prophecy*). Anyone who concerns themselves with climate change runs into this paradox: the dominant discourse of climate change, the one which has a virtual monopoly in the sphere of world politics, points to the *future*. From a sociological perspective, however, climate change is already here in the *present*, and is transforming the political, economic, technical-scientific, legal, military and cultural landscapes fundamentally and with rapid speed. That is, risk is a matter of anticipation of present-futures (Beck 1992 [1986]; Adam and Van Loon 2000).

At the same time, climate change has moved from 'subpolitics' to 'superpolitics': the potential of the issue of climate change is so enormous that it is capable of reshaping and transforming the social and political landscape. No political party dares to look as if it is ignoring climate change. It is an extremely effective mobilizer of concern, as the Australian federal elections of 2007 showed. Droughts were being linked to manmade global warming and the then-ruling coalition of the Liberal Party and the National Party was a bit slow in learning to incorporate the right 'climate change politics' into its political language and suddenly faced decisive defeat at the polls. For those voting who experienced the drought, whether it was the result of manmade climate change or not, knowledge and vocabulary to put it in those terms had come from social movements, scientists, the media and politicians. These subpolitical forces were marginal forces, often ridiculed for their apparently extreme vocabulary, and initially not well connected. Now though, their concerns have suddenly been promoted to 'superpolitics'. Al Gore, for example, received a Nobel Prize for his slideshow on climate change. Neither he nor his allies are particularly powerful actors, yet they managed to make a significant contribution to re-shaping the present political agenda on a global scale.

How did the global construction of the 'indisputable fact' of climate change become possible?

In order to answer the question of how the global social construction of the 'indisputable fact' of climate change has become possible, the sociology of climate change has to be placed in a framework of manufactured uncertainties as outlined in the theory of 'world risk society' (Beck 2008). This distinguishes between a first modernity (modern, industrial, national), in which society required that risks were calculable and subject to management, and a second form of modernity (post-industrial, post-risk calculation, post-national), in which there are dangers which have an inherent tendency to run out of control. The focus is not on 'natural' hazards such as earthquakes, which have always plagued human settlements, but on what are generally believed to be *un*natural, industrially manufactured uncertainties and hazards. These move beyond political boundaries and are of the sort we are increasingly confronted with today.[5] They include uncertainties resulting from nuclear, biological and chemical production, but also from transnational terrorist networks and first and foremost, from climate change. Indeed, these new uncertainties are not simply beyond boundaries, but are de-bounding (transgressive) because they transcend existing boundaries and eventually transform them. They do so spatially (e.g. across nation-state boundaries), temporally (e.g. they are long-tailed and, in some cases, seemingly infinite, but, above all, they cross different timescales and fit onto none of them) and socially (e.g. they create controversies regarding demarcations with respect to attributions of liability, accountability, responsibility and response-ability).

Seen through the lens of 'first modernity' (the version of modernity that insists on 'linear progress' through the deployment of rational decision-making), these new uncertainties are simply negative side effects of accountable and rational activity: residual risks that can be subject to cost–benefit analysis and future control through advances in science and technology. Seen through the lens of 'second modernity' (the version of modernity that insists on non-linearity, multiplicity and virtuality and so, at best, is only capable of partial rationality), these new uncertainties delegitimate institutional authority, erode scientific rationality, create distrust in technologies and insinuate radical doubt about the future. They contribute to a stronger emphasis on the responsibility of individuals, organizations and communities to embrace more risk. They also engender a precautionary approach to a wide range of risks that have catastrophic potential. This 'age of unintended consequences' has to be distinguished from the expectation of intentional consequences. The terrorist power of uncertainty is especially strong because we do live in a risk society. Thus the different types of global risks – ecological, technological, economic and terrorist – reinforce and at the same time contradict each other, while introducing new kinds of radicalized global inequalities.

Of course, a deep and extremely powerful resistance (and opposition) to the recognition of climate change continues. Critics hold that efforts to reduce greenhouse gases would wreck the global economy. Their view is that anthropogenic warming is a myth conjured up by bad science, radical environmentalists and the anti-corporate left. Acknowledging manmade global warming also undermines the belief of neoliberalism in unregulated economic growth as the standard for evaluating economies, societies and political leaders and as a means for addressing a wide variety of problems. However, despite the flurry of publicity in the wake of the Copenhagen Conference about some minor mistakes in the IPCC's 2007 report, and increased doubts on the part of the general public, there are signs that the long-drawn-out controversy over climate change has won over a large majority of scientists, journalists, politicians, business people and entrepreneurs who now accept and take for granted that the thesis about climate change is true (for a different view on this issue see chapters 1–3). How has this happened? Our answer is: thanks to a grand coalition of science and the United Nations, the ecological conversion of major economic actors and the effect of visible environmental transformations.

Science: In reflexive modernization, everything becomes uncertain – except climate change! Astonishingly, the process of methodical doubt produces the (socially constructed) 'certainty', that mankind faces destruction unless something fundamental is done about it. The primacy of prevention, which both the IPCC reports and Sir Nicholas Stern's 2006 report for the UK government recognize, presumes it is as good as 'proven' that ongoing climate change is manmade and is rapidly producing catastrophes worldwide which are unequally distributed socially. Simultaneously, it is held that only timely action can prevent the worst. Acting now is more sensible than waiting. The overwhelming effect of the two reports depends on the constructed certainty that mankind must act, if it does not want to abandon itself to self-destruction. So, in a world risk society, in which manufactured uncertainties have become dominant, there is a *return of certainty*.

How is this possible? The global character of climate risks is giving rise to uncertainty – the framing of the global problem, issues of inequality and justice, possible organizational responses, legal under-pinnings, global economic preconditions and implications, etc. These are being processed in turn by a whole ensemble of institutions such as the International Monetary Fund, the World Bank, the World Trade Organization (WTO) and the Organization for Economic Co-operation and Development (OECD). The heads of these institutions, who are the incarnation of 'globalization from above', all know each other and often move from one organization to the next. They have close con-tacts with the national think tanks and decision-making bodies from which they are mainly recruited. A good nickname for such 'experts in matters global' would be *Mr or Mrs Network*. They are embodiments of global interdependence and global 'discourse coalitions'. Under con-ditions of indeterminate global risks, they are constantly confronted with the contradictions between the various national definitions of their work and the various definitions in terms of global regional-ism. This sets them free from 'national framings' and enables them to define the shared goals of their work pragmatically and in ongoing dialogue. It is they who also decide whether what they do explodes national assumptions, and whether it is in the global *and* national, hence cosmopolitan, interest. This means that it is possible (though not inevitable) that conceptual factories for forging cosmopolitan subpolitics may emerge that escape the constraints of the national definitions of risk politics. The Stern Report, written by a former chief economist of the World Bank at the request of the British government, and presented with considerable pomp and circumstance, is an out-standing illustration of this point.

The report's major achievement as a work of 'stage management' is not only that it transformed the 'rationale' of the climate problem but also that it turned it into an economic and political policy issue. For years scientists have been presenting compelling reasons for finally taking decisive action against global warming. The Stern Report added the decisive economic argument. Not so long ago, the associated rational construct – i.e. the way in which catastrophic climate change was 'framed' – came down to the alternative of balancing high costs today against a vague risk in the distant future. That was the *staging of a dilemma* that permitted chauvinistic national politicians and scepti-cal voters to do nothing. The 'Stern Report' turned the argument from on its head onto its (economic) feet. It showed that the costs of taking measures against global warming today are minor in comparison to the costs of doing nothing. Thus the new rationale is that what the world invests in climate protection today will be repaid with com-pound interest in the future. This robs opponents of action of the cost argument – there is no excuse left. If the newly staged 'rationale' is to acquire historical force, however, we need more than a successful demonstration of the lack of economic alternatives to preventative climate protection. In addition, an alliance of global economic actors must be forged that would have as one of its major goals to commit the nations and governments anxious about their sovereignty to the new vision of multi-state cooperation. Lingering doubt about one's own argument must be shielded against internal critics. Let us elaborate a little further on this last point.

Definition relations are relations of domination that confer collec-tive validity and legitimation on the staging of risk. In the nation-state constitution of first modernity, they are geared to 'progress'. This means that in the distribution of burdens of proof, *laissez-faire* (some-thing is safe until it has been proven dangerous) enjoys priority over the principle of *precaution through prevention* (a catastrophe endanger-ing humanity has to be prevented even if there are doubts left).[6] The Stern Report substituted the principle of precaution for the laissez-faire distribution of the burdens of proof, not as the result of an official pronouncement and debate or a vote among scientists but through the power of publicly staged arguments. Thus the relations of definition were 'revolutionized' in that now, faced with manufactured uncertainty and the threat to the planet, the principle which had previously held – 'When in doubt, opt for doubt' – was replaced by the opposite principle: 'When in doubt, opt against doubt.' In view of the potential danger facing humanity, the irreducible uncertainty of any catastrophe prognosis is played down and the option of hiding behind the protective shield of burdens of proof that cannot be satisfied is removed. In view of the threat, the known not-knowing of future catastrophes is changed into its opposite: the *construction of certainty* in order to prevent by all means what is not supposed to happen.[7] The conception of science held by the first modernity, which posits critique and doubt as absolute, but thereby prevents timely counter-action, has thus become precarious. It is replaced by a process of enlightenment and reflection. This is the case not least in areas of 'hard science', which in confrontation with the self-destructive potential for catastrophe in developed scientific–industrial civilization, reverses the relations of power of definition in order to create world society foundations for preventive action. It is worth noting that this also opens the door to a 'green neoliberalism', a 'green capitalism'.

The ecological conversion of powerful economic actors: Opposition in science, politics and the mass media to the acknowledgement of global warming gradually loses its countervailing staging power insofar as the global economy itself sees decisive political action to combat climate change as a source of new opportunities for markets and growth. This is not to say that energy companies, for example, are now born again do-gooders acting out of a humanitarian interest – they continue to pursue short-term goals that threaten long-term harm to human beings and the environment. Yet a global consensus on climate protection can also create new 'enforced markets' in the context of acknowledged global risks. The economic attraction is that the safety and precautionary principles prescribed by the state compel (worldwide in the final instance) 'consumption' of carbon-dioxide-free and energy-efficient technologies. Under a regime of 'green capitalism' composed of transnationally structured enforced markets for environmental services, ecology is no longer a hindrance to the economy. Rather, the opposite holds well: ecology and climate protection could soon represent a direct route to profits. There is a marriage of reason between global capitalism and climate mitigation in the making. The question arises: what will a 'green neoliberalism' look like? In particular, if the growth imperative is seen as a principle hostile to humanity, how will the foundations of modernization and globalization have to be rethought?

This implies an avalanche of theoretical and political problems. Climate change and other ecological problems necessitate a fundamental reframing of class issues and justice issues, combining national and global perspectives. The same is true of population development, involuntary unemployment and exclusion (to say nothing of voting patterns and the distribution of power between political parties). These are the problems post-World War II theorists and policymakers often thought would be more or less automatically solved by economic growth and technical-scientific modernization. What follows for governance? Ultimately, state politics too have to be reinvented through an active embrace of a policy of climate protection in an alliance with civic groups. The attribute 'global' and the honorific term 'climate protection' promise elevated status, weighty responsibility and the prospect of statesmanlike stature to heads of government ground down in the mills of domestic politics.

Environmental transformations: All of that alone, however, would probably not have been enough. No-one really trusts the statements of the experts any more, according to whom weather is not climate. Those people who already have the climate catastrophe in their heads can 'see' that specific natural transformations – for example the increasing number of once-in-a-century river floods, the receding glaciers, the decrease of sea ice in the polar regions – are concrete manifestations of global climate risk. For sectors of the global population who do not share this belief or cannot afford to – in Africa, East Asia, eastern Europe or South America – climate catastrophe is nothing, a non-thing, a hysteria or a new strategy of Western imperialism to maintain global inequalities. As with any religion, the belief in climate risk produces its heretics, agnostics, mystics, non-believers and ignorant, as well as heretical secularists who do not want to have anything to do with any I'm-saving-the world messianism. The perception of risk becomes more influential the more evident it becomes that global risks elude calculation. Culturally determined views and assessments become decisive and replace the supposedly fact-based knowledge of experts.

We are at present experiencing an invasion of politics by culture. The diverse risk tendencies in the West are converging. The international environmental organizations have achieved definitional power over climate protection. They have been rewarded for their global reach and their cultural 'Red Cross consciousness' with almost limitless trust: there is no opposition to saving the world.[8]

Problematic for nation-state politics is the fact that it can only compensate for a loss of legitimacy by embracing a cosmopolitical endorsement of risk since the national frame no longer promises security. The old institutions come chasing after the needs of the world population, which is withdrawing its trust from them. This paradox is at the heart of the theory of world risk society. It stands in clear opposition to the two most important alternative[9] theoretical approaches to understanding risk, which currently inform the most important critical research programmes in this area, namely the tradition of Mary Douglas (Douglas and Wildavsky 1983; Douglas 1994) on the one hand, and that of risk governmentality (inspired by Michel Foucault) on the other. These approaches are undoubtedly important when it comes to understanding definitions and politics of risk. Their achievement and persuasiveness lie in having decoded risk as a *site of struggle*.

For social scientists following Douglas's (Durkheimian) cultural theory, the main conflict is between those groups operating in the political and institutional domains delimited by the state and the market. Risks are coupled with allocation of blame in an attempt to stabilize or destabilize the system, depending on what gain is sought. (Social) science operates as an ally, but not as a key stakeholder in a confrontation between different political epistemologies (e.g. Rayner 1992; Scott 2000).

For social scientists extending Foucault's governmentality thesis, the principal focus of attention is on the ways in which risks provoke specific modalities of regulation, surveillance and discipline (Scott-Jones and Raisborough 2007; Van Loon 2007). Here rhetoric is far less central than in Douglas's work: what matters instead is the organization of regulatory regimes. Risks enable the delimitation of domains of governance; they legitimate technical–scientific interventions and they unleash the force of the will to know(ledge). Such a perspective allows us to see that it is not the political epistemologies of risk cultures but the emergent systems of governance that inaugurate specific modes of epistemic politics serving an essentially nihilistic systemic closure.

What both perspectives share is a sensitivity to the political nature of risk-construction. However, whereas for Douglas the determining factors lie in the nature of the social system itself, for Foucauldians it is abstraction that drives risk society. But neither perspective avoids the error of viewing risk in part – or even exclusively – as an ally of the powerful rather than as unreliable or even as a potential antagonist, a hostile force confronting the nation-state (and expert systems).

Everyone is searching for a degree of security which has been lost. But the nation-state trying to deal with global risks on its own is like the drunk on a dark night, trying to find his wallet in the light of a street lamp. When asked, 'Did you really lose your wallet here?' he replies, 'No, but at least I can look for it in the light of the lamp!' Given the intolerable conditions of world risk society, the older critical theory of Foucault may be accused of affirmation and of being antiquated. The same holds true of large parts of a sociology which has focused on class relations in the welfare state. Such approaches underestimate global inequality and disarm the communicative cosmopolitan logic of global risks.

Climate change and radicalized global inequalities

Anyone wishing to uncover the relationship between world risk and social inequality will inevitably have to engage with the concept of risk. Risk and social inequality, indeed risk and power, are two sides of the same coin. Risk presumes a decision, therefore a decision-maker, and produces a radical asymmetry between those who take and define the risks, as well as profit from them, and those who are assigned to them, who have to suffer the 'unforeseen side effects', perhaps even pay for them with their lives, without having had the chance to be involved in the decision-making process. Where and for whom is the functionality, the attraction of the 'globalization' of risks? In this case too, there is an evident relationship between risk and power. Often the danger is *exported*, either spatially – to countries, whose elites see an opportunity for themselves – or temporally – to the future (time) of unborn generations.

National boundaries do not have to be removed for this flourishing export of dangers to take place; their existence is a precondition of it. It is only because these borders are like walls, restricting sight and relevance, persisting both in people's heads and in law, that what is done with deliberation remains 'latent' and a 'side effect'. Money is saved, if the risk is transported to a place where safety standards are low and the arm of the law cannot reach, in particular the arm of one's own national law. This is as true of the export of torture as it is of the export of waste, dangerous products and controversial research. Dangers are accordingly 'exported' – to low-safety countries, low-wage countries, low-rights countries. From the cosmopolitan perspective, the distribution of 'latent side effects' follows the pattern of the exploitation of marginal, peripheral regions where law is weak and need is great, because here civil rights are a 'foreign phrase' (or a luxury that means little to an empty or sick stomach). Here, too, elites have an interest in retaining the position of largely unresisting 'side effect countries' and of the 'latent' maximization of dangers in the interests of a maximization of profit.

The non-perception of risks or the unwillingness to perceive them increases with the lack of alternatives in human existence. The risks are passed on to a place where they are not appreciated or not taken seriously. The acceptance of dangers in such countries is not to be equated with agreement. Their concealment and the accompanying secrecy are the product of deprivation. Put differently, dangers are not accepted: they are imposed. And it goes unnoticed, thanks to the power to present processes as if nothing of importance is happening.

The dismissal of risks in states, in which poverty and illiteracy are especially widespread, does not mean, therefore, that these societies are not integrated into world risk society. In fact, it is the other way round. The first law of the social inequalities of climate risk is: *pollution follows the poor*. Those peoples and countries that contribute least to the acceleration of climate change are going to be the ones most affected by climate catastrophes. The new sociological narrative of climate change, therefore, has to insist on the need to extend the issue of inequality beyond the misleading and narrow field of calculations based on GNP or 'income per head'. And it has to concentrate on the fatal attraction of poverty, social vulnerability, corruption, humiliation, accumulation of dangers and denial of dignity – the factors determining attitude, conduct and group integration, fast growing in importance in world risk society.

It is consequently necessary to reframe social inequalities beyond 'methodological nationalism' (that is, beyond the aforementioned nation-state/society model). This reframing involves three crucial points:

- class is but one of the historical forms of inequality;
- the nation-state is only one of its historical frames;
- 'the end of national class society' is not 'the end of social inequality', but just the opposite: the radicalization (or globalization) of inequalities, nationally and transnationally (Beck 2007).

What we are witnessing here at the beginning of the twenty-first century is a kind of repetition, though this time on a planetary scale, of the process noted by Max Weber in the origins of modern capitalism and which he analysed as the 'separation of business from household' – in other words, the emancipation of business interests from all existing sociocultural institutions of supervision and control. Today it is the turn of the nation-state to be cast in the role of the households of the past and of the defender of parochialism.

The essence of this second stage of modernization is *the separation of power and politics*. In the course of its struggle to limit the social and cultural damage done by the first stage of modernity, the emergent modern state was able to develop institutions of politics and governance in accordance with the (postulated) merger of power and politics *within* the territorial union of the nation-state. The marriage of power and politics (or rather their cohabitation inside the nation-state) is now ending in divorce, with power partly evaporating up(wards) into cyber space, partly flowing sideways to the apolitical markets and in part becoming 'subsidiary' to the 'life politics' of newly 'enfranchised' individuals. Now, however, there is no equivalent of the 'sovereign nation-state' in sight, actually or potentially capable of taming the negative dynamics of world risk society. To sum up: we now have power free of politics and politics devoid of power. Power is already global; politics remain national/local. Territorial nation-states are local dustbins, garbage removal and recycling plants for the encroaching (climate) risks and catastrophes.

As is shown by the disturbances which regularly accompany the protests of social movements at meetings of the World Trade Organisation (WTO), the international regimes regulating trade, finance and the distribution of resources are acquiring ever greater importance in the distribution of global risks. International risk management is even acquiring increasing influence over national risk policy. An example of this development is the way the European Union is extending its key position in the risk management of European nation-states. The weakening of national structures and the strengthening of transnational non-governmental organizations of global civil society point in the same direction.

The crucial questions concerning the framework and norms of cosmopolitan accountability and responsibility crystallize in these contexts. Andrew Linklater (2001) talks of 'cosmopolitan harm conventions', by which he means intergovernmental agreements and treaties that transform the infliction of cross-border injuries and damage into crimes subject to prosecution and punishment. In this area too, initial proposals for a cosmopolitan law of risk as part of international law are being developed (Strydom 2002; Mason 2005; Apel 1988). As Linklater (1998) puts it, condemnation of 'transnational harm requires a commitment to regard insiders and outsiders as moral equals . . . Transnational harm provides one of the strongest reasons for widening the boundaries of moral and political communities to engage outsiders in dialogue about matters which affect their vital interests' (p. 84).

The 'cosmopolitan moment' of climate change, or the ruse of history

What is meant by the 'cosmopolitan moment'? For the first time in history, every population, culture, ethnic group, every religion and every region in the world is living in the shared present of a future that threatens one and all. In other words, if we want to survive, we have to include those who have been excluded. The politics of climate change is necessarily inclusive and global – it is cosmopolitan *realpolitik*. Two radically different models of climate policy appear to be emerging. One adheres to the formula 'Climate protection doesn't hurt.' The idea here is to try and lower greenhouse gas emissions in a consumer- and voter-friendly way by pursuing bold innovations in ecology and technology, in line with the old logic of progress. However, keeping a seemingly realistic eye on the power of the powerful (the automobile manufacturers, for instance) runs the risk of overlooking the power of the powerless. Climate change forces us to recognize that the only way of setting up effective checks is through fairness and equality. Only by taking account of the others – the poor – in our own decision-making can we protect ourselves effectively from the consequences of climate change. Thus cosmopolitan *realpolitik* is the politics of listening and the politics of global justice.

The alternative model is based, therefore, on the realization that climate change, if taken seriously and thought through to its logical conclusions, entails a *political paradigm shift*. Only a broad-based coalition that includes 'old Europeans', eco-conscious Americans, underdeveloped countries, developing countries, civil society movements and powerful factions of global capital can win back national sovereignty in a world risk society that is ecologically fragile and vulnerable to terrorist threats. It is not a matter of undermining, let alone abolishing, nation-states. Rather, it is a matter of restoring their capacity to act effectively at all – i.e. in collaboration with one another. Thus cosmopolitan *realpolitik* is about *empowering* national societies and states. Sociology's task (in this context) is to enquire and to analyse how global risks can be deployed as mobilizing forces to make us encounter the other, to make us see that our problems are connected to theirs, that climate change and social inequality and injustice are linked. Hence the cosmopolitan moment resides in the first instance in the necessity of including cultural others throughout the world.

This is equivalent to the claim that the *sociological* concept of cosmopolitanism (Beck 2006; Beck and Grande 2007) refers to a particular social way of dealing with cultural difference. It is distinguished, for example, from *hierarchical exclusion* (as encountered in past and present racist thought and practice), from the *universalism* that declares the dissolution of differences, from the *nationalism* that levels differences and simultaneously excludes them in conformity with national antagonisms, and from the *multiculturalism* that is understood and practised as plural monoculturalism (usually within the national framework). Cosmopolitanism differs from these forms by virtue of the fact that, as we have seen, it makes the inclusion of others a reality and/or its maxim.

There is, of course, a world of difference between cosmopolitanism as 'reality' and as 'maxim'. In the normative sense (maxim), cosmopolitanism means *acknowledgement* of cultural otherness, both internally and externally. Differences are neither hierarchically ordered nor dissolved but are accepted as such, and even viewed positively. However, at the beginning of the twenty-first century such conditions are nowhere near being accepted anywhere in the world. But what can unite human beings of different skin colour, religion, nationality, location, pasts and futures, if not *acknowledgement*? The answer proposed by the theory of world risk society is: the traumatic experiences of the enforced community of global risks that threaten everyone's existence. The recognition of the reality of the threat, however, by no means inevitably encompasses the recognition of otherness.

We must, therefore, make a distinction between a world in which the plurality of others is denied, ignored or condemned, even though that plurality cannot be expunged, and a world in which this plurality is *acknowledged* and in which all share in the commonality of difference. The 'cosmopolitan moment' of world risk society means, first, the human condition of the irreversible non-excludability of the culturally different. We are all trapped in a shared global space of threats – without an exit. This may produce very contradictory responses, including re-nationalization, xenophobia, etc. Only *one* incorporates the *acknowledgement* of others as equal *and* different – namely, normative cosmopolitanism.

World risk society forces us to recognize the plurality of the world that the national outlook was able to ignore. Global risks open up a moral and political space that can give rise to a civil culture of responsibility that transcends borders and conflicts. The traumatic experience of vulnerability shared by all and the responsibility for others arising from that, not least for the sake of one's own survival, are the two sides of a belief in world risk.

The principle of almost *boundless inclusion*, as regards both groups and topics, is reminiscent of analyses of the public sphere such as those provided by Hannah Arendt (1958), Jürgen Habermas (1991) and, more recently, Roger Silverstone (2006). Interestingly, the cosmopolitan moment engages with both the top and the bottom of the social hierarchy: not only the voiceless, but also the powerful, are addressed and called to account. Accordingly, with the declaration of 'imminent danger', the light of publicity shines into even the darkest corners of power and the most hermetic areas of decision-making.

Nevertheless, global risk public spheres have a completely different structure from the 'public sphere' explored by Jürgen Habermas. Habermas's ideal public sphere presupposes that all concerned have an equal chance to participate and that they share a commitment to the principles of rational discourse. Involvement in the *threat public sphere* is involuntary and is emotionally and existentially determined. In this case it is terror that breaks through the armour of anonymity and indifference, even if for most people it is images that are the source of terror. It is not a matter of commitment or of rationality. Potential bearers of responsibility who hide behind 'systemic constraints' are hauled before the court of global public opinion via the media. Without regard for social status they are criticized mercilessly and convicted of self-contradiction. Images of horror do not produce cool heads but they do give rise to cross-border compassion. False alarms, misunderstandings, condemnations are all part of the story. In these risk public spheres, too, pressure mounts to volcanic proportions.

Threat public spheres are impure; they distort, are selective and stir up emotions and anger. They make possible more, and at the same time less, than the public sphere described by Habermas. They are more like the picture of 'Mediapolis' so minutely and sensitively drawn by Roger Silverstone (2006) and the one sketched by John Dewey in *The Public and Its Problems* (1988 [1954]). In the latter, Dewey defends the thesis that it is not actions but their *consequences* that lie at the heart of politics. Although he was not thinking of global warming, BSE or terrorist attacks, his theory can be applied perfectly well to world risk society. A global public discourse does *not* arise from a consensus on decisions, but rather out of *disagreement* over the *consequences* of decisions. Modern risk crises are constructed out of just such controversies over consequences. Although there are some who insist on seeing an overreaction to risk, risk conflicts do indeed have an enlightening function. They destabilize the existing order but can also be seen as a vital step toward the construction of new institutions. Global risk has the power to confuse the mechanisms of organized irresponsibility and even to expose them to political action.

Egotism, autonomy, autopoiesis, self-isolation – these are key terms used to describe modern society in sociology and public and political debates. The communicative logic of global risk must be understood according to precisely the opposite principle. World risk is *the* unwanted, unintended obligatory medium of communication in a world of irreconcilable differences in which everyone is turning on his own axis. Consequently the public perception of risk forces people to communicate who otherwise do not want to have anything to do with one another. It imposes obligations and costs on those who resist it, often even with the law on their side. In other words, large-scale risks cut through the self-sufficiency of cultures, languages, religions and systems as much as through the national and international agenda of politics; they overturn the priorities of the latter and create contexts for action bringing together camps, parties and quarrelling nations that know nothing about one another.

The anticipation of catastrophic side effects, for example, means that big companies increasingly meet with anticipatory resistance to their decisions. No power plant can be built without protests from residents close to the planned location, no oilfield can be explored without critical scrutiny by transnational non-government organizations, no new medicine can be acclaimed without the known and unknown risks being listed. In other words, global risks ensure an involuntary democratization. They also, however, ensure unexpected alliances. US industry wants far more climate protection and is forming alliances with environmental groups. The heads of major US corporations agree that an active climate policy is absolutely indispensable and want to move the government in this direction. This ecological conversion is the outcome of intensive cooperation between environmental groups and industrial lobbies since 1999. It is, of course, also a matter of securing an early advantage in the global competition for the massive increase in the business of environmental technology on the road to green capitalism.

The dilemma of Green politics or: how to modernize modernity

What is so striking about climate change is the paradox of a universal consensus around a potentially catastrophic future as 'matter of fact' and an absence of consensus on political and everyday practices of how to live in accordance with these facts – that is, how to avoid the impending global catastrophe. That raises the key question: what is paralysing, blocking the enthusiasm for an ecological turn in politics that would tackle the problem at the roots? Why is there no storming of the Bastille of environmental destruction threatening mankind, no Red October of ecology? Why does the worldwide acknowledgement of the disastrous consequences of manmade climate change not arouse the same vital anger and moral outrage – a new optimism, new ideals and an inspiring democratizing euphoria – as the preceding tragedies of poverty, tyranny and war? Why has the ecological question become entangled in an ethical–religious *mea culpa*? Why is it always a matter of confessing the 'sins' of technology, of industrialism, indeed of modernity and its emancipation, and of swearing (false) oaths to stop, to turn back? Why is the conversion backward-looking (a *noli me tangere*), failing to produce *the vision of a marriage of reason between modernity and ecology*, linking technological inventiveness, concern for nature, inclusion of the cultural other and the cosmopolitan issue of justice, and arguing for a 'better modernity'?

The attempt of the Green movement to combine nature with politics ultimately ended in tragedy. The triumphal march of the Green movements of renewal and revival began with a split between two paths which in German got the nicknames 'Fundi' and 'Realo' (fundamentalist and realist). With the prospect of catastrophe, anti-modern fundamentalism gained power and influence in the public sphere.

Fundis: Millions of well-meaning souls decided to have themselves publicly whipped for their former notion of dominating nature, for their unbridled hubris, and they swore to themselves and to others that from now on they would do something that is impossible: to leave no footprints behind, no matter where they went. Anyone who wants to resist climate change by dropping out of modernity might as well try to cure an inflammation of the lungs with cardiac arrest.

Realos: By portraying a bleak future for the human race in the name of 'indisputable facts', 'realistic' Green politics has succeeded in de-politicizing political passion to the point that citizens are left with nothing but gloomy asceticism, a terror of trespassing on nature and a diffidence toward industry, innovation, technology and science. The tragic consequence is that 'realo-politics' has left Green politics in the deep freeze, and this happened at the very time when the world climate discourse was forcing open the self-imposed limits of Green politics, creating new universal obligations and so opening the politi-cal horizon to 'other modernities', including Green ones.

The alternative 'fundis' or 'realos' is out of date, since in retrospect both have deprived politics of breath. Both founder on the concept of 'boundaries' – even if in quite different senses: one talks about the limits of technology, limits of domination of nature, etc.; the other points to the immanent limits of the political system, limits of capital-ism, limits of the nation-state, etc. Both – fundis and realos – behave like Green souls who have passed the sign 'Don't cross here!' What has happened to the inspiring 'We shall overcome!' which enthuses modernity? Emancipation is the word. Either ecological concerns will succeed in being at least as powerful as the modernizing urge or they will repeatedly fail to assert themselves. The blocking point is this: the whole endeavour of political ecology is presented as a matter of *learning our limits*, even though it is the very notion of limits that, para-doxically, has constrained or even paralysed politics.

There is (once again) a third way between fundis and realos, and that is the path of *modernization of modernity*. What counts is abolishing, overcoming these self-imposed limits within a concept of the limits of Green politics, in order in this way to release anger, courage, energy, imagination, and awaken the enthusiasm needed to break up this self-blockade of a civilization which threatens to be defeated by its 'victory crises'.

Bruno Latour writes:

> For a European and certainly for a Frenchman, such an endeavour is especially timely since they tackle this philosophical issue as a psycho-social question, namely as a question of emotion, of feeling, as if they had sensed that the gamut of political passions triggered by the eco-logical crisis was much too narrow to deal with the massive dimension of the problems – or at least much too weak compared to those that reli-gion, war, protest, art, may unlock. They try to tune in to another tone of political emotions, those necessary to *redevelop*, or, to use another expression . . . to modernize modernization . . . Environmentalists, in

the American sense of the word, never managed to extract themselves from this contradiction that the environment is precisely not what lies beyond and should be left alone –this was on the contrary the view of their worst enemies! – but what should be even more managed, taken up, cared for, stewarded, in brief, integrated, internalized in the very fabric of their polity . . . If I am right, the breakthrough consists in no longer seeing a contradiction between the spirit of emancipation and their catastrophic outcomes, but to take it as the normal duty of *continuing* to take care for the unwanted consequences all the way, even if this means going always further and further down into the imbroglios. Environmentalists say: 'From now on we should limit ourselves,' post-environmentalists exclaim: 'From now on, we should stop flagellating ourselves and take up explicitly and seriously what we have been doing all along at an ever increasing scale, namely, intervening, acting, wanting, caring.' In one case, the return of unexpected consequences appears as a scandal (which it is for the modernist myth of mastery); in the other, they are part and parcel of any action. (Latour 2008)

A Green politics which wants to do justice to the dimensions of climate change must modernize modernity – that is, overcome the false alternatives of retreat or accommodation.

Climate politics, for example, cannot be contained within the old logic of national/international politics. This is good news in bad times: climate politics gives us an opportunity to reconfigure power in terms of a '*cosmopolitan realpolitik*'. The policy action strategies disclosed by global risk are rudely overturning the order created by the neoliberal coalition between capital and the state. Climate risks *empower* states and civic movements, because they reveal new sources of legitimation and possibilities of action for these actors; on the other hand, they *disempower* globalized capital because the consequences of investment decisions create climate risks, destabilize markets and activate the power of the sleeping consumer giant. There is, therefore, an alternative option to neoliberal politics in both the national and global arenas: to connect civil society to the state, and that means creating a *cosmopolitan form of statehood*.

To put it more concretely: the cosmopolitan scope for action which the state has regained *extends* its influence in both the domestic *and* the foreign domains through activity and (modes of?) governance in transnational networks to which other states – but also NGOs, supranational institutions and transnational corporations – belong. Thus the cosmopolitan state, freed from scruples concerning sovereignty, uses the unrecompensed cooperation of other governments, non-governmental organizations and globally operating corporations to solve 'national' problems.

This optimistic construction could of course easily collapse under its own weight. It is fragile because the costs and benefits of an active climate change policy are unequally distributed, internationally and nationally, and because the burning question of justice in a radically unequal world is at the heart of distribution struggles. The costs will hit existing generations hardest, whereas the benefits will fall to the grandchildren of our grandchildren. The wealthiest countries must demonstrate the greatest willingness to compromise even though they are not the most vulnerable to the effects of global warming. In order to strike the necessary global deal, the agreement of the United States is most urgently needed, even though – and because – it would have to pay China, its arch-rival, enormous sums to make it carbon-dioxide-free, at the very point in history that the huge Far Eastern country is poised to overtake the United States economically and to become a centre of world power. It is clear that there are good reasons why cosmopolitan *realpolitik* is less attractive to superpowers, which believe in autonomy, and attractive to European and other, smaller, powers, which believe in cooperation and interdependence. The consequences are obvious: The crisis deepens – and so does the gap between words and capabilities.

Notes

1. See Weber (2002: 123ff., 245f.).
2. See, among others, Beck (1992 [1986]); Giddens (1990, 1999); Harvey (1989); Dunlop (1993); Adam (1998); Jänicke (1993, 1995); Dickens (1992); Eder (1988); Ewald (1991); Strydom (2002); but also Latour (1993).
3. The panel estimated uncertainty based on levels of scientific evidence and agreement, which they used in 'confidence' judgements about the veracity of models, analysis or claims – i.e., from 'very high confidence' (90 per cent) to 'very low confidence' (10 per cent) – and of the 'likelihood' of future outcomes (from 'virtually certain' (99 per cent) to 'exceptionally unlikely' (1 per cent)); see Intergovernmental Panel on Climate Change (2007).
4. Whereas this might have sounded like a mere assumption eighty years ago, requiring profound philosophical investigations such as those of A. N. Whitehead (1978), it has by now become so obvious and ubiquitous that it is taken as simple common sense.
5. For example, whereas two decades ago a tsunami would be seen as a completely natural phenomenon, the recent tsunami of December 2004 was immediately linked to climate change and a narrative of causation related to human activity.
6. In security terms, one is guilty until proven innocent (Kruger, Magnet and Van Loon 2008).
7. It has to be noted that this only affects certain relations of risk definition, namely those that have invoked a governmental response. Many forms of risk production, for example in the realms of genetic engineering, nanotechnology, nuclear physics and biochemistry, have expanded and accelerated in the face of continued uncertainty, with an increasing (or in some cases exclusive) reliance on technological fixes and a general postponement of developing solutions to some future in which knowledge will have sufficiently increased to reduce uncertainty and its associated risks to an acceptable minimum.

8. The case of the Brent Spar and the role of Greenpeace is a clear example of this. This shows the fundamental danger of the fusion of epistemology and politics which is so vehemently professed by critical realists: disagreement is undesirable, if not impossible – one simply agrees or one is invalid in a moral sense (i.e., mad, criminal).

9. 'Alternative' is here meant in opposition to the critical realist hegemony which prohibits the very fundamental questions regarding the ontology of risk and simply urges us to reject constructionism as a folly.

Bibliography

Adam, B. (1998) *Timescapes of Modernity*, London: Routledge.

Adam, B., Beck, U. and Van Loon, J. (eds.) (2000) *The Risk Society and Beyond: Critical Issues for Social Theory*, London: Sage.

Adam, B. and Van Loon, J. (2000) 'Introduction', in B. Adam, U. Beck and J. van Loon (eds.), *The Risk Society and Beyond: Critical Issues for Social Theory*, London: Sage, pp. 1–31.

Albrow, M. (2007) *Das Globale Zeitalter*, Frankfurt: Suhrkamp.

Apel, K. O. (1988) *Understanding and Explanation: A Transcendental-Pragmatic Perspective*, Cambridge, MA, and London: MIT Press.

Arendt, H. (1958) *The Human Condition*, Chicago: The University of Chicago Press.

Beck, U. (1992 [1986]) *Risk Society: Towards a New Modernity*, trans. M. Ritter, London: Sage.

Beck, U. (2006) *Cosmopolitan Vision*, Cambridge: Polity Press.

Beck, U. (2007) 'The Cosmopolitan Condition: Why Methodological Nationalism Fails', *Theory, Culture & Society*, 24 (7–8).

Beck, U. (2008) *World at Risk*. Cambridge: Polity Press.

Beck, U. and Grande, E. (2007) *Cosmopolitan Europe*, Cambridge: Polity Press.

Bell, D. (1999) *The Coming of Post-industrial Society: A Venture in Social Forecasting*, New York: Basic Books.

Benjamin, W. (1968) 'The Work of Art in an Age of Mechanical Reproduction', in H. Zohn (trans.), *Illuminations*, London: Fontana, pp. 219–53.

Clarke, N. (1997) 'Panic Ecology: Nature in the Age of Superconductivity', *Theory, Culture & Society*, 14.

Dewey, J. (1988 [1954]) *The Public and Its Problems*, Athens, OH: Ohio University Press and Swallow Press.

Dickens, P. (1992) *Society and Nature: Towards a Green Social Theory*, Philadelphia: Temple University Press.

Douglas, M. (1994) *Risk and Blame: Essays in Cultural Theory*, London: Routledge.

Douglas, M. and Wildavsky, A. (1983) *Risk and Culture*, Berkeley, CA: University of California Press.

Dunlop, J. T. (1993) *Industrial Relations Systems*, revised edn, Boston, MA: Harvard Business School Press.

Eder, K. (1988) *Die Vergesellschaftung der Natur – Studien zur solazien Evolution der praktischen Vernunft*, Frankfurt am Main: Suhrkamp.

Ewald, F. (1991) 'Die Versicherungsgesellschaft', in U. Beck (ed.), *Politik in der Risikogesellschaft*, Frankfurt am Main: Suhrkamp, pp. 288–301.

Giddens, A. (1990) *The Consequences of Modernity*, Cambridge: Polity Press.

Giddens, A. (1999) *Runaway World: How Globalization is Reshaping Our Lives*, London: Profile.

Habermas, J. (1991) *The Structural Transformation of the Public Sphere: An Inquiry into the Category of Bourgeois Society*, Cambridge, MA: MIT Press.

Harvey, D. (1989) *The Condition of Postmodernity*, Oxford: Basil Blackwell.

Intergovernmental Panel on Climate Change (2007) *Climate Change and Water*, IPCC Technical Paper No. 6, Geneva: IPCC; available at: www.ipcc.ch/pdf/technical-papers/climate-change-water-en.pdf.

Jänicke, M. (1993) 'Über ökologische und politische Modernisierungen', *Zeitschrift für Umweltpolitik und Umweltrecht*, 2.

Jänicke, M. (1995) *The Political System's Capacity for Environmental Policy*, FFU-Report 95–4, Berlin: Forschungsstelle für Umweltpolitik.

Krimsky, S. (1992) 'The Role of Theory in Risk Studies', in S. Krimsky and D. Golding (eds.), *Social Theories of Risk*, Westport, CT: Praeger, pp. 3–22.

Krimsky, S. and Golding, D. (eds.) (1992) *Social Theories of Risk*, Westport, CT: Praeger

Kruger, E., Magnet, S. and Van Loon, J. (2008) 'Biometric Revisions of the "Body" in Airports and US Welfare Reform', *Body and Society*, 14 (2).

Latour, B. (1988a) 'Mixing Humans and Non-humans Together: The Sociology of a Door-closer', *Social Problems*, 35 (3).

Latour, B. (1998b) 'Ein Ding ist ein Thing: A Philosophical Platform for a Left European Party', *Concepts and Transformation*, 3 (1/2).

Latour, B. (1993) *We Have Never Been Modern*, Hemel Hempstead: Harvester Wheatsheaf.

Latour, B. (2005) *Re-assembling the Social: An Introduction to Actor–Network Theory*, Oxford: Oxford University Press.

Latour, B. (2008) 'It's Development Stupid! Or: How to Modernize Modernization' available online.

Linklater, A. (1998) *The Transformation of Political Community*, Oxford: Blackwell.

Linklater, A. (2001) 'Citizenship, Humanity and Cosmopolitan Harm Conventions', *International Political Science Review*, 22 (3).

Luhmann, N. (1995) *Die Soziologie des Risikos*, Berlin: De Gruyter.

Lupton, D. (1999) *Risk*, London: Routledge.

Lyon, D. (2007) *Surveillance Studies: An Overview*, Cambridge: Polity Press.

Macnaghten, P. and Urry, J. (1998) *Contested Natures*, London: Sage.

Mason, M. (2005) 'Conceptualising Environmental Democracy', in M. Redclift (ed.), *Post-Sustainability?* London: Routledge.

Parsons, T. (1965) 'The Normal American Family', in S. Farber, P. Mustacchi and R. H. Wilson (eds.), *Man and Civilization*, New York: McGraw Hill, pp. 31–50.

Rayner, S. (1992) 'Cultural Theory and Risk Analysis', in S. Krimsky and D. Golding (eds.), *Social Theories of Risk*, Westport, CT: Praeger, pp. 33–115.

Rose, H. (2000) 'Risk, Trust and Scepticism in the Age of New Genetics', in B. Adam, U. Beck and J. Van Loon (eds.), *The Risk Society and Beyond: Critical Issues for Social Theory*, London: Sage.

Rostow, W. W. (1959) *The Stages of Economic Growth: A Non Communist Manifesto*, Cambridge: Cambridge University Press.

Scott, A. (2000) 'Risk Society or Angst Society: Two Views of Risk, Consciousness and Community', in B. Adam, U. Beck and J. Van Loon (eds.), *The Risk Society and Beyond: Critical Issues for Social Theory*, London: Sage.

Scott Jones, J. and Raisborough, J. (2007) *Risk Identities and the Everyday*, Farnham: Ashgate.

Silverstone, R. (2006) *Media and Morality: On the Rise of the Mediapolis*, Cambridge: Polity Press.

Stern, N. (2006) *Stern Review on the Economics of Climate Change*, Cambridge: Cambridge University Press.

Strydom, P. (2002) *Risk, Environment and Society*, Buckingham: Open University Press.

Urry, J. (2003) *Global Complexity*, Cambridge: Polity Press.

Van Loon, J. (2002) *Risk and Technological Culture: Towards a Sociology of Virulence*, London: Routledge.

Van Loon, J. (2007) *Media Technology: Critical Perspectives*, Maidenhead: McGraw Hill / Open University Press.

Weber, M. (2002) *The Protestant Ethic and the Spirit of Capitalism*, ed. and trans. S. Kalberg, 3rd edn, Los Angeles, CA: Roxbury.

Whitehead, A. N. (1978) *Process and Reality: An Essay in Cosmology*, ed. D. R. Griffin and D. W. Sherburne, corrected edn, New York: The Free Press.

Part 2

SOCIAL JUSTICE AND SUSTAINABILITY

7

Social Justice and Sustainability: Elastic Terms of Debate

Onora O'Neill

The title of this chapter links two of the most protean terms of current political debate (for an overview, see Dobson 2007). This is immediately apparent from the fact that nobody claims to be against social justice, or against sustainability. These terms are seen as beyond criticism, contemporary versions of motherhood and apple pie, but of course more abstract and lofty (which in the eyes of some makes them quite superior). But if these notions are too elastic, there may not be much that is substantive to be said in their favour (or against them), ubiquitous though they are in current discussions. So, rather than contenting myself with obeisance to these ideals, I shall try to say a bit about the coherence and possibility of combining certain aspects or versions of social justice and sustainability.

Why are the terms popular? The term 'social justice' is, I think, popular because it suggests that we are thinking about justice that extends beyond civil and political justice, to social and economic arrangements at large. But if we are to take social justice seriously we need to know what possibilities lie beyond civic and political justice, whether they supersede or replace civic and political justice, or whether we are still to take these seriously. I think that the received answer is that we are looking at a *supplement*, or some would say a *completion*, of civic or political justice. Using the idiom of human rights, now the approved idiom, we should take the full range of human rights seriously: justice demands that we aim to have it all. In particular, most who use the phrase 'social justice' have in mind the importance for justice of greater equality (Arneson 1989; Cohen 2008). In the following, I shall say something about aiming for equality – while noting that there are other social goods that are quite often thought of as aspects of social justice such as solidarity or dignity.

Leaving those aside, we may note that there are countless *possible* equalities (Sen 1980; Gosepath 2007 [2001]), but not all of them matter. Some equalities are logically impossible (equal success, equal enjoyment of positional goods[1] – see Hirsch 1976); others are logically but not really possible (equal height or health); others are possible in both ways, but trivial (equal hair length or equal frequency of hair-cut). The equalities that discussions of social justice *may* be able to say something useful about must be *at least* logically and really possible, and, I take it, non-trivial. Debate has typically been about rather abstract equalities: some are thought of as falling under political and civic justice, such as equality under the law (Hart 1961), equal political rights or equal protection against unfair discrimination (Rawls 1999 [1971]; Nussbaum 1999; Young 2000); others are thought of as a matter of equalizing other social arrangements (Dworkin 2000). Advocates of social equalities are often divided on whether it is *equal process* or *equal outcomes* that matter (some blithe spirits simply think that both should be achieved, see Cohen 1989; Temkin 1993).

On the one hand we find advocates of equal opportunities demanding *equal process* in education, employment or healthcare: they are committed to fair process and anti-discrimination. On the other hand we find advocates of *equal outcomes* in education and economic life, who think that, even if results cannot be the same for all individuals, still they should be equalized for each social group. Most debates on these matters take a narrow view of what constitutes a social group, and think that we should measure and seek to rectify or reduce inequalities between genders, between (some) ethnic groups and between (some) income groups, but not those between other groups (Young 1990; Kymlicka 1995, 2007). Because equal outcomes for individuals or groups are remarkably hard to achieve, those who think them desirable often settle for what they take to be more attainable surrogates – such as *distributions of outcomes* that are more equal in some respect (e.g. raising the level of the least well-off (as in Rawls's second principle[2] – see Rawls 2001: 42–3); limiting the gap between the least and most well-off on some dimension). Here, I will not question the distributivist assumption that has dominated so much discussion of social justice – but I think it is ripe for discussion (see O'Neill 1986–2008 for an alternative approach).

The term 'sustainability' is, I think, popular because of its association with environmental protection (see Dryzek, Downes, Hernes et al. 2003; Dobson and Saiz 2005; Smith and Pangsapa 2008): we should aim for sustainable ecosystems, sustainable agriculture, sustainable forestry, sustainable fisheries and sustainable energy generation. But should we also aim for sustainable activities and development which (depending on one's focus) are thought of as including or requiring sustainable growth, businesses, finance and economics; government, charities and schools; travel, tourism and aviation; consumption, procurement, investing and marketing; architecture, design and fashion;

homes, cities, construction, concrete and drainage systems. A little googling will reveal lots more.

Cut to the chase: first consistency

The terms 'social justice' and 'sustainability' are both highly indeterminate: in my trade we call such phrases 'incomplete predicates', because they can be completed in many ways. You can at least *in theory* aim for *equal opportunities* and *equal outcomes*, but not all specific completions are compossible. You can at least in theory have *sustainable growth* and *sustainable agriculture* – but at certain points choices will be needed. Any achievable configuration of social justice and any achievable configuration of sustainability will require us to sacrifice – if you think the term gentler, to *trade off* – some forms of social justice and sustainability to achieve others. Moreover, if we aim *both* for social justice and for sustainability, we shall need to aim not merely for a configuration of each that is internally coherent, but for a configuration of the two that is coherent: we might find that we have to trade off some forms of equality for some forms of sustainability. Moreover, if we are committed to further aims – for example, solidarity or spiritual or aesthetic ideals – the range of compossible forms of social justice and sustainability may be further constrained (O'Neill 1996; Berlin 1997). Unless we recognize this, we are only playing with the rhetoric of social justice and sustainability, rather than thinking seriously about either.

In making these points I have said nothing yet about the *feasibility* – or to be blunter the *difficulty* – of achieving configurations of social justice and sustainability that are in principle possible, given various starting points and various assumptions. The practical constraints are huge, and discarding combinations of aims that are not compossible, or compossible only with extreme difficulty, is just a beginning.

A First step

However, I do not believe that the costs of advocating impossible or improbably difficult combinations of aims is sufficiently widely recognized in current public debates. I shall focus on this problem briefly.

There are many who advocate conceptions of social justice that combine equal procedures (non-discrimination) and equal (or more equal) outcomes. They may call for more *equal outcomes* and for *fair process*, and in some cases for greater *choice*. It seems that all three UK political parties are rhetorically committed to these improbably difficult combinations of commitments in the delivery of public services.

Yet, in most circumstances, fair process – i.e. no unfair discrimination – in dealing with differing cases cannot produce equal outcomes. Most obviously, demands that schools deliver equal educational results or that universities achieve equal access cannot be met without unfair discrimination. Still less can they be met when young people are offered choices – as in schools and universities – which differentiate their achievements and fitness, not to mention preferences, for various further activities. There is *no* chance that fair process or choice, or both combined, will generally lead to equal outcomes, just as there is *no* chance that imposing equal outcomes is generally possible without limiting choice and relying on unfair forms of discrimination.[3] Similarly in employment, where individual choice will produce differing pools of applicants, and meritocratic demands for fair process will require that we take account of their qualifications and experience, (to) different(iate) candidates for jobs, promotion, and redundancy will preclude equal results.

So the first questions to ask, if we think equalities are needed for social justice, are: *which* equalities matter, and *which* are compossible? Then we need to ask which are compossible with other goods, which are practically achievable, and which we should pursue. It is as incoherent to demand fair process and equal outcomes as it is to assume that differential outcomes are evidence of unfair discrimination.

Similar points can be made about the compossibility of different aspects of sustainability. As soon as we ask just which activities should be sustainable across which time periods, choices must be faced. A business may be economically sustainable across the medium run, but contribute levels of pollutants that make certain areas unsustainable for agriculture across that time period. A level of population growth may be sustainable across a defined time period, but not for an indefinite future. Design or fashion may be *more* sustainable, but probably not as sustainable for the environment as having *less* design and *less* fashion. Aviation that is *more* environmentally sustainable may be much *less* sustainable than *less* aviation. Sustainable concrete may be *less* sustainable than *less* concrete. And so on.

The practical point

I do not intend these comments as counsels of despair, but as counsels of realism. In the NICE (*Non-Inflationary Constant Expansion*) years we may sometimes have talked as if we could have it all. Among political and social theorists, that outlook has been sustained by the domination of human rights rhetoric in the vast majority of discussions of social justice and of many environmental issues. A focus on rights foregrounds recipience and entitlement, at the cost of leaving it unclear and often unspoken what must be done by whom if any rights are to be realized, and what the necessary conditions are for getting it done (see O'Neill, 1996, 2000, 2001). Efforts to realize rights – to make them justiciable – are spoken of as if we can take it for granted that there is some coherent way to combine a plurality of (supposed) rights, and it is only a matter of ingenuity to find a combination of requirements and prohibitions, incentives and restrictions that works. One result has been a tide of complex and detailed legislation, regulation, guidance and codes of practice that aim to fix innumerable obligations and to adjust them to one another in ingenious ways. The hope has been that these interlocking requirements will somehow secure and realize the full range of rights – or supposed rights – for all in all circumstances. It seems to me that in current circumstances we need a sharper and more realistic approach to achieve a coherent range of social justice and sustainability. I will suggest one implication for thinking about sustainability, and one for thinking about social justice.

Realism about sustainability begins with thinking about the environment. Without the necessary natural environment, all else fails (see Caney 2009). If we are to think seriously about sustainability, we need to accept that many activities and developments now dubbed *sustainable* may only be sustainable for a somewhat longer period than alternative or established versions of the same activities and developments. Sustainable concrete and fashion may be more sustainable than some other sorts of concrete and fashion, but a more sustainable environment may still do better with less of both. Short of demonstrable neutrality (or better) in the use of scarce resources or damaging technologies, many activities are less than sustainable in the long run. This suggests that we should try to be more parsimonious in speaking of technologies or activities as sustainable, and careful to state the assumptions under which, and the time period for which, they are judged sustainable.

Realism about social justice begins with thought about the necessary conditions of human survival. This simple thought has many corollaries. Realistic thought about social justice would, I suggest, no longer marginalize questions about population growth with a complacent assumption that we will somehow ingeniously achieve social justice for escalating populations in degrading environments. I do not, of course, mean that the way that population growth is reduced must be by the sorts of coercive measures that have given population policies in China (and more sporadically elsewhere) a bad name. There are other anti-natalist policies that can be, and are not being, implemented. Realism about social justice for our times will also demand sober focus on possible configurations of social justice that are feasible from where we are. This will demand an acute and realistic focus on the means at our disposal and their effective deployment. Do we have an adequate range of knowledge and skills – scientific, technical, institutional and human – to achieve needed changes? How will we obtain them if we do not yet have them? Do we know how to deploy and combine them? What are we willing to sacrifice to achieve sustainable social justice?

Notes

1. Positional goods are goods whose desirability reflects comparative judgements about the amounts others have of the same types of goods. Some examples include social status, talent or a house with a nicer view.
2. The second principle reads as follows: 'Social and economic inequalities are to satisfy two conditions:
   a. They are to be attached to offices and positions open to all under conditions of *fair equality of opportunity*;
   b. They are to be to the greatest benefit of the least-advantaged members of society (the *difference principle*).'
3. Choice in public services was initially advocated on the basis of a quite different supply-side argument that it would drive up standards – a different thought.

Bibliography

Arneson, R. (1989) 'Equality and Equal Opportunity for Welfare', *Philosophical Studies*, 56.

Berlin, I. (1997) *The Proper Study of Mankind: An Anthology of Essays*, ed. H. Hardy and R. Hausheer, London: Chatto & Windus.

Caney, S. (2009) 'Climate Change and the Future: Discounting for Time, Wealth, and Risk', *Journal of Social Philosophy*, 40 (2).

Cohen, G. A. (1989) 'On the Currency of Egalitarian Justice', *Ethics*, 99.

Cohen, G.A. (2008) *Rescuing Justice and Equality*, Cambridge, MA: Harvard University Press.

Dobson, A. (2007) *Green Political Thought*, 4th edn, New York: Routledge.

Dobson, A. and Saiz, A.V. (2005) *Citizenship, Environment, Economy*, New York: Routledge.

Dryzek, J. S., Downes, D., Hernes, H. K. and Schlosberg, D. (eds.) (2003) *Green States and Social Movements*, Oxford: Oxford University Press.

Dworkin, R. (2000) *Sovereign Virtue: The Theory and Practice of Equality*, Cambridge, MA: Harvard University Press.

Ekins, P. (2000) *Economic Growth and Environmental Sustainability: The Prospects for Green Growth*, London: Routledge.

Gosepath, S. (2007 [2001]) 'Equality', *The Stanford Encyclopedia of Philosophy*; available at: http://plato.stanford.edu/entries/equality/#EquofRes.

Hart, H. L. A. (1961) *The Concept of Law*, Oxford: Clarendon Press.

Hirsch, F. (1976) *The Social Limits to Growth*, London: Routledge & Kegan Paul.

Kymlicka, W. (1995) *Multicultural Citizenship: A Liberal Theory of Minority Rights*, New York: Clarendon Press.

Kymlicka, W. (2007) *Multicultural Odysseys: Navigating the New International Politics of Diversity*, Oxford: Oxford University Press.

Nussbaum, M. (1999) *Sex and Social Justice*, Oxford: Oxford University Press.

O'Neill, O. (1996) *Towards Justice and Virtue: A Constructive Account of Practical Reasoning*, Cambridge: Cambridge University Press.

O'Neill, O. (2000) *Bounds of Justice*, Cambridge: Cambridge University Press.

O'Neill, O. (2001) 'Agents of Justice', *Metaphilosophy*, 32 (1–2).

Rawls, J. (1999 [1971]) *A Theory of Justice*, Cambridge, MA: Harvard University Press.

Rawls, J. (2001) *Justice as Fairness: A Restatement*, ed. E. Kelly, Cambridge, MA: The Belknap Press of Harvard University Press.

Sen, A. (1980) 'Equality of What?' in *The Tanner Lecture on Human Values*, vol. I, Cambridge: Cambridge University Press, pp. 197–220.

Smith, M. J. and Pangsapa, P. (2008) *Environment and Citizenship: Integrating Justice, Responsibility and Civic Engagement*, New York: Zed Books.

Temkin, L. (1993) *Inequality*, Oxford: Oxford University Press.

Young, I. M. (1990) *Justice and the Politics of Difference*, Princeton: Princeton University Press.

Young, I. M. (2000) *Inclusion and Democracy*, Oxford: Oxford University Press.

8

Changing Values for a Just and Sustainable World

Peter Singer

The aim of this chapter, as well as the overarching goal of my latest book *The Life You Can Save: Acting Now to End World Poverty* (Singer 2009), is to address a wider audience than simply the academic one. The underlying hope is that ordinary people will find reasons to change their behaviour once my arguments are laid out properly. The main themes of the piece are primarily two. What does a just world look like? What is the role of sustainability, with a particular emphasis on climate change, in such a world?

Global poverty

According to the World Bank, 'world poverty' refers to the circumstances of people who simply do not have enough income to meet their basic needs (Narayan, Patel, Schafft et al. 2000). The definition provided by the Bank has now slightly shifted: the current figure does not put the poverty line at $1 a day but at $1.25 (although since the $1.25 is calculated in constant 1993 dollars, it is equivalent to $1.75 today) (World Bank 2008).[1] The important thing to understand is that this poverty line does not refer to exchange rates values. Rather, the poverty line refers to real purchasing power. The difference is crucial: those below the poverty line in developing countries do not dispose of the equivalent of $1.75 at the exchange rates that prevail between the local currency and American dollars. Instead, they are going to get whatever it is in the local currency which buys the same goods and services as one can buy for about $1.75 in the US today. That may equate, in currency exchange terms, to as little as 50 US cents.

In the world we live in, around 1.4 billion people have to survive on less than this sum (World Bank 2008). If you are living on so little, you are likely to be undernourished, and not likely to have safe drinking water; you probably can't send your children to school, and can't afford even the most basic health services (Narayan, Patel, Schafft et al. 2000). Your children are likely to die from diseases that don't exist in the Western world (or if they do exist they are not fatal, and easily cured). Your life expectancy may be below fifty rather than seventy-seven as it is in the rich nations.

According to UNICEF, 9.2 million children died from avoidable poverty-related causes in 2007 (McNeil 2007). Terrible as it is, this figure shows some improvement when compared to the 10 million that were dying annually just a few years ago. It is important to stress such progress: too many people have grown cynical and simply think that poverty is just like a black hole. The current figure is even more important when compared to the same figure for past decades: forty-nine years ago, 20 million children a year would die of preventable causes (McNeil 2007). The progress has been steady and significant. That said, even as we discuss this issue, 25,000 children still die prematurely every single day.

On the other hand, in the rich world we have roughly a similar number, maybe a billion people, living at a very high level of affluence. Most of these people are citizens of rich nations. But some of them are in nations that are not affluent as a whole, like China, India and Brazil. The level of affluence enjoyed by this category of people is only comparable to that of the wealthiest and most aristocratic a century or so ago. In fact such a comparison is not even a correct measure of what wealth can presently signify: it's never previously been possible for large numbers of people to travel in winter to warm climates and enjoy a holiday there, or to have fresh fruit and vegetables all year round, or to be able to control the temperature of their environment at the touch of a button.

In 1972 I wrote an article called 'Famine, Affluence and Morality' (Singer 1972) which started off with a story about seeing a toddler falling into a pond, apparently about to drown. You can save the toddler in the pond, so the story went, if you rush in immediately with all your clothes on. But you're wearing a very expensive pair of shoes and they're going to get ruined if you do rush into the pond to save him. Most people would save the child no matter what would happen to their clothes. Moreover, most people would also find a negative response to our thought experiment (that is, someone who simply says 'I didn't put the child in the pond, it's not my responsibility to save him') morally outrageous and perhaps even to be showing some major moral defect. What most people think when presented with our thought experiment is that, if you leave the child to drown, you are morally defective in some important way. To compare the value of a pair of shoes with a human life makes you some kind of moral monster (see Singer 1981; Unger 1996).

While I'm glad that people do think that way, this simple story can bring us back to what we were discussing in the previous paragraphs: all of the 1 billion or so affluent people in the world, which includes us, have the ability to save some of those 25,000 children who are dying every day from poverty-related causes. We have the ability to do that by giving to an aid organization which is effectively reducing that death toll. Some aid organizations do so directly – for instance, by providing villages with safe water so their children don't get diarrhoea or providing bed nets against malaria, or supporting health clinics where you can take your child when he or she does get sick. Others do it indirectly, working against this death toll by helping people to get themselves out of poverty in various ways, such as giving them small loans so that they can start businesses, giving them better seeds so that they can grow more food or other crops that they can sell in order to obtain some income, or providing some infrastructure so that they can sell what they're already making at markets where they can get better prices for them. There is a wide range of activities, all of which can effectively reduce poverty and hence its death toll.

Obviously there are questions and doubts about the reality and extension of such effectiveness, but if we momentarily assume that aid can be effective, then the question is: if we don't do something toward that end, aren't we in the same position as the person who says 'I don't want to spoil my shoes and so I'm going to walk past the child'? The symmetry is striking because the cost of expensive shoes and clothes could be enough, if given to aid, to save a child's life (GiveWell 2007).

In *The Life You Can Save* I go into some details about those figures. I draw on work done by GiveWell, an independent charity evaluator that has analysed the performances and figures from a number of aid agencies. Although numerous figures appear in the debate, by almost any standard or measure US$ 1,000 (or the price of a very expensive pair of shoes or of an expensive suit) is likely to be enough to save a life (GiveWell 2007; Easterly 2006). Sometimes the figures presented are much lower. Yet one should be wary of very low figures since they might not take into sufficient consideration the real costs of providing aid. For instance, in the case of diarrhoea, if you can get a child to a health clinic you can save that child's life with a very simple treatment called oral re-hydration therapy (see Gerlin 2006). The treatment itself costs about 30 cents, but that doesn't mean that for a donation of 30 cents you can save a child's life, because you have to have the health clinics for the children with diarrhoea and you have to make it possible for people to get there, or you have to send health workers out to the villages to distribute these kits in case they'll be needed. Not every kit saves a child's life. Similarly in the case of anti-malaria bed nets there are figures stating that for $10 you can buy a bed net and save a child's life. Once again, for $10 you can buy a bed net but not every bed net saves a child's life: you have to distribute a significant number of them before you can expect that one of them will actually make the difference. GiveWell estimates that $800 in donations could be enough to save a life (2007). On the other hand, Jeffrey Sachs provides a much lower figure of around $400 (Sachs 2005). What seems to matter, though, is that in both cases the order of magnitude is comparable, and the amount of money used is more or less similar to what many people in the affluent world spend on their shoes or suits.

Yet – and this is important – I don't just want to rely on the parallel with the child in the pond, simply in order to provoke a certain intuitive response. In general, in terms of ethical methodology, I am suspicious of intuitive ethical responses. We can construct an argument whose premises relate to our 'child in the pond' and yet which withstands our critical scrutiny even once our more immediate moral response has passed. The first premise of our argument clearly relates to the example of the child in the pond:

First premise[2]

1) The death of a child is bad.

Second premise

2) If it is in your power to prevent something bad from happening, without sacrificing anything nearly as important, it is wrong not to do so.

Third premise

3) By donating to aid agencies, you can prevent suffering and death from lack of food, shelter and medical care, without sacrificing anything nearly as important.

The last premise (*premise 3*) is the factual premise that I more carefully developed in *The Life You Can Save*. The conclusion from our premises is that, once we accept them, then:

Conclusion

We ought to prevent the deaths of children affected by global poverty (*premises 1–3*). Such deaths are a great bad whose prevention would come at relatively small cost to us.

The question is whether those premises are true. I believe the vast majority of people would share the acceptance of the first two premises. Libertarians may reject the second (Narveson 2003). I think there are good reasons why we shouldn't accept the libertarian perspective. Essentially, this view is: 'I've earnt my money and therefore what I do with it is my business.' This doesn't account for how much we benefit through the good fortune of having grown up in a society in which it's possible to earn your money and live reasonably well, and, conversely, it does not consider the fate of those who were unlucky enough to be born in very different circumstances in which, no matter how hard one tries, the level of comfort that we have is unattainable.

There is also a problem with the assumption that looms large behind the libertarian argument, namely: 'I've earnt my money and I'm living without violating any one else's rights.' That's the libertarian claim: as long as I don't violate anyone else's rights, I don't have obligations to others. But as we will see when we get to the issue of climate change, I think it is almost impossible to live in a developed country without affecting other peoples' lives (especially the lives of people in developing countries) in such a way that could easily be described as violating their rights.

I return now to the most controversial of our premises, the factual one. Can we really say that aid works? There are certainly many critics of aid. In *The Life You Can Save* I discussed the work of William Easterly (2006). More recently, similar conclusions have been reached by Dambisa Moyo, a Zambian economist, in her book with the telling title of *Dead Aid* (2009). Moyo, like Easterly, argues that aid is not effective. What is striking about both Moyo and Easterly (and many other authors who provide similar arguments) is that they are mainly concerned about government and multilateral – that is, World Bank, IMF, etc. – aid programmes, and not about NGO aid. In fact, Easterly barely mentions NGOs while Moyo explicitly states that that's not part of the topic of her book. Hence most of their criticisms are not directed at the claim I need to make for my argument. I am not going to suggest that the right action to perform is to transfer resources to the World Bank. My attention is focused mainly on private organizations whose efficacy is not challenged by arguments about the effectiveness of government or multilateral aid.

Even on the issue of government aid, however, Easterly refers to trillions of dollars that we have spent on development aid, and implies that the results we obtained were negligible (2006). But, as we have seen at the beginning of the chapter, the data from UNICEF are actually encouraging, and the fact that – despite population growth – the number of children dying from preventable causes has more than halved in the past fifty years should count as a form of success. Of course, many would question the link between aid and the reduction of the death toll. Some, for instance, would insist that the real benefits have come from the globalization of the economy and the liberalization of trade (Wolf 2004). These arguments certainly contain some truth. For example, I agree that trade has been a major factor in reducing poverty in countries like China and India. But on the other hand, in terms of reducing the child death toll, certainly some aid programmes have been effective.

Furthermore, we should be sceptical about the real significance of Easterly's figures (Singer 2009: 105ff.). By that, of course, I don't mean to question their veracity, but rather their real importance. Easterly refers to trillions of dollars. That seems, at least initially, a vast amount of resources. Yet, if we look closer, we will notice that the resources were given over a time-span of about fifty years. The trillions of dollars are an aggregate figure that represents the whole of the developed world. Eventually this class of countries would, over a period lasting decades, have trillions in aggregate measures of almost all of their financial projects. More to the point, when you look at such figures in terms of a proportion of how much we've earned, the results are far less impressive (see United Nations Human Development Report 1995; Organization for Economic Co-operation and Development 2008). We have been giving about a quarter of 1 per cent of gross domestic product (in other words, 25 pence for every £100 that we earn), which I don't think can be described as a strong commitment to one of the most pressing moral issues regarding international justice. Even if we reverse the perspective and try to grasp whether the amount of resources per recipient (or potential recipient) has been important, we would find out that our commitments (from the wealthy) have been less than spectacular. In fact our aid programmes have been so proportionally small that they constitute no good evidence about what significantly more generous efforts might have achieved.

If we consider aid as a percentage of gross domestic product, or GDP, we find that the average country effort is around 0.45 per cent (that is, less than half of one per cent of GDP per year).[3] Note that the average country effort doesn't reflect accurately the amount of aid as a percentage of world GDP. The latter is 0.28 per cent. The discrepancy is due to the (perhaps counterintuitive) fact that the largest economies also give the least, as a percentage of their income.[4] Neither the US nor the UK make it to the world per country average (albeit by different margins). On the other hand, the more generous developed nations are, as usual, the Scandinavian nations, with the Netherlands and Luxemburg coming close behind. Note, however, that even the highest of them is still donating less than $1 in every $100 that it earns.

Let's try to understand such figures in terms of the Millennium Development Goals (MDGs), which we promised to meet in 2015 (UN

2000). All major world leaders promised that by then we would have, among other things, reduced by half:

a) the proportion of the world's people in extreme poverty;
b) the proportion of the world's people who suffer from hunger;
c) the proportion of the world's people without sustainable access to safe drinking water;

but also have:

d) ended sex disparity in education;
e) ensured that children everywhere can take a full course of primary schooling.

These are reasonably ambitious goals. I am referring to them because we have, again from Jeffrey Sachs, an estimate of what it would cost to meet them (2005).[5]

The figure gives us an upper estimate of around $190 billion (in 2008 US dollars). On this basis, the MDGs are quite feasible if we look at them from the aggregate perspective of the world and its economy as a whole. The estimate also tells us that we might be able to achieve the MDGs privately – that is, through individual donations. I will assess this argument later, but it is useful to keep it in the back of our minds for the time being.

One common objection to the argument from the drowning child is that it demands too high a level of giving (see, for example, Murphy 2005). To save a particular child is a one-off enterprise; you ruin one set of clothes but can then go back to your previous life. In the case of global poverty, however, unless other people are willing to behave in the same way as you are (that is, saving children from preventable death), you are committing yourself to perpetual reiteration of your rescue (Appiah 2006). And we have evidence that most other people, in fact, are not doing enough. If you need $1,000 to save every single child (or perhaps a little less) and if others are not willing to provide the same scale of effort, you are committed by the drowning child analogy to provide help directly insofar as you are not sacrificing something nearly as important. So it seems that if, after having given $1,000, you were still in a comfortable position and could still afford a few small luxuries, you shouldn't be buying them, because another $1,000 will save another child and so on. Does this mean that you have to keep impoverishing yourself until you get to the point where a further donation would lead to the sacrifice of something extremely significant? Many have argued that, if these are the consequences of my argument, then the argument must be fallacious, since it describes a morality for saints rather than one for ourselves: what I am asking, so they say, is supererogatory in such a way that it makes our moral duties unsustainable and unreasonable (see Cullity 2004; Miller 2004; Hooker 2000).

Here, an appeal to Christian tradition might be useful to show that my moral outlook is not so far from that of other thinkers, even quite conservative ones, as is often implied. It is difficult to depict the Catholic Church as a radical organization. Yet Thomas Aquinas, one of the pillars of Catholicism when it comes to moral doctrine, would have shared my commitment. Aquinas argued, many centuries ago, that we owe as a natural right, to those who cannot meet their basic needs, what we have in superabundance (Aquinas 1929: Q.66, A.7). By superabundance he meant any situation in which we have more than we require to provide for our own needs, to make reasonable provision for future needs, and to provide for the needs of our dependents. Aquinas goes on to say that property exists in order to provide for our needs and so, if somebody can't provide for their needs, they have a right to take from those who have in superabundance (1929). As a result, if someone in need takes from someone in superabundance, that is not even theft, but rather legitimate acquisition of something that the one in need has a right to retain against another in superabundance.

One might argue that an appeal to Aquinas runs the risk of appearing far from our experience both culturally and in time. So perhaps the contribution of John Locke is more relevant to our times and temperament. Locke is surely one of the central figures of Anglo-Saxon political philosophy, and has had a huge influence in the United States. Interestingly, his views on charity and property are strikingly similar to those of Aquinas, namely: 'charity gives every man a title to so much out of another's plenty, as will keep him from extreme want where he has no means to subsist otherwise' (Locke 1967: 1st Treatise, sec. 42). The latter is not a quote often associated with Locke because it is from the first treatise on government, not the second treatise, which is the one that political theorists always read. The first treatise is mainly dedicated to discussions about the divine right of kings which are no longer of interest, but on the issue of charity Locke's view is more radical than the argument I have offered.

In the final chapter of *The Life You Can Save*, I take an approach that may go some way toward meeting the objection that the argument is excessively demanding. I draw a distinction between the views we can consider justified when we argue about the nature of our duties toward others and the views that we can sensibly think will be adopted by most people as a basis for action. My ethical standpoint is one that judges what we do in terms of its consequences. It is possible, then, that if the standard proposed by my argument is *perceived* as excessively demanding – whether or not, by the standards of philosophical argument, it really is – the public might react in just the opposite way from what we think would be best. People might think that if this is what morality requires, then they just cannot commit themselves to trying to act morally, and so they may do nothing for the poor. If we are looking for the adoption of a public morality on the subject, and if we believe in some form of consequentialism, this is something we have to take into consideration. Advocacy is in itself an act, and it must be judged by its real-world results rather than simply by its content.

If we accept such a view of advocacy, what we ought to do is to make the best possible attempt to put forward a standard that will achieve the best consequences in this particular context. In short, we should propose a standard that will raise the largest amount of resources for fighting world poverty. From a practical point of view, this involves advocating a much lower threshold of donations.[6] In *the Life You Can Save* – both in the book and on its associated website, www.thelifeyou cansave.com – I suggest such a standard, with a sliding scale according to how much one earns. The website also gives you the possibility of pledging to meet the standard for your level of income. An impressive body of psychological research has shown that people are more likely to give if they see that others are giving as well (see Lichtenberg 2004; Shang and Croson 2009). Eventually, if a large number of people pledge to meet the standards given on the website, this can be expected to have an effect on those who are potentially interested and need some form of incentive to participate and get involved.

Once we get to the real numbers my approach proposes, the results are astonishing. According to the standards I propose, roughly 90 per cent of the population in the affluent world ought to give no more than 1 per cent of its income to reduce global poverty, and even the super-rich, who earn millions each year, ought to give no more than one-third of their income. Even with such a modest amount for most people, the aggregate figure adds up to $1.5 trillion a year. It is important to compare this sum to what Jeffrey Sachs estimated to be necessary in order to meet the MDGs. As you will recall, Sachs argues that what is needed to attain the Millennium goals is $190 billion, or roughly 15 per cent of the figure that would come from everyone giving in accordance with my suggested levels. Two things should be noted here. First, a 1 per cent donation on income is not exactly a large commitment to be asking for. If one decides to commit any given amount of personal resources to global poverty at all, it is likely that 1 per cent percent of one's income will not appear as an unreasonable standard.

Second, note that the difference between the two figures (1.5 trillion and 190 billion) is so large that it is compatible with a serious underestimation on the part of Sachs. Even if the real figure is up to six times the figure he puts forward, it could be raised from affluent people without great hardship. With the standard of donation I advocate, not only could we meet the MDGs easily, but we could go further, and this without stretching our imagination about what people may be reasonably prepared to give, if the social environment is an encouraging one.

In sum, we really do have the possibility of dramatically reducing world poverty, and that's what we ought to do. We ought to promote a public standard like the one I propose, in the hope that we can change the public culture so that people will regard this as part of what it is to live an ethical life. Often we tend to accept that the essence of an ethical life is that we obey our negative obligations toward others. What it means to be 'ethical' is simply to abstain from cheating, from stealing, from beating up one's family, assaulting others, murdering others, and so on. While these are certainly one part of what we ought to do (or not to do), our public vision of the ethical life should also include more positive commitments toward the things we ought to do and not simply the things that we ought to abstain from doing. The definition of what a good person is should include such things as helping to reduce preventable deaths at what would be a very small cost for the individual.

Climate change

The other great issue concerning justice in the world today is climate change. I see climate change as an issue of justice, as a simple, moral question in a way that's parallel to one of these very familiar ethical problems that we have in our daily lives. Suppose you have an apple pie and you have twenty people who each want a slice of it. How do you divide up the pie fairly? Or, changing our angle on the subject, what would clearly be an unfair way of dividing up the pie? If we believe that, prima facie, each is entitled to the same amount of pie as is anybody else, then a division that gives a very big slice to one of the twenty people and small slices to the remaining nineteen seems obviously unfair. Of course, it might be the case that what seems prima facie justified, an equal division of the pie, is not in fact a correct representation of the entitlements that people can claim to have for some of the pie. But, in order for that to be so, we would need an argument to bring us to that conclusion.

The atmosphere is a common resource: nobody owns it, no nation or company. It wouldn't make sense, for instance, to say that Britain owns the atmosphere above British soil because such divisions are made impossible by the fact that – as we were all vividly reminded by the disruption to air traffic caused by the 2010 eruption of Iceland's Eyjafjallajökull volcano – what is emitted over one country does not stay over that country. The atmosphere is also a scarce resource. This is one of the essential points that we have come to realize as a result of our knowledge of climate change. We can no longer assume that the atmosphere is just a means to provide us with oxygen to breathe, because it has also the crucial role of absorbing the greenhouse gases we produce. The scarcity kicks in, and the problem of climate change begins, when we realize that the possibilities for absorbing such greenhouse gases are limited and the consequences of not taking into consideration such limits are potentially disastrous (Singer 2002: 15–20).

Hence, we need a principle of justice to decide how to allocate this limited capacity to absorb those waste gases. Naturally, there are various principles that one could propose for this task (see Singer 2002, 2006). My present aim is not to go through all of them. The crucial point, though, seems to concern those nations who are taking more than seems compatible with their fair share. Take the example of the US: it is home to about 5 per cent of the world's population while it uses about 25 per cent of the atmosphere's limited capacity to absorb greenhouse gas emissions (Hayes and Smith 1993). Even intuitively, that seems to raise some questions about fairness and justice.

Some people may say that this is a situation that has developed historically and we haven't really known about the problems of climate change during the period in which a lot of the damage to our atmosphere was done. But, at least since 1992, we have acknowledged the problem (United Nations 1992). Just as with the Millennium Development Summit, almost all the nations in the world signed on to a statement at the Rio de Janeiro 'Earth Summit' agreeing to stabilize greenhouse gases at a level low enough to prevent dangerous anthropogenic interference with the climate system. So, at least since then, we've known what the problem is, we've known what we need to do about it and, indeed, we have promised that we would do it.

Unfortunately this is a promise that has not been kept. We have continued not only to maintain our pre-Rio summit emissions but to increase the levels of greenhouse gas emissions. Although not all nations have done so, most developed countries have. In particular, the United States certainly has (*Los Angeles Times* 2000). As a result, most experts currently believe that it is going to be extremely difficult to hold climate change at a 2 °C increase above pre-industrial surface temperatures. The latter was seen by many scientists as the goal we would need to achieve in order to avoid dangerous anthropogenic interference in climatic evolution. This was the concrete target we fixed in Rio and it is quite possible that we will not be able to hold to it. At the moment, the actual target for our impact on world temperatures is slightly higher than 2 °Celsius. Now, the experts tell us that it is somewhere over this margin where we are likely to engender the aforementioned dangerous anthropogenic interference. While there is no certainty on where exactly that point is, the closer we get to the higher end of the danger zone, the more likely it is that something very serious is going to happen. What is important to realize is that what we currently see, the changes in climate that we have gradually witnessed during recent years, are only 25 per cent of the changes that will occur once the full consequences of the gases that have *already been released* are unleashed. If the latter piece of information is only partially accurate, the potential damage from climate change that we will have to deal with in the near future is serious enough to warrant deep concern.

I spend part of each year in Australia, which allows me to get a better sense of climate change than would be possible by staying in the US or Europe. Over the past twelve years, southern and south-eastern Australia have seen significant changes in rainfall patterns. Local people used to call it a drought, but it has gone on much longer than the usual cycle of drought and flood and it is fair to say that the terminology of 'drought' is no longer appropriate. We – and I include myself since it is where I come from – are running very short of water. As a result, various things that we used to do have changed. If you live in the cities you notice it in many ways. For instance, except for two hours a week, you are not allowed to water your garden unless you collect grey water from the shower or have a tank to store whatever rain falls on your roof. As a consequence, many people are installing tanks, or shower in buckets and carry the water out to their garden. Nor are you allowed to wash your car with a hose. Showering for longer than three minutes is considered unethical. These are unpleasant constraints.

But the reduction of water supplies has also had more serious consequences. Australia used to have a rice-growing industry which relied on irrigation. In several recent seasons, there simply wasn't enough water to continue such activity, and that has been a contributing factor to the recent sharp increase in world rice prices. Less water has also been very bad for those rural areas that depend on water from the Murray–Darling irrigation system, the biggest river system in Australia, which is no longer able to provide enough for such communities.

Nevertheless, Australia is an affluent country and nobody is starving because of climate change. If you can't grow rice, maybe you can shift to growing something else that doesn't require so much water, or as a last resort you can leave the land and go to the cities. Even if you can't find a job in the cities, you'll get enough social security for you to have somewhere to live. You're not going to starve, you still have healthcare, you still have access to safe drinking water. If similar things happened in sub-Saharan Africa – and as climate change continues, they are likely to happen somewhere in that region – there would be no such support for the poor and the dispossessed. Given the benchmark of comparison of what has happened to Australia, the likelihood of hundreds of millions of people becoming refugees is high. If people rely on rainfall to survive, a change in the pattern of such falls (a diminution or a change in frequency or location, which can have similar effects) can displace them. The situation really could not be more serious.

Going back to our normative question, then, what principle of justice should we use to allocate the capacity of the planet to absorb our greenhouse gases? There are many possibilities but I cannot address them all in this chapter. One could use as a starting point the historical responsibility of the developed nations (see the discussion in Singer 2002: 27ff.). But in order not to complicate our analysis with ideas concerning historical responsibility, I will focus on the present. One principle, which at least has a prima facie case for being a fair one, is equal shares (Singer 2002: 35ff.). This is the principle that you're likely to use if you carve up the apple pie, and assume that none of those wanting a slice made the pie, or provided the flour and the apples. Now, of course, somebody must have provided the apples and the flour, and somebody must have baked the pie, and these people might claim a greater share of the pie with some reason. But, continuing our analogy, we can say that nobody has provided the atmosphere. This means that nobody seems prima facie entitled to have more than an equal share of its capacity to absorb our greenhouse gas emissions.

So, unless there is a sound counter-argument, equal shares would seem to be a just way of producing a sustainable climate. This means, of course, not equal shares per country, which would be absurd given differences in population, but an equal share for every person on the planet. What is left to do then, is, first, to work out the total quantity of greenhouse gases that can safely be emitted. Several national leaders have put forward the goal, to be achieved by 2050, of reducing greenhouse gases to 80 per cent of 1990 levels. Once we have that total figure of emissions, we simply divide it by the world's population, and calculate what each person's share of the total is (see Singer 2002: 35–6). Lastly, one has to allocate each country its greenhouse gas quota, which will be the number of its residents multiplied by the per person share.

What would be the consequences of such a proposal? Going back to our previous example, the United States, with 5 per cent of the world's population, produces 25 per cent of the world's emissions, so even if we were just to maintain present emissions – and not return to 80 per cent of 1990 levels – the US would have to cut its emissions to one-fifth of what they are today. But, so the argument goes, that's clearly impossible. No nation could implement such changes within a reasonably short timeframe.

Fortunately, there is a solution that makes it possible to provide even such a drastic adjustment without causing an economic catastrophe: the creation of a mechanism for trading carbon emissions. Such a mechanism would enable the heavy polluters to buy emission quotas from low emitters. Since it is the rich nations that emit more greenhouse gases, this would also have an impact, incidentally, on producing a more just world (see Sachs 2008). A global emissions trading scheme would amount to a transfer of resources from the rich to the poor, which, for the reasons that I discussed earlier in the chapter, would be a good thing in itself, as long as the money was used for the benefit of the people in poor countries. The ethics of climate change provides further, and independent, reasons to transfer resources from high-income to low-income countries. The other advantage of this trading scheme would also reside in the structure of incentives it would provide to poorer countries. The latter would be encouraged to keep their emissions low so that they continue to have something that they can trade – namely, their unused quota of carbon emissions.

There are, as I have already mentioned, problems in transferring money to corrupt governments. There are also problems that are related to the so-called 'resource curse' issue.[7] In order to address this problem, one could imagine the creation of a system of trust funds. The trustees would be responsible for the delivery of the benefits from the carbon trade scheme to the people of the country that had sold the quota. If they judged that the circumstances did not permit the delivery of the funds in a way that would benefit the people, the money could wait in the trust fund for that country until the government is judged equipped and sufficiently well-intentioned to improve its people's wellbeing. Naturally, the issue is complex and many difficulties can be anticipated, but ultimately they are soluble, and need to be solved.

A further objection to the trading scheme for emissions is that it could, potentially, create incentives for population growth. If quotas are attributed on a per capita basis, a growing population implies a greater quota. So would countries deliberately encourage population growth in order to increase their quota? If they did, of course, that would reduce the quota for everyone else, and might lead to a disastrous further increase in the world's population. But there is a practical response to this incentive problem. We can simply modify the incentive structure by using a baseline constituted by projections of population growth for all countries by 2050 (see Baer et al. 2000).

We could use the UN projections to create such a baseline. Pegging emission quotas to estimated population in 2050 would reverse the incentive for population growth, since one is actually providing an incentive for countries to keep their populations below the baseline. This is so because, as long as countries keep their population below that level, they'll have a higher per capita allowance than if the population grows to or exceeds that level.

Another objection that it is worth considering is that some countries need to use more energy than others merely to meet the basic needs of their population. For example, Canadians will need to use comparatively more resources than Brazil to keep warm during winter. But does this mean that the rest of the world should subsidize Canadians for their cold winters, in effect imposing the cost of Canadians' choices about where to live on other nations? In a world that is exceeding the safe limit of greenhouse gas emissions, living in cold climates is a costly business, but the costs can be reduced with insulation, more efficient heating, putting on warmer clothes and lowering the heat. Parallel changes can be made, of course, by people who move to hot climates and rely on air-conditioning to keep cool. If such costs fall anywhere except on the people who use the heating or cooling, it will reduce the incentive people have to be as modest as possible in their energy use, and will impose costs on others who are living in places that are inherently more sustainable.

As in the case of poverty, our advocacy must map onto what we believe to be realistic enough to have good results in the world as it exists. Are people really going to accept the per capita standard we are proposing? In this respect, it is interesting to note that, in recent years, the concept of equal per capita shares has been endorsed not only by nongovernment organizations, but also by such senior politicians as German Chancellor Angela Merkel, who has acknowledged that, at least in the long term, this is the right way to go.

On the other hand, developing countries' leaders such as President Yoweri Museveni of Uganda have come up with their own perspective on the situation. 'You are causing aggression to us by causing global warming', Museveni said at an African Union meeting in Addis Ababa in 2007; 'Alaska will probably become good for agriculture, Siberia will probably become good for agriculture, but where does that leave Africa?' (Museveni 2007). Perhaps 'aggression' is too strong a word to use here, for it implies that one is deliberately harming others, or attacking them in some way. The affluent world is clearly not deliberately enhancing climate change. Yet, while climate change is not our purpose, our use of energy based on fossil fuels, and our heavily meat-based diet, are continued with the knowledge that they lead to greenhouse gas emissions far in excess of what our fair share of the atmosphere would be. Here, as indicated at the beginning of this chapter, we can see how the libertarian argument unravels. Our knowledge of the consequences of climate change, together with our understanding of the atmosphere as a common resource, means that our behaviour is culpably violating the basic human rights of people in developing nations. We are taking more than our fair share, and this implies dire consequences for others. Here the libertarian's case falls because it is impossible to claim that there are no rights violations involved in greenhouse gas emissions. Whatever the implications of a libertarian position are, it should be acknowledged that, in the twenty-first century, they include at the very least an obligation to a carbon neutral lifestyle.

A concluding word

A final image that I want to leave you with combines rather neatly both topics dealt with in the present chapter. Paul Allen co-founded Microsoft with his high-school friend Bill Gates. Although he pulled out earlier than Gates, he still has a (post-global financial crisis) fortune of around $10 billion. Allen has owned what was once the largest private yacht in the world, one built at a cost of $200 million.[8] What should we think about someone who spends $200 million on a private yacht when there are 25,000 children starving *every day* and when that sum could do a lot of good for those children or for other causes vital to the future of our planet and the sentient beings on it?

We ought to be developing a culture that says: this is disgraceful. To spend that much money on yourself, on your private pleasures and on those of a few family and friends, is in itself a disgrace, but it is even more so if you don't balance it with major support for the relief of poverty or the struggle for a sustainable way of living for all. Nor is Allen's yacht an environmentally friendly means of transport. Despite the name, these 'yachts' don't have sails. On the amount of diesel fuel used in just one hour by the engines of Allen's yacht, a Volkswagen Jetta diesel could travel 269,000 kilometres. No individual can justify so large a carbon footprint.

Notes

1. The poverty line is given in 1993 US dollars. The fact that the reference year is 1993 makes the present value of the poverty line somewhat larger in current nominal terms, yet in current US dollars, it is still less than $2 a day.
2. The argument as it is presented in the text is a slightly modified version of the one presented in Singer (2009: 15–16).
3. The figure is for the year 2007.

4. That is, the first figure is an average that is not weighted by the size of each country's economy. If, for example, the US, with a GDP of (hypothetically) $100, gives 0.2 per cent, and the Netherlands, with a GDP of $10, gives 0.8 per cent, the unweighted average donation for these two countries is 0.5 per cent of GDP. If, on the other hand, we take into consideration the relative size of the two economies the weighted average is (0.2% x 100 + 0.8% x 10)/110 = 0.25% (circa).

5. Sachs's estimate is 124 billion in 1993 US dollars. In 2008 dollars, the figure is roughly 50 per cent higher and thus around $190 billion.

6. Although one which increases as your income goes up, as in a progressive tax regime.

7. 'The resource curse' refers to the inverse correlation between the possession of abundant natural resources (e.g. oil) and economic growth. Possible explanations have focused on a number of factors such as the decline in competitiveness in other sectors, increased incentives for corrupt institutions, or the volatility of revenues, all of which seem to have some link with an economy based on natural resources.

8. For more on Paul Allen's yacht, see 'Paul Allen's Yacht', www.yachtcrew-cv.com/paulallen.html.

Bibliography

Appiah, K. A. (2006) 'The Politics of Identity', *Daedelus*, 135 (4).

Appiah, K. A. (2007) *Cosmopolitanism: Ethics in a World of Strangers*, New York: Norton.

Aquinas, St T. (1929) *Summa theologica, Second Part* (QQ. XLVII–LXXIX), London: Burns, Oates & Washbourne.

Baer, P. et al. (2000) 'Equity and Greenhouse Responsibility', *Science*, 289 (29 September).

Cullity, G. (2004) *The Moral Demands of Affluence*, Oxford: Oxford University Press.

Easterly, W. (2006) *The White Man's Burden*', New York: Penguin Press.

Gerlin, A. (2006) 'A Simple Solution', *Time*, 8 October.

GiveWell (2007) *Report on International Aid Charities*; available at: www.givewell.net/.

Hayes, P. and Smith, K. (eds.) (1993) *The Global Greenhouse Regime: Who Pays?* London: Earthscan.

Hooker, B. (2000) *Ideal Code, Real World: A Rule-Consequentialist Theory of Morality*, Oxford: Clarendon Press.

Lichtenberg, J. (2004) 'Absence and the Unfond Heart: Why People Are Less Giving Than They Might Be', in D. Chatterjee (ed.), *The Ethics of Assistance: Morality and the Distant Needy*, Cambridge: Cambridge University Press.

Locke, J. (1967) *Two Treatises on Government*, Cambridge: Cambridge University Press.

Los Angeles Times (2000) 'U.S. Carbon Emissions Jump in 2000', 11 November, p. A36.

McNeil, D. (2007) 'Child Mortality at Record Low: Further Drop Seen', *The New York Times*, 13 September.

Miller, R. (2004) 'Beneficence, Duty and Distance', *Philosophy & Public Affairs*, 32.

Moyo, D. (2009) *Dead Aid: Why Aid Is Not Working and How There Is Another Way For Africa*, New York: Allen Lane.

Murphy, L. (2005) *Moral Demands in Nonideal Theory*, New York: Oxford University Press.

Museveni (reported by A. Revkin) (2007) 'Poor Nations to Bear Brunt as World Warms', *The New York Times*, 1 April.

Narayan, D., Patel, R., Schafft, K., Rademacher, A. and Koch-Schulte, S. (2000) *Voices of the Poor: Can Anyone Hear Us ?* Oxford: Oxford University Press for the World Bank.

Narveson, J. (2003) '"We Don't Owe Them a Thing!": A Tough-minded, But Soft-hearted View of Aid to the Faraway Needy', *The Monist*, 86 (3).

Organization for Economic Co-operation and Development (2007) *Statistical Annex of the 2007 Development Co-operation Report*, Paris: OECD; available at: www.oecd.org/dataoecd/.

Organization for Economic Co-operation and Development (2008) *OECD Donor Aid Charts*, Paris: OECD; available at: www.oecd.org/countrylist/.

Sachs, J. (2005) *The End of Poverty*. New York: Penguin Press.

Sachs, J. (2008) 'Using Carbon Taxes to Pay for Development', *FT.com*, 24 September; available at: http://blogs.ft.com/mdg/2008/09/24/using-carbon-taxes-to-pay-for-development/.

Shang, J. and Croson, R. (2009) 'Field Experiments in Charitable Contribution: The Impact of Social Influence on the Voluntary Provision of Public Goods', *The Economic Journal*, 119 (540).

Singer, P. (1972) 'Famine, Affluence and Morality', *Philosophy and Public Affairs*, Spring (1).

Singer, P. (1981) *The Expanding Circle*, Oxford: Clarendon Press.

Singer, P. (2002) *One World: The Ethics of Globalization*, New Haven, CT: Yale University Press.

Singer, P. (2006) 'Ethics and Climate Change: A Commentary on MacCracken, Toman and Gardiner', *Environmental Values*, 15 (1).

Singer, P. (2009) *The Life You Can Save: Acting Now to End World Poverty*, New York: Random House.

Unger, P. (1996) *Living High and Letting Die*, Oxford: Oxford University Press.

United Nations (1992) *Report of the United Nations Conference on Environment and Development, Rio de Janeiro, 3–14 June 1992*, vol. I, Resolution 1, Annex 1; available at: www.unep.org/Documents.multilingual/Default.asp?DocumentID=78&ArticleID=1163.

United Nations (2000) *Millennium Development Goals*; available at: www.un.org/millenniumgoals/.

United Nations Human Development Report (1995) *United Nations Development Programme*, New York and Oxford: Oxford University Press.

Wolf, M. (2004) *Why Globalization Works*, New Haven, CT: Yale University Press.

World Bank (2008) 'New Data Show 1.4 Billion Live on Less than US$ 1.25 a Day, but Progress against Poverty Remains Strong', World Bank Press Release, 26 August; available at: http://go.worldbank.org/.

9

The Ends of Justice: Climate Vulnerability beyond the Pale

Michael Mason

It was the fifth successive year of drought in Yatta District, with the winter rains yielding 180 mm – 40 per cent of average annual totals for the arid landscape of the Hebron hills, which fill out the southern flank of the West Bank. Abdallah Al Tabaneh gestured at his herd of 140 sheep and goats, complaining that the parched rangelands had supported only fifteen days of grazing that season, so that he was forced to buy concentrated feed and tankered water for his animals. At the time of our conversation, in May 2009, he was paying 50 New Israeli Shekels (NIS) a month (almost US$ 13) for 2,500 litres of water and facing concentrated feed prices in excess of NIS 2,000 (US$ 510) a tonne. The rain-fed barley and wheat that traditionally provided fodder for the Bedouin herds was stunted, increasingly overrun by spiny shrubs unpalatable even to goats. For Abdallah the recurrent drought was unprecedented in the living memory of the 500 Bedouin households of this region, with profits from herding plummeting. Yet herd sizes had increased significantly in the past ten years (with sheep numbers tripling to 90,000 in 2008), as non-Bedouin households turned to breeding small ruminants to cope economically in the face of Israeli movement restrictions. Since the onset of the *Second Intifada* in 2000, Israeli work permits had been very difficult to obtain for West Bank Palestinians.[1]

In the nearby village of At-Tuwani, the 240 inhabitants were receiving water deliveries from international humanitarian agencies. The sole spring serving the community had seen its winter peak output drop from 30 m³/day to 4 m³/day in the past five years. Saber Akhurini, the head of the Village Council, attributed this loss to a long-term reduction in rainfall as well as the growing extraction of groundwater by residents of the adjoining Israeli settlement of Ma'on, established in 1981 on occupied Palestinian land. At-Tuwani's farming community has seen over 1,500 dunums (150 ha) of agricultural land appropriated by the settlers, who regularly subject the villagers to physical and verbal assaults: the victims include Palestinian children who walk from other villages to At-Tuwani School. Local olive-pickers and shepherds are continually harassed and have even been shot at from Hill 833, an Orthodox Jewish outpost to the east of At-Tuwani. In May 2009, villagers reported that, in the previous month, Israeli settlers had destroyed the yield from 100 dunums of their planted barley and beans.[2] No settlers have ever been prosecuted for property destruction or violence against the villagers of At-Tuwani. Indeed, the Israeli Civil Administration in control of this region recognizes only 30 dunums of the original village area of 110 dunums. Outside this narrow space, the local mosque, school and a new Spanish-financed community water cistern all face Israeli demolition orders.

It is not surprising that we should encounter high social vulnerability in the occupied Palestinian territory (oPt),[3] or that such life experiences largely remain out of sight to the mainstream Western media. Whatever the reasons for this under-reporting, we might nevertheless expect that our prevailing notions of social justice would allow us to examine the threats to human wellbeing and alleged abuses of authority noted above, indicating that this state of affairs is unlikely to be fair or right. We can draw confidence from the knowledge that, at least in the academic world, the most prominent liberal theories of justice, as discussed below, reach out and address the interests of those most disadvantaged. As Peter Singer argues convincingly in this volume, while there are significant challenges in applying our notions of social justice to climate change, we also have the theoretical resources to ensure that we can take into account the justice impacts of climate stresses for the most vulnerable peoples. Finally, our democratic intuitions would insist that justice claims are tested openly, that all evidence is shared and that all views are equally respected.

Yet I argue in this chapter that if the litmus test for the moral credibility of a liberal framework of social and environmental justice is its ability to accommodate the victims of multiple and/or enduring injuries, then it must reckon with the unredeemed justice claims of a people under occupation for over forty years. This is more than the empirical inclusion of a particular ledger of grievances; for reasons given below, it disrupts the conceptual perimeters of liberal theories of justice – the 'ends of justice'. By itself, the problem of climate vulnerability generates issues about the bounds of justice, including duties to those deemed most vulnerable to present and future climate hazards. In the next section, I outline the issue of climate vulnerability in poorer countries. This is followed by an overview of two leading liberal theories of justice as applied to those most likely to be burdened by the impacts of climate change.[4] I then show how the Palestinians, who can plausibly make claims to being amongst the peoples most vulnerable to climate change, nevertheless remain beyond the pale of climate concern – both in a legal and geopolitical sense. Their exclusion as legitimate subjects for climate justice demonstrates the arbitrary and abrupt delimiting of the international discourse on climate vulnerability.

Climate vulnerability in developing countries

For the Parties to the United Nations Framework Convention on Climate Change (UNFCCC), developing countries are the most vulnerable to adverse climate change impacts, because they have higher sensitivity and lower adaptive capacity than industrialized countries. The UNFCCC obliges Parties to take into account the specific needs of particularly vulnerable developing countries in addressing the adverse effects of climate change, while the Kyoto Protocol provides a financial mechanism to assist such countries in climate adaptation. Under the Nairobi work programme adopted by the UNFCCC in 2005, developing countries are supported in undertaking vulnerability and adaptation assessments to enhance the effectiveness of their responses to climate change and variability (UNFCCC 2007: 10–11). Recent interest in climate vulnerability is also shared by the Intergovernmental Panel on Climate Change (IPCC), which sponsored an international research project – Assessment of Impacts and Adaptations to Climate Change (AIACC) – to conduct studies of adaptation and vulnerability in forty-six developing countries.

In this important research, vulnerability is taken to mean the propensity of people or systems to be harmed by hazards or stresses, which is determined by 'their exposures to hazard[s], their sensitivity to the exposures, and their capacities to resist, cope with, exploit, recover from and adapt to the effects' (Leary, Adejuwon, Bailey et al. 2008: 4). There is a claim that climate change is altering exposures to climate-related hazards, understood as extreme weather events (e.g. flooding, extreme heat, droughts) which may trigger various societal shocks (e.g. food productivity falls, population displacements). What the IPCC labels 'key' vulnerabilities to climate change – those meriting policy attention as symptomatic of 'dangerous anthropogenic interference' with the climate system (UNFCCC Article 2) – are seen to depend on the magnitude, timing and distribution of climate impacts (Schneider, Semenov, Patwardhan et al. 2007: 784). While early IPCC formulations favoured biophysical framings of climate impacts and ecosystem vulnerability, it is now recognized that vulnerability to climate change properly extends to the socioeconomic and political conditions that affect how communities cope with the impacts of climate-related hazards. This has led to a more integrated understanding of vulnerability, which is designed to capture the role of non-climatic pressures on individuals and groups who are also facing climate hazards (Adger 2006; Patt, Schröter, de la Vega-Leiner et al. 2009). This broader vulnerability perspective is the one adopted in this chapter.

Climate vulnerability thus denotes the idea of exposure to climate-related hazards in the context of biophysical and social vulnerability, as well as in relation to response capabilities in both the short term (coping) and long term (adaptation). Efforts to derive single metrics of vulnerability to global climate (and environmental) change typically falter in the face of substantial scientific uncertainties and, more importantly, the value-laden nature of vulnerability assessments (Barnett, Lambert and Fry 2008). Vulnerability is about values perceived to be at risk by affected communities, who bring diverse preferences and ethical judgements to bear in sociopolitical evaluations of particular climate impacts. As the IPCC elaborates, open deliberations on climate impacts are likely to feature value judgements about the acceptability of potential risks, and potential adaptation and mitigation measures, taking into account such wider themes as development, equity and sustainability (Schneider, Semenov, Patwardhan et al. 2007: 784).

Equity considerations are unavoidable given the differential vulnerability of populations and groups exposed to climate hazards (Thomas and Twyman 2005). The IPCC has long maintained that the geographical regions at greatest risk tend to be developing countries at low latitudes, because of higher susceptibilities to damage. This general claim is supported empirically by recent global reviews of climate vulnerability (Leary, Adejuwon, Bailey et al. 2008; Schneider, Semenov, Patwardhan et al. 2007), demonstrating that developing countries at low latitudes are particularly vulnerable to predicted water resource impacts (e.g. flooding, reduced water availability and quality) and food supply impacts (e.g. falls in farming productivity) – impacts which increase in severity with greater projected increases in global mean temperature by 2100. However, the mapping of aggregate vulnerability patterns in the tropics and sub-tropics can displace scientific and policy attention away from key vulnerabilities facing poorer populations in distinctive sub-regions including, for the purposes of this chapter, the eastern Mediterranean.

At least in terms of exposure to climate change, Palestinians in the Gaza Strip and the West Bank face disruptive climate impacts alongside the populations of other semi-arid territories in Western Asia. In the eastern Mediterranean sub-region, climate predictions are compromised by deficits in meteorological data and uncertainties regarding the incorporation in climate models of region-specific conditions and processes (Mellouki and Ravishankara 2007). Nevertheless, climate simulations recently undertaken with three regional models have delivered generally consistent results (GLOWA–Jordan River Project 2009; Kitoh, Yatagi and Alpert 2008; Somot, Sevault, Déqué et al. 2008). Over the course of this century, and depending on the global emissions scenario employed, there is predicted to be: (i) a decrease in precipitation of up to 35 per cent (with significant seasonal variation), (ii) a significant warming of between 2.6 °C and 4.8 °C, and (iii) a tendency toward more extreme weather events. For the population of the oPt, the biophysical impacts expected from these trends include an increased probability of flash floods, droughts, desertification and saline intrusion into groundwater (United Nations Development Programme (UNDP) 2010: 9–13).

By themselves, of course, climate impacts say little about the vulnerability of affected populations or groups. In the scholarship on environmental vulnerability, there is a growing interest in the ways in which vulnerability is constituted by multiple processes interacting across different spatiotemporal scales. More precisely, hazards acting on people and systems are seen to arise from influences outside and inside the area of immediate exposure although, given their complexity, their particular character is usually specific to that area (Barnett, Lambert and Fry 2008: 105; Turner, Kasperson, Matson et al. 2003: 8077). This conceptual insight has far-reaching methodological implications insofar as vulnerability analysis is thereby compelled to engage with human–biophysical conditions and dynamics that spiral out from locales and regions of high-level concern. Arguably, these implications have still to be fully grasped. For example, a common finding in the AIACC work on climate change and vulnerability was that socio-economic and political processes are pivotal in accounting for the harm caused by climate impacts, but these non-climatic drivers were mainly derived by comparing discrete national-level studies (Leary, Adejuwon, Bailey et al. 2008). A revealing contrast is provided by Roberts and Parks (2007: 103–32), who undertook a cross-national analysis of over 4,000 climate disasters from 1980 to 2002 to test proximate and structural causes of human vulnerability: their contention that the root causes of climate vulnerability lie in enduring constraints on the development space of poorer countries invites the critical scrutiny of global political and economic structures.

Indeed, the climate vulnerability of developing countries is inseparable from, and exacerbates, global disparities in wealth and relative power: the most disadvantaged face a disproportionate burden of climate-related risks even though they are least responsible for contributing to dangerous levels of greenhouse gases, and have received little or no benefit from the economic activities causing climate change (Vanderheiden 2008: 78). In the next section, I summarize the challenges to two competing liberal theories of social justice posed by the high levels of climate vulnerability experienced by populations in many poorer countries. I argue that, while these justice frameworks profess to have conceptual resources to register the justice claims of those most disadvantaged, there are critical domains of climate vulnerability that escape their reach.

Climate vulnerability and the ends of liberal justice

Under the UNFCCC, the overriding duty imposed on Parties is that they prevent dangerous interference with the climate system (Article 2). Arguably the main articulation of justice pertinent to differential climate vulnerability relates to the legal acknowledgement in the Convention of the inequitable impact of climate change within and across generations, including the recognition that measures for mitigation and adaptation also entail different allocations of costs between states. UNFCCC Article 3.1 expresses succinctly the normative idea informing these concerns: 'The Parties should protect the climate system for the benefit of present and future generations of human-kind, on the basis of equity and in accordance with their common but differentiated responsibilities and respective capabilities. Accordingly, the developed country Parties should take the lead in combating climate change and the adverse effects thereof.'

There is a general understanding of distributive justice at work here, which divides obligations for action on the basis that industrialized (Annex I) Parties both are more culpable for global warming and have greater capacity for limiting anthropogenic greenhouse gases and adapting to the harms caused by climate change. The concept of common but differentiated responsibilities, which is also invoked in the Preamble and Article 10 of the Kyoto Protocol, has wider currency in international environmental law. While the principle sets broad parameters for international burden-sharing on climate change action, its justice-oriented implications for UNFCCC Parties nevertheless remain under-specified (Brunnée 2009: 324–8); this is evident in conflicting interpretations between industrialized and developing country Parties over the nature and scope of assistance due to vulnerable populations regarding climate change mitigation and adaptation.

These disagreements not only indicate that international climate negotiations have left unresolved divergent interpretations of equity under the UNFCCC framework, they also point to treaty commitments which reveal the inequitable treatment of vulnerable developing countries. In the first place, the asymmetry of bargaining power in climate negotiations is manifest in the greater decision costs borne by participating poorer countries, whose shortcomings in technical and administrative capacity are reinforced by their political marginalization in the global political order. This suggests a *procedural injustice* at odds with the international legal norm prescribing equality of treatment for sovereign states (Roberts and Parks 2007: 14–19). Secondly, while the principle of common but differentiated responsibilities would seem fairly to oblige industrialized country Parties to be the first to undertake reductions in greenhouse gas emissions, its operationalization in the Kyoto Protocol has also triggered *distributive injustices* to poorer countries. For example, the designation of 1990 as a base year for emission reduction commitments under the Protocol exempts greenhouse gas emissions preceding this starting-point, to the obvious advantage of countries already industrialized.[5] Similarly, the Protocol's Clean Development Mechanism, which is designed to foster green technology investment in developing country Parties, is arguably constraining the economic development space in these states, insofar as transnational companies are investing in carbon reduction opportunities that may not reflect host country economic priorities (Schreuder 2009: 191–3).

Can those liberal theories of justice featuring egalitarian maxims find normative space for those most disadvantaged by climate change? If we turn to John Rawls's (1999a) theory of justice – the seminal modern expression of social contract theory – there is, of course, in the difference principle an explicit rule for the structure of society that justifies inequalities only if they are to the greatest benefit of the least advantaged.[6] The difference principle applies to the allocation of so-called 'primary social goods' (e.g. income and wealth, rights and liberties), the distribution of which is deemed necessary for citizens to participate fully in society. While Rawls said little on environmental problems, it has been suggested that a healthy environment should be included as one such primary good in his schema of justice (e.g. Bell 2004a). Yet, as Vanderheiden (2008: 79) argues, the capacity of the atmosphere to absorb greenhouse gases at safe levels for human wellbeing is essentially a finite good, and current atmospheric levels of greenhouse gases preclude the equalization move recommended by Rawls where there is pronounced inequality: that is, maximizing the allowances of the primary good to the least advantaged. Even if we accept atmospheric absorptive capacity as a primary good, historic inequalities in global greenhouse gas emissions could, under the difference principle, invite carbon-intensive allowance transfers that would be unsafe for human wellbeing. To retain the egalitarian intent of the difference principle but also effectively to address climate change, the irreversibility of dangerous climate change justifies instead regulatory priority being given to dramatic curbs on the carbon footprint of industrialized countries, accompanied by substantial adaptation assistance to vulnerable populations.

The Rawlsian theory of justice also falters in the face of the spatio-temporal dynamics of climate change. Significantly, Rawls judged the difference principle not to be applicable between states, deriving principles of international justice from what liberal and non-liberal societies would find to be mutually acceptable for global co-existence (1999b). This includes the assumption that states are responsible for the environmental integrity of their territories, although there is no obligation for international environmental cooperation. As Bell (2004b: 142–3) observes, this renders the Rawlsian global compact ill-suited to addressing climate change, as the common property attributes of the global atmosphere are simply ignored. Furthermore, the one principle of international co-existence from this framework that might give moral consideration to the plight of populations with high climate vulnerability – the duty to assist other peoples burdened by unfavourable conditions (Rawls 1999b: 105–13) – is restricted to institutional capacity-building: the toleration of global inequalities of wealth under Rawls's 'law of peoples' blunts the effectiveness of this principle as a means of allocating the costs of climate change mitigation and adaptation (Bell 2004b: 145).[7]

If the Rawlsian framework struggles with the spatial extension of distributive justice to climate harms, there is at least the prospect of environmental justice between generations. From his domestic specification of a social contract, Rawls (1999a: 251–9) posits a principle of 'just savings' – that mutually disinterested individuals, in the original position, would agree that it is rational for them to pass to succeeding generations both reasonably just institutions and a level of capital and wealth sufficient to meet the social minimum for the least advantaged. Present generations would agree to this, he claims, by their representation of family lines (with duties to their immediate descendants) and a wish that all earlier generations in their domestic society had followed the principle. The just savings principle includes constraints on current consumption to conserve and regenerate the capacity of the natural world to sustain its human population (1999b: 107), which leads some to register its relevance for determining inter-temporal climate justice (Brunnée 2009: 321). However, the long-term, cumulative onset of global climate change disrupts the model of a neat succession of national governments or populations preserving safe climatic conditions for their own vulnerable descendants. Simon Caney has pinpointed this inter-generational *loss of control* of climate benefits and burdens, with domestic populations affected by the decisions of previous members of other societies (2006: 273). Indeed, until recently, populations could not even have *recognized* the climate harm to future generations being caused by carbon-intensive pathways of economic development. Thus, the just savings principle cannot capture essential facets of justice for climate-vulnerable future generations.

Climate vulnerability seems thus to fall outside the moral parameters of Rawlsian social justice. What of the major liberal egalitarian alternative to social contract theory – the capabilities approach associated above all with the work of Martha Nussbaum (2006) and Amartya Sen (2009)? The capabilities perspective understands global (and domestic) social justice in terms of social entitlements compatible with the equal dignity of human beings, whereby people are able adequately to secure minimal thresholds of core capabilities. These core capabilities are freedoms to accomplish things deemed necessary for a dignified life, such as being able to achieve bodily health and integrity, as well as control over one's environment (Nussbaum 2006: 76–8). For Nussbaum, being able to live with concern for and in relation to animals, plants and the world of nature is a core capability, although she examines its justice implications with reference to the species-specific entitlements of animals rather than any analysis of climate change or other global ecological interdependencies. Nevertheless, the capabilities approach has been employed by Wolf and de-Shalit to address those involuntary social and environmental risks which, they claim, entrench disadvantage for vulnerable people. Drawing on almost 100 extended interviews conducted in Israel and Britain, Wolf and de-Shalit contend that exceptional vulnerability compounds disadvantage by compelling individuals to undertake harmful coping strategies, giving as one example the plight of poor Bedouin herders in southern Israel exposed routinely to contaminated water, because of political constraints on their ability to move (2007: 67–8).[8]

Surprisingly, Wolf and de-Shalit do not consider the role of global and transnational flows of harm in entrenching social disadvantage, which weakens their commentary on environmental justice. Where capability theorists have considered the value of their approach for tackling global inequalities, the Rawlsian focus on primary goods serves as a foil: capabilities are viewed as a richer conceptual repertoire for locating social positions than resources alone, reflected in an outcomes interest in human development rather than wealth creation and transfer (Nussbaum 2006: 283–4; Sen 2009: 260–3). Nussbaum has provided the fullest account of a capabilities perspective on global justice, arguing for a global equality of opportunity in which a minimum threshold level of capabilities, for all persons, extends beyond national political communities to humanity as a whole (2006: 291–5). In the most developed account of her position, global warming is briefly mentioned as an example of a type of collective harm that justifies the allocation of institutional responsibilities to states and corporations for promoting human capabilities across national boundaries; and effective international environmental regulation is presented as one of the necessary layers of a 'thin system' of decentralized global governance for protecting core human capabilities (Nussbaum 2006: 308, 320). Nussbaum's principles for a minimally just global order include also a priority principle directed at poor and developing countries – that there is a substantial redistribution of resources from prosperous nations to poorer ones. In this way the capabilities approach has a greater redistributive ambition at the global level than the Rawlsian approach.

At the intergenerational level, there is also the claim that the capabilities perspective can better protect the ecological wellbeing of future generations than invoking a just savings principle or the kindred notion of sustainable development – that the needs of the present generation should be met without compromising the ability of future generations to meet their own needs (World Commission on Environment and Development 1987). Sen (2009: 248–52) argues that environmental sustainability should be reconfigured to encompass sustainable freedom – the preservation or expansion of current freedoms and capabilities without compromising the capabilities of future generations. In other words, each generation acts as a trustee for the core capabilities of succeeding generations. This suggestion has the virtue of integrating environmental protection considerations into human development thinking: it would therefore seem appropriate for capturing the hybrid socioecological character of climate vulnerability. As with social contract theory, though, it is by no means clear that a capabilities approach can grasp the particular risk profile of climate change, including the non-substitutable sink capacity of the atmosphere in regards to greenhouse gases (and other pollutants). As there is no priority accorded in the capabilities approach to the ecological conditions necessary for human survival (as might be provided, for example, by a human right not to suffer from the disadvantages caused by climate change: Caney 2005), there is little guidance available on how to address the inevitable tensions and trade-offs between the capabilities of the present vulnerable and of the future vulnerable. In a world of escalating climate adaptation costs and global governance failure on climate change, this leaves the capabilities perspective seemingly unable to generate special obligations of climate justice.

The brief overview above of two prominent liberal perspectives on social justice suggests that, despite their egalitarian intentions and interests in wider communities of justice (transnational and intergenerational), climate vulnerability is not yet ensconced within the scope of their moral concern. I have highlighted conceptual challenges associated, above all, with the unprecedented threat of dangerous climate change (as defined by the IPCC), particularly to the least advantaged. In the last section of this chapter, I indicate how one population with high climate vulnerability remains beyond the geopolitical pale of international climate concern. The Palestinian 'exception' to the UNFCCC discourse on climate responsibility exposes vividly the moral shortfall in its constituent norms of climate harm prevention and procedural equity.

The occupied Palestinian territory: beyond the pale of (climate) concern

Across all fields of human security, the high social vulnerability of the Palestinian people is widely acknowledged by the international community. Following the end of the *Second Intifada* in 2005, expectations were raised that socioeconomic conditions would improve in the West Bank and Gaza, but recent trends reveal instead a sharp deterioration. UN surveys indicate a deepening of poverty: by 2008 48 per cent of Palestinians in the West Bank and 70 per cent in Gaza were judged to live below the poverty line (UNDP 2009; see also United Nations Relief and Works Agency for Palestine Refugees 2009). There are also serious problems concerning secure access to affordable food and water. In 2008 25 per cent of the West Bank population and 56 per cent of the Gaza population were deemed by the Food and Agriculture Organization (2008) to be food secure, while the daily water consumption for three-quarters of Palestinians was estimated to be 60–100 litres per person for domestic use (Zeitoun 2008: 14), which compares with a World Health Oganization minimum daily standard of 100 litres per person for direct consumptive and hygiene needs. According to the UNDP, food and water insecurity in the oPt are likely to be exacerbated by forecasted climate change, on account of worsening environmental conditions for the domestic agricultural sector (which consumes 66 per cent of Palestinian withdrawn water) and a fragile water supply infrastructure. For both the agriculture and water sectors the political and economic constraints of a belligerent occupation severely restrict the development of Palestinian resilience to present and future climate hazards (UNDP 2010: 68–9).

Of course, it is the fact of belligerent occupation that renders Palestinian climate vulnerabilities *legally* beyond the pale of responsibility of Israel and the international community. In the first place, this has to do with the contested scope of international humanitarian law within the oPt, which Israel maintains is not *de jure* applicable to the West Bank and Gaza, while at the same time undertaking to comply *de facto* with the provisions of the Fourth Geneva Convention and customary law governing belligerent occupation (Dinstein 2009: 20–5). The stance of the international community is less ambiguous: the applicability of the Fourth Geneva Convention to the oPt – including the designation of Israel as an occupying power – has consistently been affirmed by the High Contracting Parties to the Geneva Convention, as well as the United Nations Security Council (UNSC). However, as I note below, even the acknowledgement that international humanitarian obligations hold in the West Bank and Gaza leaves little space for the consideration of environmental justice claims by the occupied.

Secondly, Palestinians are *physically* cast away from, and beyond, dignified treatment by literal pales, which recall the derivation of the noun from *palus* (stake) meaning a protective fence defending a settlement. For Israel this refers to various material manifestations of a 'security fence' or barrier complex constructed first along the border with Gaza in 1987 in response to the *First Intifada*, and then, since 2002, as a Separation Barrier from the West Bank (eventually to reach a planned 763 km), running mostly within the Palestinian side of the Green Line, and encompassing major Israeli settlements in occupied territory. Outside the constitutional protections afforded to Israeli citizens are the Emergency Regulations imposed on the oPt: these empower the State of Israel to declare closed military areas, exercise arrest without trial, expel and even execute individuals (Pappe 2008: 148). The Emergency Regulations have given rise to a pervasive set of controls and movement restrictions which intrude into Palestinian daily life. Gazans also face economic sanctions and a blockade, imposed after the January 2006 victory of Hamas in the Palestinian Legislative Elections, then tightened further in September 2007 following the declaration by Israel that the Gaza Strip was a 'hostile entity'. Operation Cast Lead, the Israeli military offensive of December 2008 – January 2009 in the Gaza Strip, was only the most recent, albeit shocking, example of how Palestinians have been collectively exposed to the securitized and highly asymmetrical effects of occupation.[9]

It is recognized in international law that states have a legitimate right to protect their populations, and the State of Israel has consistently invoked self-defence to justify its extensive use of coercive force against Palestinians perceived to threaten its citizens, though even the US has been uncomfortable with the Israeli propensity to favour disproportionate military actions. The routine use of violence against Palestinians by the Israeli state unsettles the assumption of liberal justice theories that constitutional democracies are inherently pacific (e.g. Rawls 1999b: 8). Indeed, Israel has been presented as a prime example of the 'state of exception' taken to be constitutive of the Western political system: that is, the unexamined foundation of political authority on unaccountable sovereign violence (Agamben 2005). Those individuals and groups excluded from membership of the state (the exiled and the bandits) serve at the same time to constitute the 'other' by which the normalcy of national citizens is measured. It is not difficult to view the treatment of Palestinians in these terms, reaching back to the exiled and refugees of 1948, recording the displaced of 1967 and then registering more recent victims of Israeli state and settler violence (e.g. Lentin 2008; Hanafi 2009). The state of exception of Israel's constant emergency footing has justified multiple contraventions of international humanitarian law, such as the domestic incarceration of 8,000 Palestinians, many without charge or under military detention orders. In the midst of the 'war on terror', which has seen liberal democracies suspend civil liberties and freely scatter derogations from due legal process, the enduring state of exception in Israel and the oPt seems to have been confirmed as the juridical paradigm of Western political authority.

Proponents of the state of exception thesis treat as hypocritical any liberal formulation of international justice that does not concede the bogus universalism of its appeals to a common humanity. Yet it is the existence of cosmopolitan norms in international law that at least gives moral weight to the justice claims of those vulnerable to social and environmental injury. Thus, the prospects for *international distributive justice* in assisting Palestinians to meet climate adaptation burdens caused by other global actors find support in those harm prevention rules with currency in international humanitarian and environmental law. For example, customary and treaty-based humanitarian obligations on Israel as an occupying power oblige it not to degrade or destroy property and resources indispensable to the survival of the Palestinian population, including agricultural areas, drinking water installations and irrigation works. Any such infrastructure oriented to food and water security becomes more critical should climate change significantly increase the physical scarcity of water, especially if movement restrictions continue to restrict economic development options for the oPt. From an international environmental law perspective, Palestinians already benefit indirectly from UNFCCC obligations on Parties effectively to prevent dangerous climate change. Insofar as customary norms of environmental harm prevention are acknowledged as pertaining to climate change, the high climate vulnerability of the oPt would justify also international assistance for Palestinian adaptation measures as a form of direct damage prevention (Verheyen 2005: 35).

The weak enforceability of both international humanitarian and environmental law is of course the key institutional deficiency hindering the reach of cosmopolitan rules of harm prevention. At the level

of state responsibility, international obligations to assist climate adaptation are more practically relevant to the immediate wellbeing of
the Palestinians than states' mitigation duties under the UNFCCC. In
the absence of Israeli compliance with key humanitarian obligations
– including those pertaining to food and water security – the international community continues to pour substantial aid into the oPt,
committing $4.48 billion in March 2009 at the donors' conference
in Sharm el-Sheikh to assist vulnerable sections of the Palestinian
population and to carry on strengthening the Palestinian National
Authority (PNA). The need to address climate risks barely registers in
these donor commitments, even though international humanitarian
organizations have now identified climate change as the most important emerging humanitarian challenge for the global community
(Office for the Coordination of Humanitarian Affairs / International
Federation of Red Cross and Red Crescent Societies / World Food
Progamme 2009). Humanitarian assistance in support of Palestinian
adaptation to climate change would logically target the disaster
risk-reduction capacity of the PNA, which suffers from a number of
structural weaknesses (Al-Dalbeek 2008). Integrating climate risks
into national disaster risk reduction is necessary for building climate
resilience in the oPt, but would inevitably be compromised by the far-
reaching limits to administrative and judicial authority of the PNA set
by the Israeli occupation. This unyielding reality perpetuates both the
need for, and ultimate ineffectiveness of, international assistance to
the Palestinians (Le More 2008).

The high thresholds of (potential) harm necessary to trigger state
obligations under international humanitarian and environmental
law leave unchecked the ongoing effects of the occupation that serve
to increase the climate vulnerability of Palestinians. Some of these
arise from Israel's *de facto* control of Palestinian natural resources
– from Gazan fisheries and natural gas reserves to the groundwater supplies of the three transboundary aquifers underlying the
West Bank.[10] Combined with the numerous restrictions on the free
movement of goods and people, this control smothers development
pathways out of vulnerability. For example, to take the critical issue
of physical water scarcity forecast to increase under climate change,
Israel consumes six times the Palestinian withdrawal from shared
freshwater resources (Zeitoun 2008: 57–8). For the crucial Western
Aquifer Basin, which is the largest groundwater resource between the
two territories, Israeli prohibition of new Palestinian wells and access
restrictions to existing Palestinian wells caught on the Israeli side of
the Separation Barrier are significantly reducing supplies of agricultural water for the northern West Bank (Trottier 2007: 121). Sari Hanafi
(2009), who subscribes to the state of exception theory, has termed

'spacio-cide' the creeping dispossession and degradation by Israel of Palestinian living spaces, which he claims has undermined the material conditions of a viable Palestinian state. Spacio-cide also disables the means by which Palestinians have historically coped with climate hazards – e.g. changes in agricultural land use, settlement locations and livelihood choices during times of drought – and which, with an end to occupation, could serve as cultural templates for effective adaptation to new climate stresses (UNDP 2010: 68–9). The Israeli erosion of the material and social conditions by which Palestinians cope with climate (and other) hazards has unjust consequences for the distribution of adaptation costs between the two territories, yet its insidious agency slips past the watch of international norms of humanitarian and environmental harm prevention.

The humanitarian safeguards against harm offered by the international law of belligerent occupation operate in acknowledged conditions of coercion – the civilian population has not consented to be occupied. In a protracted period of occupation, as for the oPt, this suggests the firm exclusion of the occupied from *international procedural justice* in the sense of their participation and recognition as citizens of a sovereign state with formal equality in the global community. Just as norms of environmental protection are sidelined by the particular (*lex specialis*) rules governing military occupation under the laws of war, political norms of collective self-determination and human autonomy seem effectively suspended. Avoiding here the state of exception rests on the expectation that the international community will make good its commitment to facilitate a comprehensive Israeli–Palestinian peace settlement in which two democratic states live side by side in peace, with recognized borders (e.g. UNSC Resolution 1850). Prior to any such final settlement, is there any scope for the Palestinians to determine collectively their own climate vulnerability with a view, if necessary, to seeking adaptation assistance from the international community?

It is the absence of state sovereignty for the Palestinians that precludes their political representatives from signing up to, and participating in, the UNFCCC – the most important international regime for allocating state duties regarding climate change mitigation and adaptation. To be sure, following the proclamation of the 'State of Palestine' by the Palestinian National Council in November 1988, 'Palestine' was recognized as an entity by the UN General Assembly (UNGA Resolution 43/177) and has since been afforded rights and privileges of participation in the work of the UN system (UNGA Resolution 52/250). This unique diplomatic identity – between a non-state and a state – has allowed PNA actors to represent the oPt in areas where they have particular expertise and authority; thus the Palestinian

Environmental Quality Authority participates as an observer in a number of multilateral environmental agreements (e.g. the 1994 UN Desertification Convention and the 1976 Barcelona Convention for the Protection of the Mediterranean). Supported by the Arab League, the PNA has sought Palestinian observer status at the UNFCCC, but so far with little success:[11] there has been little appetite, outside Arab Parties to the Convention, to pull the highly charged issue of Palestinian climate vulnerability within the orbit of a treaty sustained still by a fragile global consensus between Northern and Southern states. As the occupying power in the oPt, and also a Party to the UNFCCC, Israel could reasonably be expected to represent the interests of the Palestinian population in avoiding climate-related harm forecast to affect vital interests in water and food security, but the issue of Palestinian climate vulnerability is absent from Israeli national statements on adaptation to climate change (e.g. Office of the Chief Scientist 2008). Without any direct representation, on an ongoing basis within the UNFCCC, of Palestinian vulnerability to climate-related harm, they remain beyond the pale of the international climate regime – frozen out, for example, from access to the financial mechanisms available under the UNFCCC to support climate adaptation activities in poorer countries.

The procedural injustice that is the exclusion of Palestinian representatives and interests from the international climate regime is founded, of course, on a more general denial of national self-determination. It has been noted that participatory failings in global decision-making on climate change are intertwined with the *lack of recognition* of the needs of vulnerable peoples (Paavola, Adger and Huq 2006). In the Palestinian case, where ethnic identity has been forged by collective and individual experiences of oppression, injury and humiliation at the hands of an occupier – one whose own singular ethnic ideology (Zionism) precludes the treatment of Palestinians as equals – cultural recognition is fraught with violence. This is the case internally as well as externally: the political and often bloody polarization of the population into factions – pro- and anti-PNA, secular versus religious, refugee versus non-refugee – has frustrated moves to present a unified governing authority (Jamal 2007). The efforts of the international community have often made matters worse: the ongoing dependence of the Palestinians on substantial flows of humanitarian and development assistance has fostered corrupt, clientelistic networks, as well as bending domestic institutions to donor preferences and political interests. It would be unwise to imagine that the development of a Palestinian position on climate justice would not be affected by these broader political currents and power relationships. Yet the international community is obliged at least to recognize the right of

Palestinian political representatives to address the potentially dangerous impacts of climate change on their vulnerable population.

Conclusion

So over-determined is the vulnerability of Palestinians to physical and
psychological harm that consideration of the dangerous effects from
potential climate change represents, paradoxically, an entitlement
– the luxury to attend to impacts to wellbeing that are uncertain
and diffuse. As noted above, climate scientists do forecast disruptive
biophysical impacts for the eastern Mediterranean, by the end of
the century, as a result of climate change, yet these predictions are
dwarfed into insignificance by the immediate and enduring injuries
caused by the Israeli occupation in the West Bank and Gaza. Indeed,
it is practically irrelevant to Palestinians if the climate hazards they
face are ultimately caused by anthropogenic greenhouse gas emissions
(climate change) or are the expressions of 'natural climate variability':
both are the effects of intangible forces outside their control. The
international allocation of mitigation and adaptation responsibilities
under the UNFCCC is a justice concern for this population only insofar
as those states more culpable for global warming, and/or more capable
of assisting poorer countries, might be obliged to assist Palestinians in
becoming more resilient to dangerous climate change. However, for
reasons already given, Palestinians are beyond the pale of the UNFCCC
process: their statelessness ensures their formal exclusion from the
international regime (including access to climate adaptation financing), while their contentious political subjectivity is viewed by key
Convention Parties as toxic to the fragile global consensus on climate
action.

   As discussed in this chapter, liberal theorists of justice with egalitarian credentials have conceptual resources for bringing the least
advantaged into the fold of moral concern, but are found wanting
when confronted both with the problem structure of climate change
and with the challenge of a protracted belligerent occupation. Both
conditions are under-examined in liberal political theory, and when
these circumstances converge, as with the climate vulnerability of the
Palestinians, the limitations are compounded. In contrast, Giorgio
Agamben's (2005) 'state of exception' thesis seems at least to throw
light on the legal and moral pales staked out by liberal political
regimes, along with the zones of exclusion they create: here the exceptional case unmasks the unacknowledged conditions of conventional
political authority, notably the arbitrary violence of a 'force of law
without law' (Agamben 2005: 39) against those seen as threatening the

security of the state. And it is the nature of Israel as a security state, on a constant emergency footing, that gives force to claims that it embodies a state of exception in its domestic polity and its occupation of the Palestinian territory. There is, of course, also a globalization of violence that feeds into, and out from, the Israeli–Palestinian conflict and structures the production of Palestinian (and Israeli) vulnerabilities.[12] However, the normative cost of Agamben's theory arguably outweighs its critical intent, for there is no escape from the state of exception, no prospect of justice. Indeed, its erasure of autonomous agency is, arguably, theoretically more corrosive than the weaknesses of egalitarian liberal approaches. Much needs to be done to rework the latter to make space for the consideration of, and engagement with, the injustices of climate vulnerability.

Notes

1. Interviews conducted by the author with Abdallah Al Tabaneh, Yatta District, and with the head of the Hebron Agriculture Department, Hebron – both 11 May 2009. The regional description here accords with a survey undertaken by the Food and Agriculture Organization (2009).
2. Interviews conducted by the author in At-Tuwani village, 16 December 2008 and 11 May 2009. The scope of Israeli settler violence in the region, and elsewhere in the West Bank, has been documented by the United Nations: see Office for the Coordination of Humanitarian Affairs (2008).
3. My use of the term 'occupied Palestinian territory' follows the accepted nomenclature employed by the United Nations in reference to a series of UN Security Council Resolutions on the Israeli–Palestinian conflict, beginning with Resolution 242 in November 1967.
4. 'Climate change' here means 'a change of climate which is attributed directly or indirectly to human activity that alters the composition of the global atmosphere which is in addition to the natural climate variability observed over comparative time periods' (United Nations Framework Convention on Climate Change (UNFCCC) Article 1.2).
5. To be sure, there is a moral case for selecting this base year, which is that, prior to 1990, polluting states can claim 'excusable ignorance' in not being aware of the climate harm being caused by otherwise legal economic activities conducted by their nationals. However, this defence becomes less plausible by 1990 when the IPCC released its *First Assessment Report*, setting out clearly the nature and scope of human-induced climate change. On 'excusable ignorance', see Caney (2005: 761–2).
6. This is within a society in which basic liberties for all are extensive and protected (Rawls 1999a: 52–6).
7. For a similarly restrained notion of international justice, which locates 'residual responsibilities' to vulnerable foreign populations, see David Miller (2007).
8. For a work (Wolf and de-Shalit 2007) preoccupied in part with the least advantaged in Israel, those subject to Israeli occupation in the Gaza Strip and the West Bank are conspicuously absent: Palestinians are glimpsed only fleetingly – as suicide bombers, Kassam missile launchers or, at best, the clients of paternalistic concern by Israeli NGOs.

9. While Israel has stated that, with its unilateral withdrawal from the Gaza Strip in September 2005, its status as an occupying power there has finished, it still retains effective control of the Strip, and acknowledged in the 2003 Israeli–Palestinian Interim Agreement that the West Bank and Gaza Strip constitute a single territorial unit: Israel therefore remains bound by international humanitarian obligations regarding belligerent occupation (Dinstein 2009: 276–80).

10. This *de facto* control stands opposed to the principle that an occupied population retains permanent sovereignty over its natural wealth and resources, as stated for the oPt in UN General Assembly Resolution 305 in December 1972: see Okowa (2009: 244–5).

11. Palestine was granted observer status at the UNFCCC COP-15 meeting at Copenhagen in December 2009, but with no access to the formal negotiations and no prospect of a more permanent observer status in the international climate convention.

12. Consider, for example, the extraordinary asymmetry of US government support for 'security assistance' in the region, with a congressional budget request in 2009 of $2.55 billion for Israel (part of a new ten-year $30 billion security-assistance agreement) and $25 million on 'non-lethal' security assistance to the Palestinian Authority: see US Department of State (2009).

Bibliography

Adger, W. N. (2006) 'Vulnerability', *Global Environmental Change*, 16 (3).

Agamben, G. (2005) *State of Exception*, Chicago: The University of Chicago Press.

Al-Dalbeek, J. (2008) *An Assessment of Disaster Risk Reduction in the Occupied Palestinian Territory*, Jerusalem: UNDP.

Barnett, J., Lambert, S. and Fry, I. (2008) 'The Hazards of Indicators: Insights from the Environmental Vulnerability Index', *Annals of the Association of American Geographers*, 98 (1).

Bell, D. (2004a) 'Environmental Justice and Rawls's Difference Principle', *Environmental Ethics*, 26 (3).

Bell, D. (2004b) 'Environmental Refugees: What Rights? Which Duties?', *Res Publica*, 10 (2).

Brunnée, J. (2009) 'Climate Change, Global Environmental Justice and International Environmental Law', in J. Ebbeson and P. Okowa (eds.), *Environmental Law and Justice in Context*, Cambridge: Cambridge University Press, pp. 316–32.

Caney, S. (2005) 'Cosmopolitan Justice, Responsibility, and Global Climate Change', *Leiden Journal of International Law*, 18 (4).

Caney, S. (2006) 'Cosmopolitan Justice, Rights and Global Climate Change', *Canadian Journal of Law and Jurisprudence*, 19 (2).

Dinstein, Y. (2009) *The International Law of Belligerent Occupation*, Cambridge: Cambridge University Press.

Food and Agricultural Organization (2008) *Social Protection in the West Bank and Gaza Strip: Working Paper 5: Household Food Security Profiling*, Rome: FAO.

Food and Agricultural Organization (2009) *Assessment of Small Ruminant Breeders in Rural Hebron, Jericho, Bethlehem and Ramallah*, Jerusalem: FAO.

GLOWA–Jordan River Project (2009) *Project 3: Climate Scenarios*; available at www.glowa-jordan-river.de/ProjectP03/HomePage.

Hanafi, S. (2009) 'Spacio-cide: Colonial Politics, Invisibility and Rezoning in Palestinian Politics', *Contemporary Arab Affairs*, 2 (1).

Jamal, A. A. (2007) *Barriers to Democracy: The Other Side of Social Capital and the Arab World*, Princeton: Princeton University Press.

Kitoh, A., Yatagai, A. and Alpert, P. (2008) 'First Super High-resolution Model Projection that the Ancient "Fertile Crescent" Will Disappear in this Century', *Hydrological Research Letters*, 2.

Leary, N., Adejuwon, J., Bailey, W., Barros, V., Caffera, M., Chinvano, S. et al. (2008) 'For Whom the Bell Tolls: Vulnerabilities in a Changing Climate', in N. Leary, C. Conde, J. Kulkarni, A. Nyong and J. Pulhin (eds.), *Climate Change and Vulnerability*, London: Earthscan, pp. 3–30.

Le More, A. (2008) *International Assistance to the Palestinians: Political Guilt, Wasted Money*, London: Routledge.

Lentin, R. (ed.) (2008) *Thinking Palestine*, London: Zed Books.

Mellouki, A. and Ravishankara, A. R. (eds.) (2007) *Regional Climate Variability and Its Impacts in the Mediterranean Area*, Dordrecht: Springer.

Miller, D. (2007) *National Responsibility and Global Justice*, Oxford: Oxford University Press.

Nussbaum, M. (2006) *Frontiers of Justice: Disability, Nationality, Species Membership*, Cambridge, MA: Belknap Press.

Office for the Coordination of Humanitarian Affairs (2008) *Unprotected: Israeli Settler Violence against Palestinian Civilians and Their Property*, Jerusalem: OCHA.

Office for the Coordination of Humanitarian Affairs / International Federation of Red Cross and Red Crescent Societies / World Food Programme (2009) *Addressing the Humanitarian Challenges of Climate Change: Regional and National Perspectives*, Geneva: OCHA.

Office of the Chief Scientist (2008) *Preparation of Israel for Global Climate Change: The Consequences of Climate Change in Israel and Interim Recommendations* [in Hebrew], Tel Aviv: Ministry of Environmental Protection.

Okowa, P. (2009) 'Environmental Justice in Situations of Armed Conflict', in J. Ebbeson and P. Okowa (eds.), *Environmental Law and Justice in Context*, Cambridge: Cambridge University Press, pp. 231–52.

Paavola, J., Adger, W. N. and Huq, S. (2006) 'Multifaceted Justice in Adaptation to Climate Change', in W. N. Adger, J. Paavola, S. Huq and M. J. Mace (eds.), *Fairness in Adaptation to Climate Change*, Cambridge, MA: MIT Press, pp. 263–77.

Pappe, I. (2008) 'The *Mukharabat* State of Israel: A State of Oppression Is Not a State of Exception', in R. Lentin (ed.), *Thinking Palestine*, London: Zed Books, pp. 148–69.

Patt, A. G., Schröter, D., de la Vega-Leiner, A. C. and Klein, R. J. T. (2009) 'Vulnerability Research and Assessment to Support Adaptation and Mitigation: Common Themes from the Diversity of Approaches', in Patt et al. (eds.), *Assessing Vulnerability to Climate Change*, London: Earthscan, pp. 1–25.

Rawls, J. (1999a) *A Theory of Justice*, revised edn, New York: Oxford University Press.

Rawls, J. (1999b) *The Law of Peoples*, Cambridge, MA: Harvard University Press.

Roberts, J. T. and Parks, B. C. (2007) *A Climate of Injustice: Global Inequality, North–South Politics, and Climate Policy*, Cambridge, MA: MIT Press.

Schneider, S. H., Semenov, S., Patwardhan, A., Burton, I., Magadza, C. H. D., Oppeheimer, M. et al. (2007) 'Assessing Key Vulnerabilities and the Risk from Climate Change', in M. L. Parry, O. F. Canziani, J. P. Palutikof, P. J. van der

Linden and C. E. Hanson (eds.), *Adaptation and Vulnerability: Contribution of Working Group II to the Fourth Assessment Report of the Intergovernmental Panel on Climate Change*, Cambridge: Cambridge University Press, pp. 779–810.

Schreuder, Y. (2009) *The Corporate Greenhouse: Climate Change in a Globalizing World*, London: Zed Books.

Sen, A. (2009) *The Idea of Justice*, London: Allen Lane.

Somot, S., Sevault, F., Déqué, M. and Crépon, M. (2008) '21st Century Climate Scenario for the Mediterranean Using a Coupled Atmosphere–Ocean Regional Climate Model', *Global and Planetary Change*, 63 (1–2).

Thomas, D. S. G. and Twyman, C. (2005) 'Equity and Justice in Climate Change Adaptation amongst Natural Resource-dependent Societies', *Global Environmental Change*, 15 (2).

Trottier, J. (2007) 'A Wall, Water and Power: The Israeli "Separation Fence"', *Review of International Studies*, 33 (1).

Turner, B. L., Kasperson, R. R., Matson, P. A., McCarthy, J. L., Corell, R. W., Christensen, L. et al. (2003) 'A Framework for Vulnerability Analysis in Sustainability Science', *Proceedings of the National Academy of Science*, 100 (14).

United Nations Development Programme (2009) *MDG Advancement in 2008*, Jerusalem: UNDP; available at www.papp.undp.org/en/mdgs/mdgopt.html.

United Nations Development Programme (2010) *Climate Change Adaptation Strategy and Programme of Action for the Palestinian Authority*, Jerusalem: UNDP.

United Nations Framework Convention on Climate Change (2007) *Climate Change: Impacts, Vulnerabilities and Adaptation in Developing Countries*, Bonn: UNFCCC Secretariat.

United Nations Relief and Works Agency for Palestine Refugees (2009) *Poverty in the Occupied Palestinian Territory 2007*, Gaza City: UNRWA.

US Department of State (2009) *Congressional Budget Justification: Foreign Operations*, Washington, DC: Department of State; available at www.usaid.gov/policy/budget/cbj2009/110415.pdf.

Vanderheiden, S. (2008) *Atmospheric Justice: A Political Theory of Climate Change*, Oxford: Oxford University Press.

Verheyen, R. (2005) *Climate Change Damage and International Law*, Leiden: Martinus Nijhoff.

Wolf, J. and de-Shalit, A. (2007) *Disadvantage*, Oxford: Oxford University Press.

World Commission on Environment and Development (1987) *Our Common Future*, Oxford: Oxford University Press.

Zeitoun, M. (2008) *Power and Water in the Middle East*, London: I. B. Tauris.

Part 3

WHERE TO FROM HERE?

10

Green Peace: Energy, Europe and the Global Order

David Miliband

This speech was delivered by David Miliband for the Ralph Miliband Lecture Series at the London School of Economics on 7 May 2008.

It is a great honour to be speaking at the LSE. To do so in a lecture series in memory of my father's contribution to the School is poignant and a little ironic. Poignant because my dad is not here to listen. Ironic because his view of the School was a mixture of fondness for the people and frustration with the institution. His view of the Labour Party was also a mixture – not of fondness and frustration but frustration and despair. So the idea that his son would be speaking at LSE as Labour Foreign Secretary would have summoned pride and prejudice in equal measure.

My dad always described himself as a socialist, but also a teacher. When people tell me that his books made a difference to them it gives me huge pride. But they also tell me they remember his classes. As a teacher, he was determined to engage the minds of his students. Perhaps surprisingly for someone of strong, in fact very strong, political views, he went out of his way to talk up and discuss alternatives to his own point of view. That spirit of openness and inquiry explains, I think, the bequest that funds the lecture series, the books and the scholarships that bear my father's name in the Ralph Miliband programme at the LSE, and which have been brilliantly driven forward by Professor David Held since 1998.

I think the origins of the programme are important. It is funded by a bequest from an LSE student. The donor, who never wanted to be named, was helped by my dad with his thesis in the early 1950s. He described his relationship with him as follows:

> I am not a socialist. I try to be open-minded and non-partisan. Ralph and I were not always in agreement about specific ends. That is unimportant. What counts is his willingness and ability to avoid doctrines and socio-political traps. His work and spirit should not become a

> mausoleum for dead thoughts, like the various churches and political
> parties that strew the intellectual landscape . . . That should clarify my
> wishes – to establish a living, breathing adjunct to the LSE traditions
> of the Webbs, R. H. Tawney, Harold Laski and all of us who came to the
> LSE in their spirit.

My dad spent nearly thirty years of his life associated with the LSE.
He gained admission a year or so after arriving in the UK in 1940, fresh
from learning English and completing his Matriculation at Acton
Technical College. After being demobbed in 1945 he came to Houghton
Street to complete his studies. By the early 1950s he was on the faculty
and stayed here until 1972.

Other speakers in this series have come from the worlds of business,
economics, and academia. I am a politician, and I want to talk about
the international politics of the issues that have dominated this series,
and, in particular, the politics of energy and the global order.

If you want to skip the lecture and know the conclusion of my
argument – I confess to using that tactic as a student – it is as follows.
We face a new resource crunch, with spiralling energy and food prices
as well as water shortages. Its origins are carbon dependence. Its consequences are not just economic and environmental, but geopolitical.
We risk a scramble for resources, with each nation pitted against the
other. The alternative is a transition from a global economy dependent
on oil and gas to a low-carbon economy with a diverse mix of energy
sources and suppliers. And the best way to set a new global course, in
fact the only real means at our disposal, is through leadership from
the European Union – the largest single market in the world, with the
clout to set global standards.

Two global orders

I want to start with what I have seen in foreign policy over the last
nine months. Two trends are visible, rubbing up against each other.
The first is a world built-in reaction to the disastrous consequences of
balance-of-power politics in the first half of the twentieth century. It
is a world where national interest is pursued through international
cooperation. It recognizes that flows of people, money and products
are making countries' prosperity and security more intertwined than
ever. And it accepts that to address the shared threats we face – from
financial instability and climate change to nuclear proliferation – we
need to work together through shared rules and institutions, from the
EU to NATO, the WTO and the UN.

The second is a world where national interest is still pursued through
competitive rivalry. Notions of interdependence and multilateral

cooperation are dismissed as a passing fad. International relations is a zero sum game where nations compete for power. From trade to nuclear proliferation, the danger is more insecurity. To emphasize, these are not competing visions of international interest on the one hand and national interest on the other. They are two different visions of how national interest is pursued. Multilateralism is not the betrayal of modern national interest, but its expression.

For much of the last decade, we have spoken as though cooperation will win over competition. We have tended to see globalization as an inevitable force sweeping all before it. But the truth is that the globalization of the twenty-first century is as fragile as the globalization of the nineteenth century – which ended on the streets of Sarajevo in 1914. Then, as now, there are big gains, often invisible, from globalization. Then, as now, there are important insecurities, often all too visible. And I believe that the resource crunch we now face is the fulcrum on which this all turns. If we fail to address the problems of scarcity and high prices in respect of fuel, food and water, the traditional paradigm of competitive, balance-of-power politics threatens to return with a vengeance. But if we succeed in finding new, innovative ways to meet the growing demand for natural resources, the newer paradigm of cooperation and collaboration will win out.

The resource crunch

Let me start by setting out what is driving the resource crunch, and how we can address it. First, a richer, more crowded world is propelling a surge in demand for natural resources. The global population is projected to rise from 6.6 billion now to 9 billion in 2050: an increase the size of the total global population in 1950. The world is facing the most rapid and the largest build-up in the demand for energy in modern history. All of the rise is coming in developing economies so that, by 2025, the global South will have higher demand for energy than the North. As India, China and other developing countries enjoy rapid economic growth, their citizens want and can afford the standards of living enjoyed in industrialized countries. They are driving more cars – 20,000 new vehicles appear on Chinese roads each day. And they are consuming more electricity – two additional coal-fired power plants each week to feed the Chinese grid.

Second, energy demand is growing at a time when the supplies of cheap oil and gas are dwindling. Oil and gas supplies are becoming far more costly to extract as more accessible reserves have been depleted and raw material prices rise. Supply is concentrated in countries whose governments directly control their hydrocarbon industries, and are developing them more slowly than consuming countries might want. Some of them might be prepared to use their natural resources as instruments of foreign policy. In the UK, as North Sea oil and gas supplies are depleted, we are becoming increasingly dependent on energy imports. As a result of rising global demand, we are seeing investment in alternatives to oil and gas. Some are better for climate change, such as nuclear and renewables. Others are far worse, such as coal and oil sands. Over the next decade, the most likely effect of growing insecurity of oil and gas is a dash for coal – a resource that is relatively cheap, abundant in many countries, but far worse for carbon emissions.

Third, we are seeing an extraordinary period of food price inflation. Rice hit $1,000-a-tonne for the first time last week. The UN Food and Agriculture Organization say food prices rose 57 per cent between March 2007 and March 2008. The World Food Programme is warning of a silent tsunami plunging another 100 million people into starvation. There have been protests at food price rises in Egypt, Morocco, Mauritania, Ethiopia, Indonesia. In Haiti, the Prime Minister was dismissed after days of deadly protests and looting.

The causes are manifold: global demand has surged, but supply has not kept pace. Higher energy prices have pushed up the costs of fertilizers and irrigation, making them unaffordable for many farmers in developing countries. Adverse weather conditions – such as a ten-year drought in Australia – are limiting the land available for food production. Biofuels, not necessarily bad in themselves but sometimes sponsored without proper concern for sustainability, have prompted the cultivation of fuel-crops where food-crops might otherwise have been grown. Meanwhile, the World Bank estimates that demand for food will rise by 50 per cent by 2030.

Fourth, 500 million people live in countries chronically short of water. By 2050 this figure is expected to rise to 4 billion. In northern China, a sinking water table means wells need to be dug much deeper and more pumping capacity needs to be installed. A falling water table and lack of power to run pumps has led to a serious shortfall of drinking water in Bangladesh's capital, Dhaka. Irrigation will become more difficult, more expensive, and more energy-intensive. Farming, both for food and for biofuels, will be affected by water shortages.

The future consequences of this resource crunch are not just economic, they are geopolitical. The main energy consumers, in particular the US and China, are competing for limited resources. There is already a scramble in Africa – the fastest-growing source of new oil in the world. The main production sites will be a source of rising tensions, whether dormant border disputes in the Gulf or countries pushing claims to their share of what could be a quarter of the world's undiscovered oil and gas in the Arctic. About a third of the world's civil wars are currently in oil-producing states, up from a fifth in 1992. And among developing countries, a country that produces oil is twice as likely to suffer an internal rebellion as one that doesn't.

Key transit routes are also increasingly important to energy security, with Turkey playing a pivotal role in bringing oil and gas from both the Middle East and central Asia into Europe; shipping routes across the Caspian and Black Seas increasingly critical to European energy security; and two-thirds of Asia's oil consumption depending on free passage through the Straits of Malacca between Indonesia and Malaysia. All the while, economic power is shifting to oil- and gas-rich states and the elites within them. The vast majority of oil and gas in the world is now supplied by state-owned companies. The revenues accruing from high energy prices can then be used to buy up foreign assets. And, as Thomas Friedman has argued, 'soaring oil prices . . . strengthen antidemocratic regimes'. Resource-rich regimes have less incentive to enter into bargains with their own people. 'No taxation without representation' is meaningless when fuel revenues negate the need for taxation.

If we are to avoid these consequences, we need to address the causes of the resource crunch. Dependence on scarce and vulnerable supplies of hydrocarbons is forcing up energy prices. Higher energy prices and pressure on land is forcing up food prices. Climate change exacerbates water shortages and the availability of agricultural land in some parts of the world. People warned of the danger of oil dependence after the 1973 oil crisis. But global warming changes the equation in a fundamental way. If climate change didn't exist, the answer would be more straightforward. We'd switch to coal and possibly oil sands too for cheaper energy and greater security of supply. But our hydrocarbon dependence – at least when the carbon is emitted into the atmosphere – exacerbates the problems I've described. It exposes us to both energy and climate insecurity. So we need to shift to low carbon, not only investing in renewables and nuclear, but also moving forward with technologies such as carbon capture and storage (CCS) to limit the damage of our continued dependence on coal.

Low-carbon transition

There is a clear pathway to a low-carbon economy that would reduce our carbon footprint and make our energy system more resilient. That is the good news. But for each of the technological changes I am going to describe, there is a major political challenge – how to share the financial burdens of a transition from carbon dependence to carbon independence. First, we need investment in energy efficiency. There is massive potential to cut our energy use and save money by insulating homes, making cars more fuel-efficient, and using less electricity. If the US, China, India and Russia had the same energy efficiency as Japan, world energy consumption would be cut by 20 per cent.

Second, we need to address energy storage as well as new energy production and infrastructure. Following the oil price shock in the 1970s, the International Energy Agency helped to develop a system of oil storage to insulate the global economy from short-term oil shocks. It is right to ask questions about how we respond to shocks in the gas sector; how we improve gas storage; how we get more investment in interconnections between countries to ensure a better match between demand and supply; and how we create the right framework to ensure new pipelines are built to reduce dependency on individual suppliers.

Third, we need to move to low-carbon electricity generation. If we could develop near-zero-emission electricity, the UK would cut its emissions by almost a third. Renewables and nuclear have a part to play here. But to meet the demand for more energy in the medium term, the world will continue to rely on fossil fuels, in particular coal, given the concern over security of gas supplies. That is why urgent investment in CCS for coal is indispensable. The technology exists, but it needs to be applied at scale to bring down costs quickly. The EU has made a commitment of up to 12 CCS demonstration projects by 2015. The UK government is playing its part by funding a competition to build the UK's first CCS coal-fired power station. We need similar investment across Europe to deliver on the EU commitments.

Fourth, a post-oil transport system need not be a mirage. As the King report set out last year, the initial steps will be through hybrid and plug-in hybrid cars combining electric and petrol engines. Biofuels can also play their part where they are produced sustainably. In the longer term, fully electric and hydrogen cars are realistic options.

Europe's responsibility

The political blockage on reforming the high-carbon economy is a question of who moves first. The UK can play a role. But it can only have a decisive effect through the EU. The UK contributes about 2 per cent of global manmade emissions; Europe contributes 14 per cent. Britain accounts for less than 4.5 per cent of global trade (in goods and services); Europe, almost 40 per cent. Europe's success in securing peace and prosperity across western Europe, and democracy in eastern Europe, leaves it ready to establish a new *raison d'être*. The answer is to go back to the future. The story of the European Union began with

cooperation on coal and steel as a way of preventing conflict and instability. Coal and steel were the critical resources needed to wage war. A
common market was seen as a preventative step. Today, Europe again
needs to avert an energy scramble leading to conflict not within its
borders, but beyond its borders. Europe's goal should be to drive a low-
carbon transition not just in Europe, but beyond – using regulation,
markets and negotiating positions that set the global benchmark. Five
priorities stand out.

First, the world needs a global carbon market to enable transfers
from rich to poor countries to help them leapfrog straight to low-
carbon energy. The EU Emissions Trading Scheme is the foundation
for this. We need to ensure its long-term future. Extend the scheme
to cover more sectors of the economy. Ensure caps are set centrally
as the European Commission have proposed rather than by member
states. And link the EU Emissions Trading Scheme to carbon markets
which are now emerging in other countries – the US, Canada and New
Zealand. A global carbon market would play a huge role in helping
developed countries find the most cost-effective sectors to reduce their
emissions, and transferring funds to poorer countries for mitigation
and adaptation.

Second, the world needs to accelerate global investment in green
technology. The EU has the critical mass to do this – and gain a
competitive advantage for European businesses in the process. EU
standards and regulations can mobilize capital investment in new
vehicles, power stations and appliances, bringing down the cost of
deploying low-carbon technology across the world. It is important to
be clear why regulation is necessary. In 1981, it was widely assumed
that oil prices would continue to rise. Instead, prices dropped steadily and investment in alternative energy sources tailed off. However
high the carbon price, uncertainty in energy prices can deter investment. That is why, alongside emissions trading, long-term targeted
regulation is often needed. That means following through on the
European Commission's commitment to reduce the emissions from
power stations. It means setting ambitious long-term regulations for
reducing emissions from vehicles. It means dynamic regulation, as
in the Japanese Toprunner programme, where minimum standards
are ratcheted up to the level of the greenest products every few years,
incentivizing manufacturers to innovate.

Third, the world needs open global markets in agriculture and
increased global investment in low-carbon R&D. The developed world's
agricultural policies cost developing countries about $17 billion each
year – about five times the amount of overseas development assistance
spent on agriculture. The EU Budget and the Common Agricultural
Policy (CAP) must be redefined for a new purpose. Despite reform, it

carries more baggage from the past than innovation for the twenty-first century. The wrong response to the challenges is to hunker down, reiterating arguments from the 1950s and 1960s about food security to justify the CAP as a model for the future. Instead, we need continued liberalization of agriculture, allowing market forces and the price mechanism to play a greater role, globally, in gradually matching supply and demand and avoiding sudden dramatic shortages and wrenching adjustments. As part of that, we must ensure the current budget review and the new EU Budget that follows align spending to priorities, and ensure spending is only used as a policy tool when it is the best tool to use. A greener EU Budget is an important part of that process. That will mean investment in low-carbon technologies and creating the conditions to enable private sector investment in infrastructure and energy grids.

Fourth, the world needs a global dialogue between producers and consumers. We must use the platform provided by the Lisbon Treaty to create a single dialogue between the EU and our key energy suppliers and trading partners around the world. People often talk about Europe's dependence; but we have a market that others want to sell into, not just demands that we need to service. Energy security is one of the compelling strategic arguments for Turkish accession and demonstrates why it is so important to drive this process forward. The EU–Russia dialogue is critical to energy security too: we are stronger if the EU speaks with one voice, engages multilaterally rather than bilaterally. The EU–China dialogue is critical to moving to a low-carbon economy: we need a low-carbon alliance between the world's fastest-growing economy and the world's biggest single market.

Fifth, the world needs a global deal on climate change. The EU has a critical role as the negotiator on behalf of twenty-seven countries. The most difficult questions will be the level of ambition we set ourselves and who should pay for mitigation and adaptation. The EU will be able to lead the way. The targets we set ourselves last year – to reduce our emissions by 20 per cent by 2030, and by 30 per cent in the context of an international agreement – place us in the vanguard of the battle against climate change. And our carbon markets will stand us in good stead when it comes to financial transfers to the developing world.

Carbon dependence is the root of the resource crunch problem. So low carbon is the heart of the answer, not just to climate change but also to energy security. And it is the best route for protecting and promoting the liberal international order which has been the basis of our peace and security over the last sixty years.

Conclusion: green is the new red

I have focused today on the geopolitical impact of our continued dependence on hydrocarbons and the challenges we face in forging an alternative path. But I have called my speech 'Green Peace: Energy, Europe and the Global Order' because I believe that the transition to low carbon promises not just environmental and economic dividends, but significant geopolitical advantages too. A world in which we succeed in building low-carbon economies and curbing greenhouse gas emissions is a world in which power and resource wealth will be dispersed. It is a world where we would all be less beholden to the fuel-rich. It is a world in which we mitigate the worst effects of climate change, and work together – through shared rules and institutions – to prevent or manage water and food shortages peacefully, and to minimize the conflict and mass migration that many are now predicting. It is, in short, a world of order where shared rules are the basis for positive interdependence, and for our continued stability and prosperity.

No sane person could be opposed to this. But it is the subject of ferocious political debate. The reason is that the means are less consensual than the ends. The shift to low carbon represents a wrenching transition in political economy, notions of social justice, and issues of international governance. In other words, this is not just an environmental project. It is a political one. It challenges ideas of national sovereignty. It challenges attachment to free markets – since carbon dependence is the world's greatest market failure. It challenges distrust of collective action. And it challenges us to tackle inequality – or there will be no global deal.

I began by talking about the two paradigms within foreign policy: the risk that competitive rivalry between nations over resources will undermine cooperation to address shared threats. I want to conclude with two paradigms within progressive politics: the social democratic tradition and the radical liberal tradition. Both these traditions have been championed at the LSE. Both had more adherents here than my father's commitment to Marxism. We will only overcome the resource crunch if we draw heavily on each: the social democratic belief in the role of the state in planning and regulation, and the radical liberal belief in the need to mobilize markets and social movements. That is what the resource crunch enjoins us to do. It is a huge project, but one which requires the spirit of social progress and intellectual inquiry that is the best of the LSE.

11

The Politics of Climate Change

Ed Miliband

This speech was delivered by Ed Miliband for the Ralph Miliband Lecture Series at the London School of Economics on 19 November 2009.

It is a very poignant moment for me to be delivering the Ralph Miliband lecture, fifteen years after my father's death. I want to use this opportunity right at the outset to pay tribute to the LSE in general, and David Held in particular, for establishing the Ralph Miliband lecture series, from a bequest by one of his students. It has established itself as a lecture series pushing the boundaries of political and social thought and it is a signal of the quality of the contributors that I find myself between Will Hutton last week and Slavoj Žižek next week.

As my brother recorded when he delivered his lecture in this series last year, my father had an ambivalent relationship with the LSE, to put it mildly. Things were never really the same for him after the troubles of 1968, and the reaction of the authorities to the student uprising. This is reflective of a very profound anti-establishment streak in him: I remember as a child him refusing an invitation to put an entry into *Who's Who*, on the grounds of the company he would have found himself in. If he had an ambivalent relationship with the LSE, the same is true of the Labour Party. He became convinced from the early 1960s that it could not be the vehicle for socialism. Some might say his sons are now proving him right.

But the best thing about him as a political influence was that, while he may have had huge problems with Labour politics and expressed outrage at many of the decisions of its leaders, he never had contempt for the process of trying to use it to make people's lives better and make Britain a more progressive place. He was a political lodestar: a point in the orbit, not always to follow, but from which to navigate. He had a profound belief in the ability of politics to change things, a belief I share. He had a fundamental optimism, not always common on the Left. Yet his optimism was based not on historical laws but on the actions of people. When it comes to the issue of climate change, it seems to me that faith in politics, optimism and belief in people as having the power to shape the world we live in are crucially important commodities. These are the values that keep me going as we face increasingly difficult challenges in our attempts to reach an international deal.

Beyond a global deal on climate change

There is no doubt that it remains a challenge to get a strong international deal which covers emissions, finance for developing countries, support for new technology, action on forestry and a clear and short track to a legally binding treaty. The world requires a comprehensive agreement that is consistent with the science and the need to limit climate change to no more than 2 degrees of warming. That means a deal which will ensure that global emissions peak by 2020 at the latest. Even more important, however, is the work of how this will be done. Implementation will have to occur not just in one country but in every country – in democracies and dictatorships, in richer countries and poorer countries, in energy exporters and energy importers – not just for a year or two, but over decades.

So I would like to take this rare opportunity to look past more immediate negotiations, and talk about what it will take to get the permanent change we need. My focus will be on the UK, not so much in terms of our transition plan and the specific policies we have already laid out and will continue to drive forward, but in terms of what might be called the grammar of politics. The argument I want to make is the following. The challenge of climate change is so great that we are all transition economies (and I use the phrase advisedly). The low-carbon challenge is such that our system of economic production and the way we go about our daily lives will have to alter profoundly. To secure that change, I think we need not just to change a set of policies but to adapt our politics.

In particular, I want to argue that what you might call the politics of 'now' finds its limits in climate change. The politics of now is about an offer to people to provide immediate improvements in their lives. It is the dominant part of the terms of trade of modern politics and, I will argue, an important part of progressive politics. But I want also to acknowledge the harder truth which is that, when it comes to the issue of climate change, the politics of now is not enough.

We need to fashion something that goes beyond the politics of now, to what you might call a politics of the common good (a phrase used recently by another Miliband lecturer, Michael Sandel). What is a politics of the common good? To my mind, it is:

- a politics that goes beyond the satisfaction of immediate wishes to treat citizens as citizens, speaking honestly about the tough choices we face;
- a politics that has at its heart the interests not only of the consumer today, not even just the citizen during their own lifetime, but looks to future generations and intergenerational justice;
- a politics that does recognize that self-interest in a broad sense is a powerful, important and empowering motivator;
- a politics that appeals to a sense of idealism about what is fair here and around the world.

The challenge

If we are to tackle climate change in the years ahead, it is clear we will need to secure change on an unprecedented scale. The change needs to be very extensive. In the United Kingdom we have pledged in law to cut our emissions by 80 per cent. That means we need our electricity and transport systems and homes to be near zero carbon. In turn, this means that we need a dramatic increase in renewable energy – we are planning for a six-fold increase by 2020. We need to dramatically reduce the energy intensity of our homes, with better insulation and more efficient appliances an essential aspect of progress. And if we are to electrify our transport and heating and allow for the intermittency of wind power, we need the total capacity for power generation to go up even as its carbon pollution goes down. The changes need to happen quickly. And the change needs to be permanent.

So the consensus for change cannot be like the 'Make Poverty History' campaign that was very effective at securing agreement at Gleneagles but less effective at building a coalition for the long term. This change needs to fundamentally rewrite the way our economy works in perpetuity. That means the case for action we have to make cannot simply rely on the idea that we are living through exceptional times. We need low carbon to become precisely unexceptional. Without that social acceptance, support for the policy won't endure in the way it needs to. To make these changes requires leadership from government, but it also requires us to build and maintain consent. To take that consent for granted is a mistake and to assume we can sustain change without it would be wrong in my view too.

The politics of 'now' is not enough

The question I would like to put forward is: what kind of politics do we need to make this happen? At the heart of modern politics is a certain way of thinking – what you might call the politics of 'now'. The politics of now, at its best, is about meeting immediate needs and improving people's lives in ways which markets alone will not do. Appeals to self-interest were at the core of many of the great progressive social movements of the twentieth century – from pensions to the NHS – and will be at the core of many of the social movements in the twenty-first century. Politics is about improving the lives of people and therefore there is nothing wrong with a politics that appeals to people's self-interest. I have seen it in my own constituency, from tax credits to Sure Start in the last decade.

But climate change poses a big challenge to the politics of now because the challenge of climate change is marked by distance: first, temporal distance. While the politics of now looks for what are sometimes called 'quick wins', when it comes to climate change there is a significant time lag between when we act and when we see the consequences of those actions. The carbon emitted at any point has effects for decades to come; hence we have seen global warming of 0.8 degrees so far but the scientists tell us that we are destined for 1.4 degrees warming on the basis of emissions already in the atmosphere. The decisions taken by countries now will not be felt in terms of their impact on the planet's warming for around twenty to thirty years. This time lag creates another sort of temporal distance: between the generation that needs to act and the generation that feels the greatest benefit. It is for good reason that some young people in the climate change movement wear T-shirts saying 'How old will you be in 2050?'

Secondly, there is geographical distance. The people who are most vulnerable to climate change, the people who will suffer first – indeed are already suffering today – are not in our neighbourhoods, our country, or even our continent. This emphasizes the sort of moral case and politics we saw in the government's advocacy of international debt relief: distinct from a direct politics of self-interest. Thirdly, there is causal distance. The nature of the threat seems very large and is the sort of thing you see in Hollywood movies. It is hard to link the specific actions that we take as individuals with this monumental problem and to believe we can really have an effect. And if the impacts of the problem are distant, the costs of tackling it are immediate. While, as Lord Stern showed, in the long run it is less costly to tackle climate change than to fail to do so, there are significant up-front costs. Even after we do all we can to make it easy to lead a low-carbon lifestyle, there remain some hard choices that cannot be tackled by a politics of 'now'. There are hard choices about our environment, for example over the issue of wind farms. There are hard choices about how we manage the transition to low carbon, because while some new industries will emerge, some old industries will lose out.

Getting past the politics of now

We need to move beyond the politics of 'now' to a politics of the common good, a politics that treats people not simply as consumers but as citizens. What does that require?

First, it needs a willingness to take the argument to people about the tough choices involved in tackling climate change. This is the starting point: a willingness to engage with people on, for example, the fact that, to deal with the problem of climate change, energy bills are likely to rise. Or that if we are to move away from high-carbon energy to low-carbon energy, we need new energy infrastructure. That openness about hard choices has to be accompanied by a sense of fairness of outcome and fairness of procedure. The test of whether we can persuade people about the low-carbon transition despite higher energy bills is whether they think there is fairness in the way energy is provided and in who pays. That is why the state has to play a strategic role in guiding change. Without strong state action, it would be too easy for the costs of tackling climate change to fall disproportionately on the poorest. As for fairness of procedure, it is at least in part about whether people feel they have a chance to have their say and their views properly taken account of. For example, when we have to build 10,000 wind turbines over the next decade, and a number of nuclear power stations, a test of the new Infrastructure Planning Commission will be whether when they consult people, they are seen to do so in a fair-minded way.

Intergenerational aspects

The second aspect of a politics of the common good is a focus on intergenerational justice. For most policy areas, it is sufficient to have a conception of justice that is intra-generational: it focuses only on the people alive today. When it comes to healthcare or education or policing, we need to keep an eye on the sort of world we are setting ourselves on a path toward in several decades' time, but it rarely needs to be a deciding factor. For climate change, the intergenerational character of the problem is perhaps its defining feature. If we only live for today, we will let climate change get out of control. We have to recognize that the society of today is a custodian of our resources for the society of tomorrow.

As a start, we need to think about the role of economics when it comes to valuing future generations. At the moment, as Lord Stern took into account, the discount rate used in even the most environmentally sensitive economic models still gives virtually no value to policy effects that are more than a couple of hundred years away. That is a long time away. It is perfectly acceptable for most areas of policy. But when it comes to carbon impacts, and the risk that the effect of policy in a few hundred years is a catastrophe for life on Earth, it may be that we should be more cautious about relying on such models. But we are going to need some more profound changes than in the way we build economic models. We need to institutionalize long-term change that protects future generations. That is why we have legislated for an 80 per cent reduction in carbon emissions by 2050, with specific markers along the way. And to ensure there are appropriate independent checks on delivery, we introduced the Climate Change Committee to take a robust external view on progress.

Yet the nature of climate change means that action in the UK alone will not be enough to protect future generations in Britain. Climate change is an intrinsically global problem – one of the hard truths is that UK action is necessary but not sufficient. This is why we need to have a global trajectory for carbon, consistent with scientific findings. And, in turn, that requires greater international cooperation. It is worth saying at this point that, despite the frustration of the UN negotiating process, it seems to me that a framework involving the UN is the only way we can embed the commitment I am talking about. There is little room for free-riders when it comes to climate change and hence we need a global approach.

The role of self-interest

The third element of a politics of the common good may seem paradoxical given what I have said about the politics of now: self-interest. But the truth is that the appeal to self-interest has been an important thread in thinking on the Left since the movement started. It was self-interest that motivated the first trade unions. It was in their self-interest to have limits on the amount of time they had to spend at work. It was in their self-interest to have better safety conditions in the mines and mills. It was in their self-interest to have pensions and access to healthcare. So, when it comes to climate change we should not hold that there is only tension between self-interest and the common good.

There are areas where an appeal to individual self-interest can support the social need to tackle climate change. There are lots of hard choices, but not everything is a hard choice. That means we have to highlight where the benefit of tackling climate change goes beyond avoiding catastrophe, and instead offers us a positive benefit. Part of the problem of our current politics of climate change is that we only talk about the costs, never the benefits of tackling it. As a Labour Party member pointed out to me, 'If Martin Luther King had said "I have a nightmare", nobody would have followed him.'

Take the issue of jobs. If the world sends a clear signal via a global deal on climate change, we can unlock a new green industrial revolution. Already low-carbon technologies are multi-billion-pound industries. If the world can make the change needed on a global scale, they will become even larger. In the UK, with the right industrial policy, that could create many thousands of jobs throughout the country. These can be high-quality high-skilled jobs: manufacturing jobs building electric cars and wind turbines; construction jobs insulating homes and building power stations; science and technology jobs developing the technology of carbon capture and storage or recyclable packaging. In my view, we don't hear this positive case enough. The call of candour means we have to be clear about the risks of inaction. But we also need to speak to people's self-interest when talking about the benefits of action. In fact, it is only by doing this that we can have the credibility to ask people to change their lifestyles when that is necessary.

Social justice

The fourth and perhaps most important aspect of a climate politics of the common good is idealism. Even after we have done all we can to build public support through candour and fairness, institutionalized intergenerational equity and spoken to people's self-interest, there will still be work to do. It is in that space, after the work of self-interest is done, that we cannot live without ideals. We need a politics of climate change that speaks to people's idealism as well as their wallets. It must chime with the ideal of the good society. In my view, the most important ideal is social justice. We do not just need to preserve our world for future generations, we need to hand over a fairer world. We need to show people how action on climate change can reduce inequality and help build a stronger, more cohesive society. That includes the elements I talked about before: energy bills, keeping costs down, ensuring fair access to the new jobs and opportunities. But it is also something bigger. I said we are a transition economy. We are. And it is at moments of transition that we have the greatest ability to shape society for the better. The central challenge is to incorporate climate change into everything we do: so it is an intrinsic part of our economic policy, our energy policy, our approach to social justice.

Conclusion

I began by talking about the need to build and maintain public support for action on climate change. I am not pessimistic. I believe that the politics of the common good that I have sketched out is very much a politics we can advance. I also believe that there is a public desire for facing up to these issues. People are concerned about not just their children, but their children's children, and so we can have the support we need for mechanisms to protect future generations. Self-interest can be a powerful and socially useful motivator. Furthermore, with social justice at its heart, we can have a low-carbon transition that maintains public support. And more than that, I think the value of this sort of politics is not limited to climate change. On issues like social care and pensions, issues of poverty and social mobility, I believe this politics of the common good has the power to motivate people to act.

Politicians have an essential role to play in building this sort of politics. But, as my father understood, it is people demanding change that has, throughout history, changed the world. Nowhere is this more true than in relation to climate change, where the Green movement has already moved opinion in so many countries. That movement will face big challenges in the years ahead as it reaches out to a wider constituency, but it is a vital part of winning the battle to create a wider consensus on climate change. And in that context, I want to leave the last words for my father, in a passage from the end of his last book: 'In all countries, there are people, in numbers large and small, who are moved by the vision of a new social order . . . It is in the growth in their numbers and in the success of their struggles that lies the best hope for humankind' (Ralph Miliband, *Socialism for a Sceptical Age*, Cambridge: Polity Press, 1994).

12

International Climate Policy after Copenhagen: Toward a 'Building Blocks' Approach

Robert Falkner, Hannes Stephan and
John Vogler

How should governments respond to the apparent failure of the 2009 Copenhagen Conference on climate change? Initial reactions by diplomats and observers were dominated by profound disappointment, even despair, at the inadequate outcome of the two-week-long negotiations. For many, the Copenhagen Accord represents what is wrong with international climate diplomacy: cobbled together by some of the most obstinate powers in climate politics, the three-page document represents little more than the lowest common denominator. In the face of a growing sense of the urgent need to act against global warming, it eschews tough and legally binding commitments on mitigation; and despite the worldwide recognition that developing countries will suffer most from climate change, the promises for funding of adaptation measures remain vague. Many more non-governmental organizations (NGOs), business leaders and others engaged in climate efforts are now looking for alternative governance arrangements outside the seemingly deadlocked diplomatic route.

Once the dust had settled, however, the tone of the debate started to change. Analysts began to note quiet relief among negotiators that Copenhagen did not cause the international process to collapse altogether. Indeed, the three-page Copenhagen Accord, however perfunctory its contents, accepted the need to hold mean temperature increases below 2 °C and explicitly endorsed the dual-track climate negotiations under the UN Framework Convention on Climate Change (UNFCCC). It contains in its Annexes the first (non-binding) pledges by all major economies to rein in emissions, including from non-Annex I countries. Furthermore, the Accord establishes the principles for a system of international monitoring, reporting and verification and paves the way for an increase in future funding for developing countries. After a brief period of stock-taking and mutual recrimination, negotiators quickly regrouped and set about preparing for the next Conference of the Parties (COP-16), to be held in Cancún, Mexico, from 29 November to 10 December 2010. It seems as if climate diplomacy is back on track, even if Copenhagen has lowered expectations.

What can be hoped for in the future international process? What should be the strategy of those wishing to strengthen international climate policy? Many, if not all, countries in Europe and the developing world remain committed to negotiating a global climate deal. They believe that only a universal and comprehensive treaty with firm commitments for emission reductions stands a chance of averting the threat posed by global warming. Other countries, including major emitters such as the United States, remain wary of this approach. They either hold that reaching an agreement on a global treaty is unrealistic or would not wish to be legally bound by such a treaty in any case. Either way, they prefer to build elements of global climate policy from the bottom up, by taking action at the domestic level. Major emerging economies such as China have similar concerns about sovereignty, but join the G77 bloc of developing countries in demanding a legally binding framework for mitigation by industrialized nations. Little has thus changed in the way in which the major players in climate politics define their interests.

In the light of these conflicting positions, this chapter reviews the options for future international climate policy. It argues that a major reassessment of the current approach to building a climate regime is required. This approach, which we refer to as the 'global deal' strategy, is predicated on the idea of negotiating a comprehensive, universal and legally binding treaty that prescribes, in a top-down fashion, generally applicable policies based on previously agreed principles. From a review of the history of the 'global deal 'strategy from Rio (1992) to Kyoto (1997) and beyond, we conclude that this approach has been producing diminishing returns for some time, and that it is time to consider an alternative path – if not goal – for climate policy. The alternative that, in our view, is most likely to move the world closer toward a working international climate regime is a 'building blocks' approach, which develops different elements of climate governance in an incremental fashion and embeds them in an international political framework.

This alternative, as we argue below, is already emergent in international politics. The goal of a full treaty has been abandoned for the next climate conference in Mexico, which is instead aiming at a number of partial agreements (on finance, forestry, technology transfer, adaptation) under the UNFCCC umbrella. For this to produce results, a more strategic approach is needed to ensure that – over time – such partial elements add up to an ambitious and internationally coordinated climate policy, which does not drive down the level of aspiration and commitment.

The rise (and decline) of the 'global deal' strategy

From an early stage, international climate diplomacy has been focused on the creation of a comprehensive treaty with binding commitments on mitigation and adaptation funding. This global deal strategy contains five key elements:

- it prescribes, in a top-down way, generally applicable policies that are based on commonly understood principles;
- it strives to develop targets and instruments of climate governance (regarding mitigation measures, carbon sinks, adaptation efforts) in a comprehensive manner;
- it is intended to be universal in its application, applying to all countries according to agreed principles of burden-sharing;
- it is universal in its negotiation and decision-making process, being based on the primacy of the UN framework; and
- it seeks to establish legally binding international obligations.

This approach builds on an established model of environmental regime-building. Since the 1970s, global environmental issues have been dealt with in a compartmentalized way by negotiating issue-specific treaties and building institutions around them (Susskind 1994). This model has proved highly successful in creating a growing web of treaty obligations and institutional mechanisms for addressing transnational forms of pollution, from marine pollution to transboundary air pollution and trade in endangered species. Over the last four decades, the number of multilateral environmental treaties has grown steadily, climbing to well over 500 today.[1]

The international regime to combat the depletion of the ozone layer is widely regarded as the most successful example of a global deal strategy (Parson 2003). The 1985 Vienna Convention created a framework for international cooperation on information exchange, research and monitoring and established the norm of ozone layer protection. The 1987 Montreal Protocol then set a specific target for reducing emissions of ozone-depleting chemicals (by 50 per cent by 1999). The Multilateral Ozone Fund, which was created in 1990 to support implementation in developing countries, received pledges totalling US$ 2.55 billion over the period from 1991 to 2009. Subsequent revisions of the Montreal Protocol succeeded in bringing forward the emission reduction schedule, with nearly all production and use of ozone-depleting substances ceasing in most industrialized countries by the late 1990s.

Given its success, it should not come as a surprise that the ozone regime served as the main model for climate diplomacy. To be sure, climate change was widely recognized to pose a more complex and costlier challenge than ozone depletion, and early on there was some debate about a universal approach versus regional or sectoral ones (Nitze 1990). But by disaggregating the problem and applying the convention-plus-protocol approach, negotiators hoped to repeat the success of the experience with the ozone regime (Sebenius 1994: 283).

Initially, the strategy seemed to pay off. The UN Framework Convention was successfully negotiated in the run-up to the 1992 UN Conference on Environment and Development in Rio de Janeiro (Mintzer and Leonard 1994). Largely due to US resistance, the Convention did not include binding commitments to emissions reductions. It did, however, establish the norm of global climate stabilization and the principle of 'common but differentiated respon-sibilities', which have underpinned international climate politics ever since. Moreover, it achieved near-universal support, with all major industrialized and developing countries ratifying it in subsequent years. In many ways, the UNFCCC resembles the Vienna Convention on ozone layer depletion, in that it inscribed a normative commitment into a legal agreement and paved the way for the negotiation of a more specific protocol with binding commitments. The latter was achieved in 1997 with the signing of the Kyoto Protocol, which included dif-ferentiated commitments by industrialized countries to reduce their greenhouse gas emissions by, on average, 5 per cent with 1990 as the base year.

The detailed construction of a climate regime was to prove much more difficult and the Kyoto Protocol only entered into force in February 2005, after a prolonged struggle to muster a sufficient number of ratifications. The Kyoto Protocol was also more limited in scope than the Montreal Protocol and its subsequent revisions. Commitments to reduce greenhouse gas emissions were of only limited environmental impact and did not extend to developing countries; and, critically, the United States failed to ratify the climate deal, thereby undermining the long-term effectiveness and future of the Protocol. Of course, the 1987 Montreal Protocol on its own would not have sufficed to deal with ozone layer depletion. Only subsequent treaty revisions brought the production and use of ozone-depleting substances to a near halt in the late 1990s. In this sense, the Kyoto Protocol served a similar purpose as a staging post on the road toward a more inclusive and demand-ing climate regime. If its mitigation schedule could be strengthened and extended to those emerging emitters that were not bound by the original emission reduction targets, then Kyoto would make a meaningful contribution to the long-term goal of climate stabilization. But what if the goal of agreeing a successor agreement to Kyoto turned out to be elusive?

The benefits of the global deal strategy

Before we turn to the tortuous history of post-Kyoto international climate negotiations, it is worth reviewing briefly the reasons why the 'global deal' strategy has been dominant in international environmental politics. There are at least four reasons why it remains central to many countries' international climate policy today.

First, a treaty that contains firm and measurable commitments that are legally binding is likely to be more effective in securing lasting emission reductions than a system of voluntary pledges. In economic analyses of climate stability as a public good, such international commitments are seen as essential if the collective action problem of 'free riding' is to be overcome (Stern 2007: ch. 21). Even if international law cannot override the sovereign right of nations, the ongoing legalization of international relations has greatly strengthened domestic compliance with international obligations. Of course, treaties cannot guarantee that states will act on their commitments. But they can create an environment in which reporting and review mechanisms enhance transparency and trust, and where the creation of compliance and enforcement mechanisms can increase the incentives for states to comply with their international obligations. The growth of international environmental law thus reflects a more profound normative change to international society, one that is 'part of a broader shift in international legal understandings of sovereignty: away from an emphasis on the rights of states and towards a far greater stress on both duties and common interests' (Hurrell 2007: 225).

Second, multilateral environmental policy focused on creating comprehensive regimes has contributed to the growth of important institutions that support global environmental governance. The institutions range from systems of generating, assessing and disseminating scientific information to national reporting instruments and mechanisms for capacity building and financial aid. Where they are based on legal commitments and universal application, such institutions not only support the objectives of specific environmental treaties but become an important feature of overall environmental governance. They support learning effects among states, with regard to the understanding of global environmental problems and the choice of effective policy instruments (Haas, Keohane and Levy 1993; Vogler 2005).

Third, the firm commitments that states enter into as part of a legally binding global deal send strong signals to private actors in the global economy enabling them to reduce transaction costs. In contrast to voluntary pledges in a highly fragmented global governance system, a comprehensive treaty-based regime increases the credibility of public undertakings to reduce pollution. This in turn can stimulate a more determined effort by the private sector to deal proactively with environmental problems early on. Such signalling is particularly important for long-term investment decisions by the corporate sector in environmentally friendly technologies and processes (Engau and Hoffmann 2009).

Fourth, even if international agreement on a global deal remains elusive, the continuous push for such an outcome helps to maintain political momentum in international negotiations. Environmental leaders routinely put ambitious targets and timeframes on the international agenda to set a high level of expectations and mobilize support for international solutions. The very fact of an ongoing negotiation process creates its own dynamics and can contribute to a more collaborative spirit among participants. As Depledge and Yamin point out, '[t]he negotiating environment of a regime enmeshes delegations in a dense web of meetings, practices, processes, and rules, generating an inherent motivation among negotiators to advance the issue' (2009: 439). This logic of institutional bargaining is evident in the two-decades-long history of climate negotiations. At various points, negotiators were able to renew momentum for an international climate deal despite setbacks such as the US withdrawal from the Kyoto Protocol in 2001.

In some sense, therefore, Copenhagen can be seen to represent just another hold-up on the long road toward the final goal, a comprehensive international treaty on climate mitigation and adaptation. But, as we argue in this chapter, the Copenhagen Conference not only revealed the lack of willingness among key actors to commit to a legally binding climate treaty; it also demonstrated that the 'global deal' strategy may have passed the point of diminishing returns. How has it come to this?

From Kyoto to Copenhagen: a road to nowhere?

The Kyoto Protocol epitomizes both the success of the global deal strategy and its shortcomings. On the one hand, it was the first climate agreement that laid down quantitative targets for emissions reductions. These are to be achieved over the first commitment period of 2008–12, by which time a new and more comprehensive treaty is meant to succeed Kyoto. The Kyoto Protocol introduced innovative instruments for achieving its overall target in a cost-effective manner, such as the flexibility of a five-year commitment period based on a mixed basket of six greenhouse gases, emissions trading, the Clean Development Mechanism and Joint Implementation. The Kyoto Protocol thus scores highly in terms of some of its political achievements. The very fact that it was adopted in the face of strong resistance from powerful states and influential business interests is in itself a sign of the success of the 'global deal' strategy.

On the other hand, in order for the Kyoto Protocol to be adopted, a number of compromises had to be built into the agreement that severely curtailed its environmental effectiveness (Victor 2001; Helm 2009). First, Kyoto exempted all developing countries from mandatory emission reduction targets. This, of course, reflected the UNFCCC's principle of 'common but differentiated responsibilities and respective capabilities'. But by creating a sharp dividing line between Annex I countries and non-Annex I countries, the question of how to include the rapidly emerging emitters from the developing world in future mitigation efforts was left unresolved. It was to resurface as a critical stumbling block in the run-up to the 2009 Copenhagen Conference.

Second, and related to the first point, the United States never ratified the Protocol, not least due to the US Senate's insistence that emerging economies also undertake mandatory emission reductions. America's 2001 denunciation of its signature of the Protocol dealt it a critical, if not fatal, blow. It removed the then-largest greenhouse gas emitter from the regime's core mitigation effort, thus reducing its environmental impact even further; it placed an even heavier political and economic burden on the other industrialized countries that sought to make the agreement work without US participation; and it cast a shadow over any future effort to negotiate a post-Kyoto climate treaty. Re-engaging the US thus became a key imperative for reviving the global deal strategy.

Third, the Kyoto Protocol suffered from several shortcomings in its regime design, including the short-term nature of its emission targets, the ability of countries to withdraw from the agreement and a weak compliance mechanism. These design faults reduced the incentives for Annex I countries to invest in mitigation efforts and undermined the willingness of non-Annex I countries to join the agreement at some future point. As Barrett argues, Kyoto 'doesn't provide a structure for both broadening and deepening cooperation over time' (2003: 374).

Despite these shortcomings, the European Union and other proactive players in climate politics have pressed on with implementing the agreement after its entry into force. In 2005, the EU created the world's first regional emissions trading system to help its member states meet the Kyoto targets. It also invested considerable political energy into the international process in an effort to secure a post-Kyoto global deal

(Vogler and Bretherton 2006). Europe's persistence in pursuing this objective played a key role in the adoption in 2007 of the Bali Road Map, which laid the foundations for the negotiation of a successor agreement to the Kyoto Protocol (Clémençon 2008). The Copenhagen Conference in December 2009 was meant to deliver the political compromise for a new international climate regime that would include commitments by all major emitters. Yet, despite the apparent success of the global deal strategy in sustaining political momentum, the conference failed to deliver the desired result.

Copenhagen not only disappointed those hoping for a diplomatic breakthrough; it also laid bare the deep fissures in climate politics that make a global deal ever less likely. The parties to the UN Framework Convention engaged in tough bargaining over nearly every aspect of the proposed rules for mitigating climate change. Rather than promote a global solution in the interest of climate protection, the major powers focused narrowly on securing their own national interest and avoiding costly commitments to emission reductions or long-term funding for adaptation. Whether Copenhagen signalled the transformation of climate politics into plain *realpolitik* will be debated for years to come (see Bodansky 2010; Hamilton 2009). What is important for our context is that the UN conference brought into sharper focus the underlying shifts that have occurred in climate politics and that, in our view, signal the end of the global deal strategy.

The growing obstacles to a global climate deal

It is a truism in international relations that long-term international environmental cooperation needs willing partners. Force and coercion are widely regarded as weak, if not irrelevant, instruments for promoting cooperative behaviour by states (Young 1994: 136; Falkner 2005), even if economic clout can in some cases be used to threaten sanctions against or offer inducements to reluctant players (DeSombre 2001). The lack of political will among major emitters must therefore count as one of the key obstacles to reaching a global climate deal. Of course, this is not a new phenomenon and has plagued international climate politics ever since the UNFCCC was adopted in 1992. But against the background of a recent surge in worldwide support for climate action, the continued reluctance of major players to move beyond informal pledges and voluntary measures has become *the* major hurdle on the way to a global deal.

There are several reasons why it has proved so difficult to overcome this obstacle. The first is that some major emitters lack the necessary domestic support or have yet to create domestic policies as the basis for meaningful international commitments. Indeed, of the five leading emitters that account for two-thirds of global CO_2 gas emissions – China, the United States, the European Union, Russia and India – only the EU has offered strong support for a binding climate treaty and has backed this up with domestic legislation. Collectively, these five major players hold the key to success in international climate politics. If all or some of these five emitters refuse to commit to international emission reductions, the chances of reaching a comprehensive and meaningful global deal are low.

Out of those five, the US has been, and remains, the pivotal player. The US has contributed most to global warming in cumulative terms, if all historical emissions are taken into account. As the world's pre-eminent state, leading economy and unrivalled military power, it bears a special responsibility for the state of international climate policy. To date, the US has repeatedly held back international efforts, despite agreeing to the UNFCCC (which it ratified) and the Kyoto Protocol (which it failed to ratify). For much of the last fifteen years, and especially under the presidency of George W. Bush, the US has dragged its feet in negotiations and rejected any mandatory emission reductions.

The US may have re-engaged in climate diplomacy under President Obama, but lack of domestic support for an international treaty continues to hold back a more proactive international role (Falkner 2010). Recent attempts to steer a domestic climate bill through a Democrat-controlled Congress have faltered, and the chances of a federal cap-and-trade system being introduced in the near future are rapidly diminishing as the political pendulum swings back toward the Republicans. More importantly for a 'global deal' strategy, the US Senate has repeatedly stipulated that emerging economies must shoulder comparable commitments to mitigate their rising emissions if the US was to ratify a future climate treaty. Having rejected the Kyoto Protocol and avoided domestic measures to limit emissions in the past, the US now faces even tougher domestic adjustment costs should it ever wish to accede to a binding international climate regime.

While the US makes its own willingness to consider an international climate deal dependent on commitments by major emerging economies, China itself remains steadfastly opposed to a mandatory mitigation regime unless the US takes a lead in controlling emissions. Just like other emerging economies and developing countries, China insists that industrialized countries bear a greater historical responsibility for global warming and that poorer countries need to catch up economically before a heavy mitigation burden is placed on their shoulders. The two largest emitters are thus locked into a 'game of chicken', in which neither side is willing to make the first significant concession.[2] For other countries, the US–Chinese relationship creates a profound political conundrum: unable to change the US or Chinese position, the push for a global deal is likely to fall at the first hurdle.

Of course, the US and China are not the only veto players. Russia, which helped the Kyoto Protocol to enter into force by ratifying it in 2004, has since kept a low profile in climate politics, playing only a marginal role at Copenhagen. India, on the other hand, has taken on an increasingly assertive role in international talks. Traditionally sceptical of demands for developing countries to contribute to the mitigation effort, it has put forward a robust defence of the Kyoto Protocol's sharp distinction between Annex I countries and non-Annex I countries. In the run-up to Copenhagen, the Indian leadership repeatedly stressed that it was unwilling to accept binding mitigation targets, echoing G77 statements against the injustice of shifting the climate mitigation burden to poorer nations. Both India and China are cognisant of the increasing attention that will be paid to their expanding carbon footprint as their economies continue on their current growth path. But they fear that they cannot achieve their long-term development objectives if they take on binding mitigation targets as part of an international agreement. Even weak intensity targets and national policy approaches are viewed with suspicion in case they lead down a slippery slope toward firm reduction targets.

Structural shifts in the international political economy have, if anything, complicated the search for a global deal by strengthening the veto power of certain laggard countries. Whereas, during the 1990s, the gap between European and American climate policy defined the main fault line in climate politics, more recently the divisions between developed and emerging economies have moved centre-stage. This shift manifests itself in climate politics in two principal ways: in the growing share of emerging economies in worldwide emissions; and in the demands that these countries are making for enhanced representation and influence within the established framework of international cooperation.

The changing distribution of global emissions is rooted in the shift in economic activity and power to emerging economies, particularly in Asia. In 2007, China surpassed the United States as the world's largest CO_2 gas emitter.[3] The country's contribution to the global enhanced greenhouse effect is difficult to measure precisely, but all estimates point in the same direction: namely dramatically rising energy consumption and emission levels for the next few decades. Business-as-usual forecasts suggest that the country's energy-related CO_2 emissions alone will make up more than a quarter of worldwide emissions by 2030. The US Energy Information Administration (EIA) estimates that China's energy-related CO_2 emissions will rise from 2.24

gigatonnes (Gt) in 1990 to 5.32 Gt in 2005 and 12.01 Gt in 2030. World emissions are estimated to climb to 42.3 Gt in 2030.[4] Overall, non-Annex I countries have increased their share of global emissions from 33.1 per cent in 1990 to 48.3 percent in 2006. Their share is expected to rise to 58.5 per cent by 2025.[5]

Against the background of a global economic transformation, the United States and China increasingly view world politics through the lens of their bilateral relationship. As the two largest emitters worldwide, with a combined share of global greenhouse gas emissions of 41.8 percent in 2006,[6] the two countries are fully aware of their central role in determining the future of climate policy. A *de facto* G2 formation between the US and China, which has already emerged in other areas of global economic relations such as finance, is beginning to play a more important role in climate politics as well (Garrett 2010: 29). Moreover, with other emerging economies flexing their muscles and asserting their national interests, the dynamics of climate negotiations have begun to change. The emergence of the BASIC group in climate negotiations – assembling Brazil, South Africa, India, and China – is the clearest sign yet of how global economic change has been translated into a new international political structure.

One of the first casualties of this alteration was the European Union's ambition to play a leadership role. As is widely recognized, the Kyoto Protocol would not have come into force had the EU not provided leadership in the 1997 negotiations and in the struggle to secure its entry into force in 2005. Europe's emissions trading system provides a model for international emissions trading under the climate treaty and remains the world's pre-eminent experiment in reducing greenhouse gas emissions through a flexible market-based instrument. The EU expected to play a leading role again in Copenhagen, having committed to comparatively demanding emission reduction targets and offered substantial financial aid to developing countries. By leading the debate on international climate policy and pioneering innovative mechanisms, the EU hoped to encourage tangible concessions by other players.

Yet, as soon as the gavel came down at the closing COP-15 plenary in the early afternoon of Saturday 19 December, the realization sank in among European negotiators that the EU had not played a leading role in the final phase of the Copenhagen Conference. While a 'Friends of the Chair' grouping of twenty-seven countries, including the EU and its most important member states, was drafting the Copenhagen Accord, it was the US President who brokered the final compromise with the BASIC countries in a separate meeting without European input. Having argued for a comprehensive deal in the run-up to the conference, European leaders were left with little choice but to endorse the watered-down version of the Accord.

The final stage of the Copenhagen Conference also brought to light the shortcomings of the UN negotiation framework. Two years had been spent in preparing for the conference, a process that had started with the adoption of the Bali Road Map in 2007. At COP-15, negotiators from over 190 countries spent a further intensive two weeks negotiating (unsuccessfully) over heavily bracketed texts, only to see a smaller group of heads of government take over and draft a compromise agreement that was not based on the official negotiation texts prepared in the preceding COP working groups. In the end, the COP plenary, the official UN forum with decision-making authority, failed to adopt the leaders' Copenhagen Accord. It merely took note of it.

The negotiations at Copenhagen were painstakingly slow and cumbersome, complicated not least by the need to agree a package deal that includes *all* elements of the climate regime (emission reductions, timetables, financing, etc.) and that is acceptable to *all* countries. As the UN Climate Convention approaches universal acceptance with a total of 194 ratifications as of 2010, it may produce a high degree of participation and legitimacy but ends up delivering a diminishing rate of return in terms of effective bargaining.

A growing number of observers now argue that UN-style decision-making based on the consensus principle has become an impediment to a post-Kyoto climate regime (Hamilton 2009). This was evident not least in the closing days and hours of the Copenhagen Conference when heads of government wrestled the initiative from their official negotiators and created a more fluid yet manageable framework for striking bargains. The use of smaller and more exclusive negotiation groups is a common feature of international environmental negotiations. But, as was to be expected, the Copenhagen Accord was criticized by some parties for its lack of ambition and legitimacy. It remains to be seen whether the new bargaining structure that emerged in the final two days of the climate summit remains a one-off event or points to the arrival of a new form of multi-track diplomacy in climate politics.

The transition toward a 'building blocks' approach

If, as we argue in this chapter, a 'global deal' strategy yields rapidly diminishing returns in the post-Copenhagen era, then the question arises as to the alternatives that are available to climate negotiators. There is no shortage of proposals on how to advance the goal of climate protection, and the academic and policy debate has produced dozens of more or less specific models for international climate policy (for an overview, see Aldy and Stavins 2010; Biermann, Pattberg, van Asselt et al. 2009; Kuik, Aerts, Berkhout et al. 2008). This is not the place to review this debate or assess specific proposals. Instead, we take a wider perspective and propose a shift in thinking on how to construct the global climate governance architecture. Our argument is that construction by 'building blocks' provides a more realistic approach to creating a workable global climate regime, even though it is not without its own risks and shortfalls. Some characteristics are shared by both the 'global deal' and 'building blocks' approaches, not least the objective of creating a strong international framework for climate action; but they also differ in important ways, primarily on the question of how to achieve this goal.

Fundamental to a building blocks approach is the recognition that, given prevailing interests and power structures, a functioning framework for climate governance is unlikely to be constructed all at once, in a top-down fashion. The approach reinterprets international climate politics as an ongoing political process that seeks to create trust between nations and build climate governance step-by-step out of several regime elements. Although dispensing with the idea of creating a comprehensive, legally binding, treaty up-front, it remains committed to building an overall international framework for climate action. It is thus closer to the 'global deal' strategy than a thoroughly 'bottom-up' model of climate governance which relies solely on decentralized national and sub-national climate measures. In other words, a building blocks approach combines the long-term objective of a global climate architecture with a dose of political realism in the process of creating this architecture.

A number of variants of this strategy have been developed in recent years. One such version seeks to advance climate stability by disaggregating the global climate governance into component parts that can be developed in a more flexible manner, involving different sets of negotiations based on varying political geometries and regime types. Heller (2008), for example, proposes the 'pillarization' of climate policy as a way of developing parallel agreements on specific, functionally defined, issues. Rather than wait for a single agreement to cover all governance mechanisms, individual agreements are developed on matters such as technology innovation and diffusion, adaptation funding, deforestation, and sectoral approaches for industrial sectors.

To some extent, pillarization overlaps with what advocates of a bottom-up model of climate governance propose (Hulme 2010; Prins, Galiana, Green et al. 2010). Critics of the UN process imagine these elements of global climate governance as self-standing, de-centralized initiatives. Instead of investing political energies in a drawn-out and cumbersome international negotiation process, countries focus on what can be done here and now, at the national level. Rather than forcing economic change toward a low-carbon future through top-down regulation, they seek to induce such change through promoting energy efficiency, introducing alternative energy sources and inducing technological breakthroughs throughout the economy (Nordhaus and Shellenberger 2010). The 2005 Asia–Pacific Partnership on Clean Development and Climate is one such example of a coalition of countries that engages in a range of bottom-up initiatives loosely grouped around the themes of energy security, air pollution reduction and climate change.

Yet, by abandoning all efforts to create an international climate regime, the bottom-up approach removes a major stimulus for developing more ambitious domestic policies, thus solidifying the lowest common denominator. It turns climate change from a political into a technological challenge and eschews the difficult distributive conflicts that are central to international climate politics. A building blocks approach would recognize that domestic policies need to be embedded in a broader international effort, within the UNFCCC or through an affiliated negotiating process.

In fact, this dual approach of advancing domestic and international policies is already evident in the pre- and post-Copenhagen process. Significant advances were made at Copenhagen in most of the areas listed above and some of them may be ready for official agreement in Cancún in December 2010. For instance, with regard to the planned instrument for avoiding deforestation (UN-REDD), the 'Paris–Oslo' process has brought together around sixty industrialized and developing countries to drive the implementation of preliminary and complementary REDD+ measures over the next three years. Its financial clout (US\$ 6 billion pledged so far) and the experiences gained from project design and management will undoubtedly speed up the forest-related negotiations under the UNFCCC.

Besides advancing such 'functional' issue-areas – including deforestation, adaptation, and technology transfer – which already benefit from a certain degree of political agreement, a building blocks model can also be applied to core regime areas such as climate mitigation through targets, timetables, and 'sustainable development policies and measures' (SD-PAMs). A promising strategy would thus rely on resolving easier problems ('low-hanging fruit') through flexible deals and addressing more complex issues at a later stage. The Copenhagen Accord already reflects this approach through its 'pledge-and-review' list of voluntary commitments from a large number of countries. While industrialized nations have put forward specific mitigation targets, developing countries have made measurable commitments on energy intensity and other 'nationally appropriate mitigation actions' (NAMAs) that do not involve costly measures which could stifle economic growth.

Given that the Accord still represents a lowest common denominator agreement with questionable long-term effectiveness, a building blocks approach would need leading countries to 'raise the bar' and push for partial agreements with a select group of parties. For example, Bodansky and Diringer (2007) have made the case for a 'menu' of mitigation actions that allows for multiple regulatory tracks and attempts to simultaneously satisfy demands for flexibility (national conditions and interests) and integration (greater reciprocity and coordination). It is also clear that such agreements would need to be designed to include appropriate incentive structures so that greater participation can be achieved over time.

With the present reluctance of the pivotal players, the US and China, to entertain stronger commitments, the responsibility for forging more ambitious coalitions may once again fall to the EU. A growing number of commentators now suggest that a 'coalition of the willing' should heed the calls from the developing world to continue the Kyoto Protocol beyond 2012 and enter a second commitment period (Grubb 2010; Tangen 2010). Besides the EU, other candidates for such a coalition include 'progressive' medium powers such as Mexico, South Korea and Indonesia, as well as existing parties to the Protocol such as Japan and Russia. Gathering enough support for a new commitment period would be far from easy, but it would cement the EU's status as a front-runner in climate governance. Moreover, it would provide a boost to embryonic regional and national carbon markets and keep alive a more ambitious regulatory framework which could, later on, become the core of a comprehensive global settlement.

Certainly, this selective approach to developing limited policy approaches is and remains a second-best alternative to an elusive global deal. By embedding such partial agreements in a global political framework, it is hoped that they will ultimately add up to a larger political architecture. How to construct a global agreement which would go beyond the very limited ambition of the Copenhagen Accord remains an open question for now. Alternative international forums and settings, such as the G20 and the Major Economies Forum (comprising seventeen members), may need to be employed in the search for global compromises between the major players in climate politics (Giddens 2009). These forums would need to provide the necessary political space to facilitate frank discussions and, potentially, strategic bargaining between the biggest emitters.

Given the need to proceed on various 'tracks', creating a coherent governance architecture out of separate and partial agreements remains a key challenge in the building blocks approach. Coherence is needed to ensure that climate policies reinforce each other rather than trigger competitive dynamics (Biermann, Pattberg, van Asselt et al. 2009). It is also of importance for the creation of transparency and trust in governmental efforts that are undertaken without a fully comprehensive and binding climate regime in place. Moreover, because building climate governance will remain an ongoing international process, the partial agreements suggested above should be designed to accommodate future deepening and broadening. The latter could be ensured, for instance, by creating 'docking stations' so that new participants can be added without great difficulty at a later stage (Petsonk 2009).

International coherence and coordination will also need to be sought with regard to measuring parties' mitigation efforts, through internationally agreed monitoring, reporting and verification systems. Progress on this front will also play an important role in scaling-up national and regional emissions trading systems to the global level. The Copenhagen negotiations have shown measurement and verification to be a highly sensitive political subject, which will require a great deal of trust-building, persuasion and reciprocal action among the major powers.

Are there any real-world analogies to the building blocks model of climate governance? Some have likened the approach to developments in the trade policy area after 1945 (Bodansky and Diringer 2007; Antholis 2009). To be sure, there are profound differences in the problem structure and political dynamics of trade and climate change. Most importantly, as Houser reminds us, 'the climate doesn't have time for a Doha-like approach' (2010: 16). Still, the procedural analogy between the evolution of the 1948 General Agreement on Tariffs and Trade (GATT) and a climate building blocks approach is instructive. The GATT was a partial trade agreement focused mainly on reducing tariffs on trade in manufactured goods. It was a second-best solution and served as a fallback position after the more comprehensive agreement on the International Trade Organization (ITO) failed to be ratified by the US. Building on the GATT, the parties gradually expanded the scope of the trade regime in successive trade rounds from the 1950s to the 1970s. This process culminated in the Uruguay Round, which expanded the trade regime to cover new areas such as services and agriculture. It integrated the various trade treaties under the umbrella of the newly created World Trade Organization (WTO). Over time, membership of the GATT, and later the WTO, grew steadily, and the commitments taken on by member states were gradually expanded and deepened.

The WTO can thus be seen to have been fabricated out of a number of building blocks that allowed countries to adjust their expectations and identify common interests in a process of repeated negotiations. The WTO was the crowning achievement, rather than the starting point, of a regime-building process. The trade regime was not meant to be created in this manner, but the failure of the ITO left no choice but to pursue a 'pluri-lateral' coalition of the willing. This was helped by the fact that expectations of commercial gains from increasingly comprehensive global trade rules mobilized a variety of domestic and transnational actors in support of the GATT/WTO. Such gains will be harder to come by in climate politics. Still, those who stand to reap 'first-mover advantages' from stronger global climate governance – for instance leading technology corporations or innovative regions such as California – can be expected to put pressure on national governments. The building blocks of climate governance thus need to be designed to create incentives for those countries still reluctant to make firm and ambitious commitments. The prospect of a lucrative global carbon market or competitive advantage in a carbon-constrained global economy would become the critical ingredient for driving forward the process of building a more comprehensive global architecture (Keohane and Raustiala 2010: 378).

Conclusions

Given the deadlock in current international negotiations, what should be the strategy of those wishing to strengthen international climate policy? Our analysis suggests that the push for a 'global deal' is producing diminishing returns and that parties may need to consider a second-best scenario. This alternative strategy is based on the idea of creating a climate regime in an incremental fashion, based on partial agreements and governance mechanisms. While the objective of a universal and comprehensive treaty with firm commitments for emission reductions remains valid, a building blocks approach is needed to realize this objective.

Our review of the international climate negotiations from the early 1990s onwards shows that the global deal strategy has been successful in driving the international process forward and creating political momentum behind global climate protection. But it has repeatedly come up against resistance by large emitters and is unlikely to succeed in bringing future negotiations to a rapid conclusion. The next conference of the parties in Mexico at the end of 2010 is not expected to produce agreement on a binding treaty. And the Copenhagen Accord points in the direction of a different international process, based on multi-level policies and initiatives. To some extent, therefore, international climate policy is already being re-defined as an ongoing process that combines parallel efforts to create partial agreements on building blocks of global climate governance.

Such a building blocks approach offers some hope of breaking the current stalemate, even though it provides no guarantee of success. It would allow for a disaggregation of the negotiations into a proper multi-track approach. This would enable parties to secure 'low-hanging fruits' and thereby avoid early and ambitious action in some areas being held hostage to failure to resolve other areas of contention. It would also separate the controversial question of the *legal* status of any agreement on climate from the need to secure a *political* consensus on a range of mitigation and adaptation strategies.

There are important drawbacks to such an approach. It would involve a departure from the established principle in international environmental negotiations that 'nothing is agreed until everything is agreed'. This principle has promoted grand bargains to be struck, based on a complex web of concessions across a range of issues and countries. The building blocks approach would prevent such a grand bargain and may thus deter parties from making necessary concessions in one area without securing other parties' concessions in others. In addition, because building blocks do not require universal participation, they may reduce the urgency of concerted global cooperation (Biermann, Pattberg, van Asselt et al. 2009: 26). A system of partial agreements and variable geometry may reinforce the logic of free-riding and heighten concerns over economic competitiveness.

Thus, the building blocks approach can only be a second-best strategy. Whether it will produce the desired results depends on the creation of an international political framework, built around the UNFCCC, which ensures that partial agreements and regime elements are connected and add up to a larger climate governance architecture. The Copenhagen Accord may well end up being the foundation for such a political framework, even if it requires further work. The danger is that moves in the direction of a building blocks approach, which are well on the way as parties gear up for COP-16 in Mexico, would lead to a disintegration of global climate policy. Preventing a collapse into a decentralized, purely bottom-up, approach is of critical importance. A more strategic approach is therefore needed for the building blocks strategy to be successful in the promotion of ambitious and internationally coordinated climate policy.

Notes

The authors are grateful to the Economic and Social Research Council (ESRC) for research funding, Clement Feger for research assistance, and Michael Jacobs, Jouni Paavola, Fariborz Zelli, Dimitri Zenghelis and members of the BISA Environment Working Group for helpful comments on an earlier version of this chapter. The usual disclaimers apply.

This chapter was first published in *Global Policy* 1 (3) in October 2010.

1. Definitions of what counts as a multilateral environmental treaty vary, and by some measures this number has risen to well over 1,000. See the International Environmental Agreements Database Project, at http://iea.uoregon.edu; accessed 23 October 2010.
2. For an early depiction of the US–Chinese relationship in climate politics as a game of chicken, see Ward (1993).
3. The Netherlands Environmental Assessment Agency was the first in 2007 to put China in first position among global emitters. See Leggett, Logan and Mackey (2008) for a discussion of the remaining uncertainties in the emissions data.
4. Energy Information Administration (EIA) emission profiles, June 2008, Washington, DC, available at: www.eia.doe.gov/.
5. Based on data from World Resources Institute: www.earthtrendsdelivered.org/taxonomy/term/64?page=1; accessed 23 October 2010.
6. Authors' calculation, based on Millennium Development Goals' Indicators, at: http://mdgs.un.org/unsd/mdg/SeriesDetail.aspx?srid=749&crid=; accessed 23 October 2010.

Bibliography

Aldy, J. E. and Stavins, R. N. (eds.) (2010) *Post-Kyoto International Climate Policy: Implementing Architectures for Agreement*, Cambridge: Cambridge University Press.

Antholis, W. (2009) 'Five "Gs": Lessons from World Trade for Governing Global Climate Change', in L. Brainard and I. Sorkin (eds.), *Climate Change, Trade, and Competitiveness: Is a Collision Inevitable?* Washington, DC: Brookings Institution Press, pp. 121–38.

Barrett, S. (2003) *Environment and Statecraft: The Strategy of Environmental Treaty-Making*, Oxford: Oxford University Press.

Biermann, F., Pattberg, P. H., van Asselt, H. and Zelli, F. (2009) 'The Fragmentation of Global Governance Architectures: A Framework for Analysis', *Global Environmental Politics*, 9 (4).

Bodansky, D. (2010) 'The Copenhagen Conference: A Post-mortem', *American Journal of International Law*, 104 (12 February); available at: http://papers.ssrn.com/sol3/papers.cfm?abstract_id=1553167; accessesd 1 July 2010.

Bodansky, D. and Diringer, E. (2007) *Towards an Integrated Multi-Track Climate Framework*, discussion paper for the Pew Center on Global Climate Change; available at www.pewclimate.org/docUploads/Multi-Track-Report.pdf; accessed 1 July 2010.

Clémençon, R. (2008) 'The Bali Road Map: A First Step on the Difficult Journey to a Post-Kyoto Protocol Agreement', *Journal of Environment and Development*, 17 (1).

Depledge, J. and Yamin, F. (2009) 'The Global Climate-change Regime: A Defence', in D. Helm and C. Hepburn (eds.), *The Economics and Politics of Climate Change*, Oxford: Oxford University Press, pp. 433–53.

DeSombre, E. R. (2001) 'Environmental Sanctions in U.S. Foreign Policy', in P. G. Harris (ed.), *The Environment, International Relations, and U.S. Foreign Policy*, Washington, DC: Georgetown University Press, pp. 197–216.

Engau, C. and Hoffmann, V. H. (2009) 'Effects of Regulatory Uncertainty on Corporate Strategy: An Analysis of Firms' Responses to Uncertainty about Post-Kyoto Policy', *Environmental Science and Policy*, 12 (7).

Falkner, R. (2005) 'American Hegemony and the Global Environment', *International Studies Review*, 7 (4).

Falkner, R. (2010) 'Getting a Deal on Climate Change: Obama's Flexible Multilateralism', in N. Kitchen (ed.), *Obama Nation? US Foreign Policy One Year On*, LSE IDEAS Special Report, London: LSE, pp. 37–41.

Garrett, G. (2010) 'G2 in G20: China, the United States and the World after the Global Financial Crisis', *Global Policy*, 1 (1).

Giddens, A. (2009) *The Politics of Climate Change*, Cambridge: Polity Press.

Grubb, M. (2010) 'Copenhagen: Back to the Future', *Climate Policy*, 10 (2).

Haas, P. M., Keohane, R. O. and Levy, M. A. (eds.) (1993) *Institutions for the Earth: Sources of Effective International Environmental Protection*, Cambridge, MA: MIT Press.

Hamilton, I. (2009) 'Lessons from Copenhagen: Has the UN Played Its Last Card?', *Carbon Positive*, 24 December; available at: www.carbonpositive.net/viewarticle. aspx?articleID=1789; accessed 17 March 2010.

Heller, T. (2008) 'Climate Change: Designing an Effective Response', in E. Zedillo (ed.), *Global Warming: Looking Beyond Kyoto*, Washington, DC: Brookings Institution Press, pp. 115–44.

Helm, D. (2009) 'Climate-change Policy: Why Has So Little Been Achieved?', in D. Helm and C. Hepburn (eds.), *The Economics and Politics of Climate Change*, Oxford: Oxford University Press, pp. 9–35.

Houser, T. (2010) *Copenhagen, the Accord, and the Way Forward*, Policy Brief PB10-5, Washington, DC: Peterson Institute for International Economics.

Hulme, M. (2010) 'Moving beyond Climate Change', *Environment*, 52 (3).

Hurrell, A. (2007) *On Global Order: Power, Values, and the Constitution of International Society*, Oxford: Oxford University Press.

Keohane, R. O. and Raustiala, K. (2010) 'Towards a Post-Kyoto Climate Change Architecture: A Political Analysis', in J. A. Aldy and R. N. Stavins (eds.), *Post-Kyoto International Climate Policy: Implementing Architectures for Agreement*, Cambridge: Cambridge University Press, pp. 372–402.

Kuik, O., Aerts, J., Berkhout, F. et al. (2008) 'Post-2012 Climate Policy Dilemmas: A Review of Proposals' *Climate Policy*, 8 (3).

Leggett, J. A., Logan, J. and Mackey, A. (2008) *China's Greenhouse Gas Emissions and Mitigation Policies*, CRS Report, Washington, DC: Congressional Research Service.

Mintzer, I. M. and Leonard, J. A. (eds.) (1994) *Negotiating Climate Change: The Inside Story of the Rio Convention*, Cambridge: Cambridge University Press.

Nitze, W. (1990) *The Greenhouse Effect: Formulating a Convention*, London: Royal Institute of International Affairs.

Nordhaus, T. and Shellenberger, M. (2010) 'The End of Magical Climate Thinking', *Foreignpolicy.com*, 13 January; available at: www.foreignpolicy.com/ articles/2010/01/13/the_end_of_magical_climate_thinking; accessed 13 April 2010.

Parson, E. (2003) *Protecting the Ozone Layer: Science and Strategy*, Oxford: Oxford University Press.

Petsonk, A. (2009) '"Docking Stations": Designing a More Welcoming Architecture for a Post-2012 Framework to Combat Climate Change', *Duke Journal of Comparative and International Law*, 19.

Prins, G., Galiana, I., Green, C., Grundmann, R., Korhola, A., Laird, F., et al.

(2010) *The Hartwell Paper: A New Direction for Climate Policy After the Crash of 2009*, Institute for Science, Innovation & Society, University of Oxford, LSE Mackinder Programme, London School of Economics and Political Science, May; available at http://eprints.lse.ac.uk/27939/; accessed 1 July 2010.

Sebenius, J. K. (1994) 'Towards a Winning Climate Coalition', in I. M. Mintzer and J. A. Leonard (eds.), *Negotiating Climate Change: The Inside Story of the Rio Convention*, Cambridge: Cambridge University Press, pp. 277–320.

Stern, N. (2007) *The Economics of Climate Change: The Stern Review*, Cambridge: Cambridge University Press.

Susskind, L. E. (1994) *Environmental Diplomacy: Negotiating More Effective Global Agreements*, New York: Oxford University Press.

Tangen, K. (2010) *The Odd Couple? The Merits of Two Tracks in the International Climate Change Negotiations*, Briefing Paper No. 59, 30 April, Helsinki: The Finnish Institute of International Affairs.

Victor, D. G. (2001) *The Collapse of the Kyoto Protocol and the Struggle to Slow Global Warming*. Princeton: Princeton University Press.

Vogler, J. (2005) 'In Defense of International Environmental Cooperation', in J. Barry and R. Eckersley (eds.), *The State and the Global Ecological Crisis*, Cambridge, MA: MIT Press, pp. 229–53.

Vogler, J. and Bretherton, C. (2006) 'The European Union as a Protagonist to the United States on Climate Change', *International Studies Perspectives*, 7 (1).

Ward, H. (1993) 'Game Theory and the Politics of the Global Commons', *Journal of Conflict Resolution*, 37 (2).

Young, O. R. (1994) *International Governance: Protecting the Environment in a Stateless Society*, Ithaca: Cornell University Press.

Index

Page numbers in *italics* refer to figures.